To Burlin

Best Wishes

Pat Ferrell

Runaway Father

>>>>>>>>>>>>>>>>>>>>>>>>>>>>>>>>>>>>>>

Runaway Father

>>

*The True Story of Pat Bennett,
Her Daughters, and Their
Seventeen-Year Search*

Richard Rashke

Harcourt Brace Jovanovich, Publishers
San Diego   New York   London

HBJ

Library of Congress Cataloging-in-Publication Data
Rashke, Richard L.
    Runaway father: the true story of Pat Bennett, her daughters, and their seventeen-
year search/Richard Rashke.—1st ed.
        p. cm.
    ISBN 0-15-179040-X
        1. Desertion and non-support—United States—Case studies.
    2. Runaway husbands—United States—Case studies.
    3. Missing persons—United States—Investigation—Case studies.
    I. Title.
    HQ805.R37   1988
    306.8'8—dc19   88-10909

Designed by Ann Gold

Printed in the United States of America

First edition

A B C D E

*For abandoned and
abused children everywhere*

*The quality of a civilization
may be measured by how it cares for
its elderly. Just as surely, the
future of a society may be forecast
by how it cares for its young. . . .*

—Daniel Patrick Moynihan

Contents

>>>>>>>>>>>>>>>>>>

Author's Note

>>>>>>>>>>>>>>>>>>>>>>>>>>>>>>>

The first names of two people have been changed for reasons of privacy—Lenora, the woman James Parker "married" after he abandoned his wife and daughters; and Beth, a family friend. Pat Bennett's lawyer's name has been changed to Victoria Gordon. The first name of Pat Bennett's cousin, David, has been changed to Joe, his middle name, to avoid confusion.

Unfortunately, the runaway father himself, James C. Parker, has declined repeated requests through his attorneys to be interviewed. Information about him comes from court records, public and subpoenaed documents, his interviews with the press, and my interviews with those who knew him.

——R.R.

Part One

>>>>>>>>>>>>>>>>>>>>>

Survival

1

>>>>>>>>>>>>> David had not come home all night. Pat waited up for him, holding dinner as long as she could. Then she cleaned the kitchen, put Christine and Andrea to bed, and crawled between the cool sheets, exhausted. Pregnant for the third time, she felt listless as August. Anemic again, she thought as her eyes blinked closed. I must remember to tell Dr. May.

In spite of her fatigue, Pat awakened every few hours, hoping to feel the security of David's warmth and hear the rhythm of his breathing. Each time she realized he hadn't come, she checked the clock, then drifted into yet another anxious dream.

Andrea began whimpering at six that morning as usual. Without opening her eyes, Pat reached over and felt David's side of the bed. It was empty, unrumpled. She tried to hold back the day with a few more minutes of sleep, but Andrea soon wailed for her bottle and woke up Christine, who padded into her parents' room in her footed pajamas.

"Daddy?" Christine said in a disappointed voice when she saw her father wasn't in bed. "Daddy?"

So the day began.

When Pat's eyes finally opened, she greeted the morning with an anger so hot it melted her pain. It had been months since David had stayed out all night, and she had talked herself into believing that he had finally sown the last of his wild oats. Now she realized for the first time in her three and a half years of marriage that what she had been calling his "restlessness" was nothing less than adultery. The admission was hard to grasp. Why would David want another woman when she was eager for him? If he loved her, how could he hurt her? And if he no longer cared, why did he still make love to her?

Pat eased herself out of bed and began her morning routine.

It was a small but comfortable two-bedroom apartment with red oak floors and plenty of light. Disney-character placemats hung on the walls in the girls' bedroom—Donald Duck, Pluto, Snow White, and Dopey. Above Christine's bed stretched a heavy cardboard choo-choo train seven feet long, which Pat had bought in a toy store. Up to a height of two feet, the walls were covered with crayon scribbles. In the middle of the room sat a tiny table and two chairs surrounded by toys. A picture window overlooked a wide strip of lawn out back, with picnic tables, a life-size toy stagecoach, and Jungle-Gym bars. Beyond the lawn lay thick woods. In the evenings, rabbits and groundhogs ventured out to feed on the grass.

The apartment was furnished with the things Pat and David had bought on credit for four hundred dollars: a matching brown tweed easy chair and couch with two imitation walnut end tables, a formica-topped dinette table with light blue vinyl-backed chairs to accent the navy blue living-room rug, a double bed with a bookcase headboard and matching dresser. Scattered throughout the apartment were mementos marking the mile-posts of Pat's twenty-three years. On the bookcase, next to her old college textbooks, sat two beer mugs, one bearing the word "Bermuda," where David had proposed to her; the other reading "Immaculata College," which she had attended for three semesters. The Boston rocker in one corner of the living room had been a gift from her friends at Jackson Memorial Hospital in Miami, where she had worked until she was eight months pregnant with Andrea. Standing somewhat out of place on an inexpensive tea cart was her grandmother's antique silver tea service.

Pat changed the girls, gave Andrea her bottle, and put her in the playpen against the wall in the living room. Then she gave Christine her early morning bath. It was one of the joys of her day and not even David's night out could rob her of that pleasure.

She had been six months pregnant with Christine when David stayed out all night for the first time. Married just over a year and a half, they were living in a cheap, off-base apartment in Camp Lejeune, North Carolina, where David was stationed as an enlisted Marine. That first time, unable to accept the possibility that David might be with another woman, Pat told herself that a soon-to-be father needed a night out with the boys. But six weeks after Christine's birth, a pregnant teenager knocked on her door, claiming David as the father and asking for four hundred dollars to cover expenses in a home for unwed mothers. Pat was shattered. She rushed into the bedroom and brought out Christine. Clutching the proof of David's love, she rocked the baby in her arms as if the touch and smell of their own child could prove the pregnant girl a liar. But as Pat paced the floor and wept, she sensed that the girl was telling the truth.

Composing herself, Pat told the teenager she would be willing to help financially once Christine was old enough to allow her to go back to work. The girl declined the offer. She had come to make David suffer, she said, not his wife.

Later, when Pat confronted him, David argued with quick, cold logic. Girls come to Lejeune all the time to shake down Marine wives by claiming to be pregnant when they aren't, he explained. They demand money and promise to leave town forever. How could she fall for such an obvious scam?

In Miami a year later, after David's discharge from the Marines and while Pat was carrying Andrea, David began staying out all night again. One day, Christine pulled out a package of condoms from the glove compartment of the car; but even then, Pat could not admit to herself that David was actually using them. A month after Andrea was born, however, a woman phoned and asked for David. As soon as Pat identified herself as David's wife, the woman's voice froze. Begging the caller not to hang up, Pat asked, was she David's girlfriend? The woman admitted she was, but said she hadn't known David was married. A few days later, Pat got a package in the mail: a stack of love letters signed "David" and a gift of fifty dollars for Andrea.

The letters burned like acid. As she raced through each page, Pat's anger rose around her like a steel wall. She went looking for David and found him in the shower. Without a word, she slid back the glass door and tossed the letters in.

This time he couldn't talk his way out of it like he had at Camp Lejeune, nor was she prepared to let him try. But what should she do? She had two children now and no job or money. Worse, she still loved David and needed him for a string of reasons she only dimly understood. She had always been the obedient, doting wife, bolstering her marriage with every available excuse. Yet after three years, even she had to admit failure, and the realization made her afraid. If David was capable of change, she would have to shock him into it.

For the first time since she had left home, Pat called her parents collect and asked for help. They agreed to send airplane tickets for her and the children and offered to hire a van to bring her things back to Washington. They promised to find Pat an apartment and cover all her expenses until Andrea was old enough to allow her to go back to work. She accepted the offer as a loan.

Pat waited until David was on a training flight for his private pilot's license. Then she had the movers empty the house of everything except David's clothes and a few pieces of furniture. She wanted him to come home to bare rooms and a lipstick message on the bathroom mirror: "Go fly a kite!"

David walked in before she could leave for the airport, and she could sense his shock. When he finally realized that she was serious about leaving, he agreed to drive her and the children to the airport.

Pat settled into a two-bedroom apartment in northern Virginia and waited for David's next move. Common sense told her he would never change. Even if he did, she knew she would never completely trust him again. But she was lonely, in love, and insecure without him. When David finally asked to join her and promised to be faithful, she decided to give him a second chance. For a few weeks all was well. But now she was pregnant again. And he had stayed out all night.

For the first time, Pat began to see why she put up with his behavior. David stayed out all night only when she was most vulnerable—either pregnant or caring for a new baby. What could she do? Her children needed a father. She *had* to believe she still loved him. If she didn't, she could never live with him. And if she walked out, where would she go? What would she do once she got there? How could she pay her way?

Now, as she waited to face him, Pat finally understood the survival game she had been playing—a game that defied logic, although millions of women had played it before her. She had convinced herself that her husband was faithful in spite of the evidence, but subconsciously she had vowed never to trust him again.

No more, she told herself. David wasn't restless, he was cheating. And he was doing it when she felt most helpless and needy. Pregnant or not, she wouldn't stand for one more night of it.

When David walked in just after seven that morning, Pat was feeding Andrea at the kitchen table. Christine sat in her little rocker in the living room, and when she saw her father, her face broke into a sunny smile.

"Daddy," she cried. "Daddy!"

Christine adored her father. The most difficult moment of her day was when he would kiss her good-bye and drive off to work. The sight of his car pulling up in front of the apartment at dusk was her reward for missing him all day. Even though she was not quite two years old, his unpredictable comings and goings the last few weeks had unsettled her. She cried more, laughed less, and seemed irritable and anxious.

This morning, David ignored Christine and headed straight for the bedroom without saying a word.

"David, where were you?" Pat demanded as she wiped cereal from Andrea's face. "I want to know where you were!"

Ignoring Pat's questions, David walked out of the bedroom and into the bathroom. Pat put Andrea back in the playpen and, while David showered, she went through his suitcoat pockets. There she found a motel receipt dated August 28, 1968. She felt her anger rise. Last night she had held his dinner, waited up as long as she could, and worried most of the night, only to find that he had spent money they could ill afford for a motel room and who knew what else. Without bothering to knock, she yanked the bathroom door open.

"What the hell is this?" she shouted, waving the motel slip in his face. When she got no answer, she tossed the piece of paper at him in disgust and slammed the door. She was not surprised at his silence. A few months earlier in Miami, David had also refused to discuss his love letters. Tearing them into tiny pieces, he had simply flushed them down the toilet. As if that would make the problem go away.

After showering, David walked back into the bedroom and began putting on his tailor-made blue suit and a clean white shirt that Pat had carefully starched the way he liked it. Pat stood just inside the door fighting back a familiar and growing panic.

"Why do you have to sleep with someone else?" she asked sadly, surprised at the sound of her voice. "What's wrong with me?"

Unruffled, David stood before the mirror and straightened his blue-and-maroon-striped necktie. No answer.

"You make me sick," Pat said, finally allowing her anger to overcome her fear and insecurity. "How can I even want you to touch me!"

David stepped out of the bedroom without a word of explanation, walked past Christine, whose eyes never left him, and slipped out the apartment door. He had not stopped long enough even to hug or kiss his daughters good-bye.

Christine stared at the door, sobbing. Pat picked her up and held her tightly. It was only seven-thirty and it promised to be a very long day.

2

>>>>>>>>>>>>> The morning dragged. By the time Pat straightened the apartment, dressed the girls, and settled down Karen and Michael, two children whom she babysat, it was ten o'clock. That was the hour when the young mothers in the building gathered on the front stoop and turned their kids loose. There were often as many as fifteen women huddled together watching twenty-five children run around the lawn like gophers.

The stoop was a place to kill time and gossip, a maternal commune with each woman keeping an eye on her neighbors' children. On muggy mornings and evenings, the women sat on the cool cement steps. In the afternoons, they sprawled on blankets under a sugar maple whose branches brushed the building when a strong wind blew. It was a pleasant place to wait for husbands to come home.

Fairmont Gardens in Annandale, Virginia, sat parklike amid apple trees, maples, and Virginia pines planted in haphazard care on stretches of weedless grass. A ribbon of blacktop wound through the lawns and flowerbeds to a four-lane highway linking the development to the rest of the world. Although there were nearly four hundred apartments in a string of two-story brick buildings, the planners had designed the space so well it was hard to tell so many people lived there.

Since David took the car to work and he and Pat rarely went out together, she felt isolated and unchallenged most of the time. Chatting with the other women, even if it was only to swap gossip, made her feel like an adult. All about the same age and all facing the same struggles, the women understood each other like sisters. This morning, sensing Pat was moody, they left her to Andrea and her private thoughts and kept a lookout for Christine, Michael, and Karen, who played on the sidewalk.

With eight anxious hours to wait for David's next move and feeling frightened and insecure, Pat slipped back into blaming herself for his behavior, no longer certain about the conclusions she had reached earlier that morning. He had stayed out all night and was angry at her, she reasoned, because she had not made a perfect home for him as a wife should.

Perfect was what she sensed David wanted. An only child raised in a tidy foster home, her husband had grown into a tidy man. He liked clean, starched white shirts. A home free of clutter. A nicely set table and dinner, hot and waiting, served by a smiling wife in a dress and makeup. And he wanted children who cried only when he wasn't home, and who didn't spit up, soil diapers, or throw toys.

Pat, on the other hand, was one of five children born to parents for whom clutter was life. She grew up feeling comfortable with dishes in the sink, babies screaming, and toys scattered on the floor. Although the neatness issue had always created sparks between her and David, she had managed to keep things on shelves and in closets until Andrea was born nine months earlier. With two children of her own, two more to sit, and a baby on the way, she was finding it increasingly difficult to have perfect children in a perfect apartment and still look attractive herself. Besides, housework was an insult. At first she had accepted it as part of the fine print of "I do." But when she couldn't keep up with the endless chores, and David complained without so much as stooping to pick up a toy, she began to show her resentment. On days when she felt especially harried or bushed, she wouldn't even try to keep up the illusion of a perfect home. If David wanted one so badly, he'd simply have to help. Or learn to put up with the mess.

The previous week, Pat knew, had almost driven David mad. Her parents had left town for a few days, and she had agreed to look after her teenage sister and ten-year-old brother, along with babysitting Karen and Michael. That gave her six children and a husband to worry about. She knew David would be unhappy with the added commotion, but she had had no choice. She couldn't turn her parents down after all they had done for her, and she and David needed the twenty dollars a week babysitting money. Pat felt the tension building between her and David all that week. It was the ironing board, however, that brought things to a head.

David had walked through the door after work one evening to the usual baby bottles in the sink and toys on the floor. Andrea was crying in the playpen as she had been doing for much of that noisy week, and the ironing board was still up between the living room and the dining area. Overwhelmed with housework, Pat had either forgotten to take it down or had left it up in unconscious protest, she couldn't say which. The clothes she had already ironed were folded and piled on the couch. In the basket on the floor sat the things that still needed ironing. On a doorknob hung David's freshly pressed shirts which had first been starched, then put in the freezer until she was ready to press them. David took one look around and walked back out the door. He returned later that night when the apartment was quiet and neat.

If only she had taken the time to fold the ironing board! Pat felt a stab of guilt as sharp as a labor pain. As usual, the guilt quickly turned to panic. Any thought of losing David left her numb. Without him to define her, she seemed to have no sense of herself. He had hinted he might take a month's furlough from the marriage to think things over, and she had even found a stack of apartment brochures he hadn't bothered to hide. But he had never talked about permanent separation, thank God. David loved Christine too much to do that. She had always been his "buddy." When he washed the car, she'd stand next to him with a little rag. When he went out, she'd beg to go along, clinging to his pants leg.

On top of it all, Pat felt so unattractive these days. Five feet four inches tall, with light blue eyes and shoulder-length blonde hair flipped up at the ends, she had a slim, hourglass figure and, even four months pregnant, weighed only 120 pounds. But now that she was showing, she felt undesirable. When she had begun to thicken with Christine and Andrea, David seemed to lose interest in her. Maybe that was why he spent last night in a motel, Pat thought. Maybe her body disgusted him.

Or maybe it was the business about college. Pat had been pushing David to get a degree ever since they married. She was determined to do everything she could, even go back to work, to give him a chance to get an education and better their lives. At Lejeune, they had taken courses in English and history and had studied together in the evenings. She found it fulfilling, fun even. When David got his discharge, she had suggested they move to Greenville and finish college together at East Carolina University on the GI Bill. But David had decided to move to Miami instead. It was a big disappointment for her; she could not understand his lack of interest in school.

Turning it over in her mind now, Pat realized that college was her ambition, not David's. Perhaps being pushed had bothered him more than she realized.

Then there was the matter of intimacy. Pat was a toucher whose eyes couldn't hide her emotions. David, on the other hand, rarely said how he felt. During their courtship, he had always found it easier to express his feelings in letters than face to face.

She had met him at his going-away party in January 1963. She was eighteen, a senior in an all-girl Catholic high school and so shy, she blushed at the slightest provocation. Pat liked David immediately. Nineteen and on his way to Marine Corps boot camp, he was tall, muscular, and meticulously dressed. He wouldn't dance with anyone else at the party and didn't want her to either. Never having had a real boyfriend before, she enjoyed feeling like the only girl in the room. At the Catholic mixers she had gone to, she had grown used to boys passing her by. She knew she had a good figure but thought her face was plain. A boy's wolf whistle would startle her; she was sure that if he saw her close up, he'd walk the other way.

David changed all that in one night. He asked her out and afterward kissed her goodnight. Their two-year courtship was a blend of love letters and occasional dates during his home leaves. The dates were fun, the letters warm and intimate. Pat married the David who wrote letters.

Once married, David seemed to slide into a pattern of emotional coolness. He disliked being fussed over and would frequently withdraw into himself. Pat often attributed his aloofness to his mother's decision to send him to his aunt to raise when he was two years old. Why she had given only him away and not his sister seemed to bother him.

Now, waiting on the front stoop, Pat grew more anxious by the hour. Before she knew it, it was lunchtime, and one by one the women began to drift away. Pat brought the four children back inside and fed them. At nap time she put Karen and Michael in the double bed, Andrea in her crib, then lay down next to Christine. While Christine slept, Pat usually dozed, but this afternoon she was too edgy to rest; she dreaded David's return yet wished he would hurry. As soon as Christine's breathing grew heavy, Pat slipped out of bed, grabbed a basket of dirty diapers, and raced to the laundry room in the basement before someone else beat her to the washers.

At four o'clock, Karen and Michael's father picked them up, and Pat began to prepare dinner. She loved baking pies and breads and experimenting with new recipes. The kitchen, with its Pepto Bismol-pink refrigerator, stove, and countertops, was the only place she had felt creative lately. Normally, she had the table set and dinner waiting when David walked in; the ritual was important to her. When Pat was a child, her father had worked two jobs and never came home for supper on weeknights. Having missed that family tradition herself, she now insisted on it for her daughters.

Lately though, David had been coming home at such unpredictable hours. She peeled the potatoes, washed the vegetables, and trimmed and seasoned the meat. Then she dressed Christine. Although Pat always made her older daughter look pretty for her father, today she took special care. She put Christine in a frilly red-and-white gingham dress and pinned her long, reddish-orange hair back with red barrettes. Then she brought Christine and Andrea outside to play with the other children.

After a week of record-breaking heat and humidity, it was an unusually pleasant August afternoon. Pat and Andrea joined the other women on a blanket under the maple while Christine waited for her father's car to turn the corner and pull up in front of the stoop. As soon as she saw the car, she would run down the sidewalk shouting, "Daddy! Daddy!" It was a beautiful moment and Pat always looked forward to it.

But not that afternoon. No matter how much she tried, Pat found it impossible to shake a sense of impending doom. None of the problems in their marriage was insurmountable, she argued to herself. Once the baby was born, she wouldn't be so tired and listless; her stomach would be flat again, and she'd exercise to tone her muscles. She would work harder at keeping the place neat for David, and in return, perhaps, he would be just a little more tolerant when she failed. If she was too clinging, she would learn to be more restrained, and maybe David would try to be more expressive. If he didn't want college, she wouldn't push him. And once the new baby was old enough, she would go back to work if he felt overwhelmed by the responsibility of three children.

When David pulled in just after six, Christine jumped off her tricycle and ran to him. Without so much as a glance at his daughter, he walked straight into the apartment building. He didn't seem angry or in a hurry. Pat picked up Andrea, grabbed Christine by the hand, and followed. By the time she reached the apartment, David was already emptying his closet, holding as many hangers as he could in his left hand.

Pat watched in resignation. There was nothing to say. When his arms were full, David walked back out to the car and returned for another load. On his second trip, Pat snatched his car keys from the dining-room table and rushed across the hall to the apartment of her friend Lorraine, who was also pregnant.

"He's leaving," Pat said. She wasn't surprised he was going, but she was furious at the way he was doing it. No explanation. No word where he was going or how long he intended to stay away. "He's taking his clothes. I'm going to keep his keys so he can't go."

"Don't, Pat!" Lorraine advised. "Don't do that. Give him the keys and let him go. You can't hold on to someone by force."

Pat went back to her apartment, put the keys on the table, and watched David empty his dresser drawer. The apartment seemed as still as a grave. Pat wasn't crying, David didn't look angry or sad, Andrea was sitting in the playpen, and Christine was watching her father pack with the same curiosity as she would watch him polish the car. David seemed cool, methodical, almost as if he were packing for a business trip.

Pat felt too defeated and worthless even to try wringing an

explanation from him. If she asked, she knew she would get upset, the kids would cry, and she would not get a straight answer anyway.

After his fourth trip to the car, David didn't come back. Numb and in shock, Pat called her mother.

3

>>>>>>>>>>>>>> "David left," Pat told her mother. She wasn't crying or shaking. She was just imparting information with a matter-of-factness that surprised even her. "He took his clothes. I guess he was fed up. I'm sure he'll be back in a couple of days. What do you think I should do?"

Pat's mother had opposed her marrying David. Twenty was too young to begin a family, especially for a girl so naïve and impressionable. She herself had never regretted waiting until she was twenty-six before settling down. And she didn't like her daughter's choice of an enlisted man with no trade or education to fall back on. When Pat had called her mother from Bermuda, while visiting David, and said he wanted to marry her then and there, Pat's mother had tried to talk her into waiting until David got a discharge and a decent job.

"Come home and give it a rest," she had advised. "If you still want to marry him after that, your father and I will give you a church wedding with all the trimmings."

Caught between David and her mother and confused, Pat chose to listen to her mother. But she had had to face David's anger; he wouldn't even drive her to the airport. Three months and a dozen letters later, Pat dropped forty-four quarters into a pay phone to talk to David for three minutes. Afraid she might lose him if she didn't agree to marry immediately, Pat told him she had changed her mind. He said he'd be home in two weeks. Pat's mother was not happy with her daughter's decision, especially since she had only one semester left in her two-year course at Immaculata College in Washington. But realizing she couldn't stop her, she gave Pat her blessing and her written consent.

When, after three years, her daughter brought the children

back to northern Virginia, Pat's mother thought the marriage was dead. Pat's reunion with David three months later left her skeptical. She had seen enough of men to know that once they walked out, they frequently kept right on going. And David, she sensed, was the walking kind.

This time, when she got Pat's call, she spoke her mind. "Get yourself a lawyer, Patsy. In the meantime, don't worry. Your daddy isn't going to leave you and the babies without."

Her mother's words made Pat realize the corner she was in. It was almost David's payday, time to do the heavy shopping. There was no milk in the refrigerator, she was nearly out of baby food, she didn't have a car, and the only store within walking distance was McDonald's. She and David had about fifty dollars in their joint checking account.

The more she thought about Andrea and Christine, the more Pat worried. If only David had left some money or promised to give her some on payday or see to it that the rent was paid. But he had said nothing; he had just left her dangling. Although she had no reason to doubt that he would take care of her and the children, especially now that she was pregnant, she didn't know how or when.

Pat put the girls to bed, waited until they were asleep, then joined Lorraine on the front stoop, feeling guilty and depressed. The evening was growing pleasantly cool and the maple leaves fluttered in a gentle breeze. Other women were inside with their husbands. Lorraine's was still at work.

"You're better off without him," Lorraine said. Gentle but firm, she told Pat the truth she didn't want to hear. "If he gets whatever it is out of his system, he might come back. If not . . . you don't need him."

Pat had looked up to Lorraine from the first day she moved into Fairmont Gardens. Slender and striking, Lorraine had the poise and self-confidence Pat lacked. Pat said little, convinced her new neighbor would think she was dull. But Lorraine found Pat bright and warm with a good sense of humor. They quickly became close friends.

Although she knew Lorraine was right, Pat couldn't bear the thought of losing David. Alone in the apartment later that evening, she convinced herself he'd be back. In a few days, he'll walk through the door, arms full of groceries as if nothing had happened, she told herself as she waited for sleep. "You look pretty," he'd say. "I missed you."

Anxious to look her best when he did come back, Pat went to the Fairmont Gardens beauty parlor the next morning for a haircut and a permanent. A twenty-five-dollar extravagance, she thought as she wrote out the check—more than a week's babysitting money—but worth it. She needed to face David with confidence, not feeling fat and beaten. Later in the day, her father dropped in with bags of groceries and baby food. Although she was grateful, Pat was embarrassed and felt a flash of anger. But guilt quickly smothered it. Her father was working two jobs to support her mother, brother, and sister. Now he had to take care of a grown daughter whose husband had decided to take a vacation from fatherhood.

Although David didn't come back that first day or the next, Pat's check did. The beauty parlor called to say it had bounced: insufficient funds. Instead of being angry at David, Pat felt ashamed. How could she tell the beautician that her husband had cleaned out their checking account and left her and two children without even enough money to wash and dry a load of diapers?

Too humiliated to call on her father again, Pat phoned Father Finley, associate pastor at Saint Michael's Church, where she had gone to grade school and where she and David had been married. It was beginning to dawn on her that she might be in worse trouble than she had imagined. If David planned to stay away for only a few days, why had he cleaned out the checking account just before payday?

Like her mother, the priest was practical. "See an attorney right away," he advised. "I suggest Phil Brophy. He's a good Catholic."

Pat was relieved to hear the priest mention an attorney. The thought of David *not* coming back had begun to creep into her mind at unguarded moments. She didn't know the church's position on legal separation, or how to go about getting one. Religion was one of her few comforts, and she didn't want to lose that too. As a child, she had prayed the rosary daily; at Camp Lejeune she frequently went to Mass and Communion during the week, and she still confessed weekly. Even though the president of Immaculata had asked her to return her school ring and had refused to let her complete the last semester of her two-year course of studies because she had gotten married, Pat had not allowed the narrow-mindedness of one nun to shake her faith.

With no idea what an attorney would advise or what he would charge, Pat could not have done better than Philip Brophy. The father of thirteen who wasn't embarrassed to drive to court in a clunker, he was so outraged at Pat's story that he took her case for twenty-five dollars.

"You have a problem," Brophy told her. "You're broke and have no income. It may be some time before your husband pays child support. What are you going to live on in the meantime?"

Recognizing that Pat was in a state of shock, Brophy told her exactly what to do. Her problem wasn't new and he told her the same thing he had told many women before. "First, move back in with your parents," he said. "Second, go out to the Juvenile and Domestic Relations Court in Fairfax and sign a petition for child support. Third, go to the county services office and apply for welfare."

Brophy's words shook the fear right out of Pat. Welfare? She didn't need welfare. David would send her money. After all, he was the father of their children. They were his responsibility and he knew it. Move back in with her parents? Never! To live with them again would be to admit total failure as a wife and mother. She would not give up what little independence she had and become a burden to them.

"In the meantime," Brophy continued. "I'll see if your husband has an attorney. Maybe we can speed things up and settle the dollars and cents out of court."

Eight days after David walked out, Pat went to the Juvenile and Domestic Relations Court wearing her prettiest maternity dress and feeling like a criminal. The counselor who helped her file a two-page petition for child support sensed her guilt.

"You're different from most of the women who come in here," he told her. "I can tell you're going to make it. Don't ever forget that. You're smart. And with those beautiful blue eyes of yours, you'll find someone."

Pat cried for the first time since David had left. The

counselor's words had pierced the armor of her shock. She couldn't believe she was actually asking the law to order her husband to pay money to feed their children. But the counselor had also told her she was smart and pretty when she felt naïve and undesirable. His words were a comfort she would summon again and again during the next few months.

If Pat felt degraded asking the court for help, it was nothing like taking a number and waiting in the welfare office. No one in her family, whose history she had traced back to the 1700s, had ever received charity or public assistance even if it had meant working two jobs as her father did. She was the first on the dole. And after spending almost two years in college with women who had moved on to careers or comfortable marriages. What would her classmates think if they saw her now? She stared at the floor, convinced that everyone in the waiting room was looking at her. Finally a clerk called her number.

Her ordeal had been for nothing. The welfare counselor told her she didn't qualify for public assistance because she had not lived in Virginia a full year.

"But I've lived here most of my life," Pat objected.

"You left the state," the counselor explained. "And you've been back less than a year. You'll have to wait three more months until mid-January. We'll do all the paperwork today. Then, as soon as you fulfill the Virginia residency requirement, you'll begin receiving your checks."

The prospect of court-ordered support, welfare, and food stamps left Pat more depressed than the thought of life without a husband. Her family's pride didn't help matters. Her mother resented the fact that Pat would even consider taking public assistance. She and her husband had always taken care of their own and always would. "Daddy will support you," she told Pat. There was an edge of anger to her voice. "We don't want you on welfare."

Philip Brophy moved as if Pat were his most important client. And to him, she was. She had young children who needed help, and it had already been three weeks since her husband walked out. He got a subpoena for David to appear in court so a judge could determine the amount of child support he'd have to pay. David immediately hired an attorney and agreed to settle out of court. Delighted with the news, Brophy called Pat.

It was Christine's second birthday and there were so many kids laughing and shouting in the apartment that Pat had a hard time hearing Brophy. She had gone out of her way to make the day special for Christine, who missed her father and had been crying constantly. When Christine played on the front lawn, she frequently ran up to parked cars, calling in her small voice, "Daddy! Daddy!" as if she expected the door to swing open and her father to step out. When Christine's loss became too painful to watch, Pat took her to a pediatrician, Dr. Carl Hanfling, who said, "Even though Christine's only two, she can understand the truth. So you might as well tell it to her." Pat took his advice, and whenever Christine cried for her father, Pat simply explained that Daddy wouldn't be coming home for a while. Now, momentarily caught up in the excitement of birthday cake, ice cream, and Kool Aid, Christine looked happy.

"David's agreed to half his paycheck," Brophy said. "That's ninety-nine dollars and eleven cents every two weeks. If you agree, I'll ask the court to write up an order."

The news made Pat lighthearted, almost happy. Although Christine was too young to understand, her father had just given her a wonderful birthday present. Half of David's salary seemed so generous; still, Pat wished that he made more than $396 a month. Her rent came to $142.50. That would leave her with $1.86 a day for food, clothes, and medical expenses. And she had no idea when David would come back. One month? Three? Well, however long he needed to think things through, she would survive and be waiting.

With babysitting money, she calculated, she could make it until early January when she would begin getting welfare to supplement David's child-support payments, if necessary. If her parents were humiliated by her receiving public assistance, well, they would simply have to swallow their pride. The new baby was due in late January. Pat figured that by mid-March, when the baby was six weeks old, she could get a job and drop off the dole. If the plan worked, all she had to do was grit her teeth for six more months at most. Back on her feet, she'd repay her parents every single dime they were giving her for food and rent. Philip Brophy had already agreed to accept a dollar a month until she had paid his twenty-five-dollar fee. She began to feel a sense of hope again. The court counselor was right. She'd make it.

The Juvenile and Domestic Relations Court accepted the settlement, ordering David to make his first payment by October 3, in effect giving him a free month. It also scheduled a hearing on December 30 to review Pat's case. But before October 3 came, Pat got a phone call from the Beneficial Finance Company demanding that she repay her $461 loan and threatening to repossess her new furniture.

"What loan?" Pat asked. "What new furniture?"

4

>>>>>>>>>>>>> Pat learned that after she left him in Miami nine months earlier, David had taken out a $745 loan in her name—for furniture.

Pat was so angry when the skip-chaser read her the loan application that she could hardly talk. It was one thing for David to clean out their checking account to buy time to think. But sticking her with a forged loan! How stupid did he think she was? The more she allowed herself to feel her anger, the more frightened of it she became. Sensing it would consume her if she let it, she quickly slammed a lid down over the feeling.

Pat knew where David worked but not where he was living. Concerned that she might get him in trouble if she called his office, she decided to ask his best friend, Bill Daniels, where David was staying. It was Bill who had thrown David's going-away party, where Pat had first met David.

Since Bill didn't have a phone, Pat called his mother, who lived next door to him. "Do you know where David is?" she asked. "He left me with the girls . . . and I'm pregnant."

"Yes, indeedy, I know where he is," Bill's mother said. It sounded as if she was speaking through clenched teeth. "Livin' right next door with my Billy. . . . You just forget David, you hear? I brought up six kids on a waitress salary. You kin do it, too."

"I only want to talk to him," Pat said.

"Well, if you must . . . I'll go and call 'im."

Bill's mother got back on the line a few minutes later. "He won't come to the phone," she said in disgust. "He says he don't want to talk to you."

Pat had left David alone for three weeks while she lived on charity. She had been willing to give him time, even to wait until October 3 for rent and food money. But getting stuck with a forged loan—when she had to borrow change just to use the washer and dryer—was the last straw.

That evening Pat asked Lorraine to drive her to Bill's house. She didn't dare ask her father, for fear he'd cause a scene.

"Don't go," Lorraine warned Pat. She knew that if Pat was torn between anger and love, her seeing David was a bad idea, loan or no loan. She could only get hurt more deeply. "Let him be."

"I can't," Pat said.

Parked next to Bill's car was a new white Chevy Nova Supersport that said David all over it. Pat's anger blew like an oil well. David had taken the few dollars they shared out of their checking account, he had walked out just before payday, he had left her without enough money even for milk, he had stuck her with an unpaid loan that amounted to more than three months' rent—and now he had bought himself a new car! His monthly payments had to be more than half of the court-ordered child support he owed.

Bill Daniels met Pat at the back door and saw the fire in her eyes. "Hi, Pat," he said sheepishly. "I guess I'm in the middle."

"I guess you are! Where is he?" Hearing the threatening tone in her voice, Bill stepped aside.

David drove Pat back to the apartment in his new car as calmly as if he were taking her home after a date. Pleased just to have him at her side like old times, Pat had buried her anger once again under a fragile feeling of security. When they got to the apartment and put the children to bed, they chatted. In spite of the reassuring words, a sadness filled the room.

David said he'd be back soon. She didn't want him to come home for the wrong reasons, did she? In the meantime, she and the girls wouldn't starve; her parents would see to that. The new car? Well, he had no choice, the old one died. She shouldn't worry about the loan, he'd handle it.

David took a few bills from his wallet, laid them on the table, and headed for the door. Pat counted the money: sixty-five dollars. Her warmth for David boiled into hot anger. She'd

be damned if he could turn his back on her! He'd bought a
new car that must be costing at least one hundred dollars a
month and he'd given her sixty-five dollars for the children as
if he were the most generous father in the world!

Pat ran after David shouting, "Sixty-five dollars! What the
hell is that? You're not going to get away with this."

Catching up with him, Pat grabbed David by the shoulder
and tried to swing him around. When he shrugged her away,
she tore his shirt, then ran past him and turned to face him.
Six months pregnant and afraid, Pat directed her anger into
her bare right foot. She kicked David hard in the shins. She
wanted to hurt him, make him cry out in pain, watch him walk
away limping—anything just so he'd react to her.

But it was Pat who let out a yelp, and David walked away
without a word. She spent the next two weeks on crutches with
a sprained ankle. When mid-October rolled by and she still
had not received any court-ordered support, Philip Brophy
called Associates Finance, where David worked. He had been
fired. No forwarding address.

Things were now bleaker than ever. Pat lapsed into a
depression so severe she thought she might be having a nervous
breakdown. Her marriage appeared to be over, and she felt
she was to blame because she had failed to keep the family
together. She had little to offer her daughters now but love.
Among her many anxieties, she worried about getting to the
hospital to have her baby, even though her father had assured
her he would be on call day and night. She slept fitfully, and
when she finally drifted off late at night, it was with a prayer
that she would never wake up.

The end of October came and went. No child support.
Likewise, Thanksgiving. At the end of November, Philip Brophy asked the court to subpoena David to explain why he had
failed to support Christine and Andrea for eight weeks. The
court issued the subpoena, but the sheriff was unable to serve
it. He couldn't find David. Bill had asked David to move out
and Pat didn't know where he was living or working.

David's foster mother apparently did. She invited Pat and
her granddaughters over for Christmas, saying David would
be there.

It never crossed Pat's mind to tell the sheriff where David would be celebrating the holiday. She could hardly have her children's father arrested during Christmas dinner.

Pat was tempted to stay home herself. She was sick with the flu and hated the thought of watching her mother-in-law shield David. The baby was due in a month and she felt as big as a house. She hadn't had money to get her hair done for the holidays and was depressed after spending Christmas Eve with two children and no husband. It was her twenty-third birthday; the next day would be her and David's fourth wedding anniversary. And as much as she wished it weren't so, she still loved him.

When Pat walked into her in-laws' home, she knew it was a terrible mistake. David was already there, trim and relaxed in an expensive three-piece suit, his white Nova parked outside. He spent the afternoon sipping bourbon and eating ham and turkey as if he hadn't a care in the world. If he knew the sheriff was after him, he didn't show it. He gave Christine and Andrea huge stuffed elephants, which they loved. Their mother had only given them clothes and plastic toys.

All Christmas Day Pat felt defeated and helpless. She was in David's family home, watching his foster mother dote on him. Everyone at dinner, it seemed, was on his side. She felt too depressed to cry. She realized David had a hold on her she couldn't shake. Away from him, she could think of things to say, feelings to express, demands to make. Around him, she faded into a shadow.

Soon after Christmas, Pat started getting phone calls from a repossessor working for the company that had financed David's new Chevy. He had missed so many payments that the company wanted the car back, but it couldn't find him. Did she know where David was living or working?

Pat told the repossessor she knew nothing and why. "If you find him, will you let me or the sheriff know?" she asked. She wanted David to feel the pinch of the law and to hear the court lecture him. "The judge wants to talk to him, too."

On January 14, the repossessor called again. "I found him," he said.

"You did? Where?"

Pat was excited. If David was arrested and forced to face

the judge, maybe he would learn that failing to support one's children was a matter the courts took seriously. More than that, Pat wanted David to experience the same humiliation and fear she was feeling. He had made her suffer; now she wanted to see him squirm. As her attorney had told her, "A month on the road gang in the middle of July would do him a world of good." She not only believed it, she prayed for it without the slightest trace of guilt. The law, not she, would punish him.

"He's working at Victory Van Lines in Alexandria," the repossessor said.

"What are you going to do?" Pat asked.

"Repossess the car."

"Not so fast," Pat said. "Someone should notify the sheriff."

"I have to tell the police I'm taking the car so I don't get arrested for stealing," the repossessor said. "I'll make sure the sheriff is there."

"Let me know?" Pat asked.

"As soon as it's over."

Late afternoon the next day, Pat got the call. "He's been arrested," the repossessor said. He went on to explain what had happened.

The repossessor had waited for the police across the street from Victory Van Lines. The sheriff had pulled up in a marked car and had gone in. Shortly afterward he had come out with David and handcuffed him. The sheriff had fished David's car keys out of his pocket and handed them to the repossessor, who unlocked the Nova, got in, and leisurely drove off.

"He was standing there in cuffs," the repossessor said. "He looked shocked to death—and he couldn't do a damn thing. It was great."

Pat felt a sweet revenge as she listened. There was only one thing David loved more than himself—his car. To take it was to cut off a leg. Good! It was about time he got a taste of what helplessness felt like. Convinced that the law had finally scared responsibility into him, Pat was sure things would be different. She was wrong.

David's foster mother paid the five-hundred-dollar bond and bailed him out of jail that evening. The next day, the judge sentenced him to ten days in jail for contempt, suspending all but two days. Victory Van Lines fired him. When he got out of the county jail, his foster mother was waiting for him with another car.

Pat dreamed of a hundred ways to get even. Slash his tires. Steal his false teeth. Hound him. Too weak to confront him directly, she phoned the mother of the teenager he was dating— the girl had signed credit card slips using David and Pat's card. She told the teenager's mother that David was married and had two children with a third due any day. She knew she was being bitchy, but she didn't care. The woman promised to keep her daughter from seeing David again. Then Pat turned all her pent-up anger on her mother-in-law. She told David's foster mother she was low class. She had spoiled David and made him the kind of father and husband he was. It was all her fault; she was as irresponsible as he was. She had hidden him from the law as if it were some kind of game, then bailed him out of jail, where he belonged, and bought him another car. She had rewarded him for deserting his children. After all that, how could she expect Pat to keep bringing Christine and Andrea over to visit!

Three days after David got out of jail in January of 1969, his third child was born. It was Richard Nixon's inauguration day, and by late afternoon the streets and sidewalks were slick with ice. Pat's parents came over to her apartment for dinner. Her mother had been helping with the cooking and cleaning for weeks. At four that afternoon, Pat began to feel labor pains even though the baby was not due for two more weeks. Her parents took her by the elbows, walked her down the icy sidewalk to their car, and drove her to her obstetrician's office. After examining her, Dr. Russell May sent her to Fairfax General Hospital. "I'll be there shortly," he said.

Pat was in labor for four hours and Dr. May spent every minute of them at her bedside, holding her hand. When he wasn't talking to her gently, he was reading a magazine, turning the pages awkwardly with his free hand.

"We talked about an anesthetic before," he told Pat at one point. During one of her checkups, he had suggested an epidural, a spinal injection. "Is that what you want?"

"How much will it cost?" Pat asked.

Although her limited insurance would cover 80 percent of

the hospital bill, it would not pay for the anesthetic or for Dr. May's fee, which came to $210. He had agreed to accept five dollars a month until she paid it off. Since she was paying another dollar a month to her attorney, Pat was concerned about getting too deeply into debt.

"I don't know, but I think around seventy dollars," Dr. May said. He seemed surprised she had asked.

"I think I'll do without."

Because she had been given an anesthetic when Christine and Andrea were born, Pat didn't realize what she was letting herself in for. She had never read anything about natural childbirth nor had she taken any classes. When the hard pains began, she changed her mind as fast as she had made it up.

"I'll take the shot," she told Dr. May.

"It's too late," he told her. "The baby's almost here."

Pat watched her baby being born in the big overhead mirror. She never knew anything could be so painful and beautiful at the same time. If she hadn't been so poor, she thought when the pain stopped, she would have missed the whole thing.

"It's another girl," Dr. May told her. He put the unwashed infant on her stomach. Pat started to laugh and couldn't stop. She felt relief that it was all over. That her daughter was normal.

A nurse wheeled Pat into the hallway where two other women who had just given birth lay on gurneys. Their husbands were at their sides, smiling and attentive. Seeing their pride and love, Pat began to cry. Even with her mother nearby, she felt alone and abandoned.

Pat dozed off. When she opened her eyes David was standing there. Convinced he had come only to humiliate and hurt her, she quickly turned her face to the wall.

"I went down to the nursery to see her," David said. "She's the healthiest-looking one. What are you going to call her?"

Pat was surprised he wanted to know. When she had seen him on Christmas Day, she had asked what he wanted to call the baby, since he had chosen both Christine's and Andrea's names. He had told her then that if she wanted a name, she should go to the phone book and pick one. It was a cruel thing to say and it had struck her with all the brutality of an ice pick.

"Marcia Ann," she said to the wall.

It seemed David had come just to spoil a special night. Pat realized he was the last person she wanted with her. He was Marcia's deserter, not her father.

"What are you doing here anyway?" she demanded. David didn't have to see her face to know she was angry. "You didn't stick around while I was carrying her. Now you want to see what she looks like. Well, you don't have a right to be here—I want you to go!"

When Pat finally stopped crying and got settled in the recovery room, a nurse came by and picked up her chart. "Oh, I see you're separated," she said. "Are you going to keep the baby?"

The nurse said "separated" as if it were a dirty word, something Pat had done that was wrong. How could anyone think she would give up Marcia after all they had already gone through together? Almost nine months of suffering and worry, fear and anger.

"Keep her?" Pat said. "Of course I'm going to *keep* her. She's my baby."

5

>>>>>>>>>>>>>> Early in 1969, Pat began receiving $249 a
month from Aid to Dependent Children. David's $198-a-month
child support was to go directly to the court, which would then
reimburse the state. Pat would never see it. Besides the monthly
check, she also got sixteen dollars' worth of free food stamps.
As long as David paid the court, Pat figured she was actually
accepting only sixty-seven dollars a month in public assistance.
If she could just swallow her pride for a few more weeks, she
was sure she could find a job as a medical secretary and make
more than welfare was paying her.

But if welfare was humiliating, Pat found the food-stamp
system utterly degrading. Soon after getting out of the hospital,
she began combining trips to the supermarket in a borrowed
car with visits to her doctor or bank. Wearing makeup and her
best dress was the only way she could face the world outside
Fairmont Gardens with dignity. If she didn't preserve her
pride, she was afraid she'd slip deeper into dependency. With
three children and no husband or job, it was her only hedge.

But Pat quickly learned that the nicer she looked in the
supermarket line, the nastier the cashiers became when she
pulled out food stamps to pay her bill. They would eye her
from head to toe, then say, "Boy, that must be nice!"

In a way, Pat couldn't blame them for being hostile. She
was young, well dressed, and looked healthy. If they had to
work behind a checkout counter, why couldn't she do the
same? Grocery shopping became a weekly humiliation. In the
supermarket Pat would say over and over, "For my children,
for my children." Finally, she stopped dressing up and took
Christine, Andrea, and Marcia shopping with her. Although
she still got dirty looks, she heard fewer unkind remarks.

The supermarket experience made her even more determined to get off welfare before she became so demoralized she could no longer fight back. David's walking out that way had all but destroyed her self-confidence as a woman and mother. Food stamps robbed her of her last shred of dignity.

As Pat saw it, she had only two choices—get back together with David, whom she still loved in spite of everything, or go to work. She tried David first. She phoned David's foster mother, asking her to have David call. When he did, she invited him to the apartment, no strings attached. Pat made it a point not to tell her parents or friends what she was doing because she knew they would get angry and try to talk her out of it. Every time she broke down in tears and said, "But I love him," they would say, "Any man who would do that to you once will do it again!"

At the apartment David seemed kind and friendly, but he didn't want to talk about coming back to live. When Pat asked if he was paying child support to the court, he said he was, but her question seemed to make him suspicious.

"Do you get those payments?" he asked.

"No," she said. "They go from the court to the welfare office."

"So you never even see them?"

Pat knew she had said the wrong thing and could almost hear him thinking, Why should I pay, if she doesn't get the money?

Then David started blaming Pat. If he was a delinquent father, he said, it was her fault. She had made Victory Van Lines fire him. What did she expect when she had him arrested in front of his boss? How could he pay if he was in jail? How could he work if she had his car repossessed? But in spite of her meddling, he said, he had found another job in the finance business. Feeling beaten and guilty, Pat didn't press him to tell her where he was now working.

Just before he left, David went into the bedroom and took the model car set he kept under their bed. As she watched him pack it up, Pat knew he wouldn't be coming back. He picked up Christine, gave her a big hug and kiss, and let her have a sip of his ginger ale. Then he put her to bed and walked out for good.

———

Pat went job hunting. Although she preferred to stay home with the children, she needed to become independent and useful as soon as possible. Comforted somewhat by the thought that she could find a good sitter in Fairmont Gardens, Pat set up an interview with the personnel director at Fairfax General Hospital, where there were openings for medical secretaries and transcribers.

The director seemed impressed by Pat's qualifications. But from there on, it was downhill.

"I note on your application you have children," he said. "What are their birth dates?

"What does your husband do?

"I see. . . . Who will take care of them when you're at work?

"Well, what if they get sick?

"I see. . . . I'm sorry, but we have no openings at this time."

Pat drove home close to tears. She got the message. Who wanted to hire a single mother of three, two of whom were still babies? Not sure what to do and discouraged that it was already March and she didn't have a decent job, she called the Juvenile and Domestic Relations Court to make sure David was paying his child support.

David had made only two of his twelve payments to date, she learned, and the court wanted to talk to him but couldn't find him. Pat felt another surge of rage, and this time she was in no hurry to bury it. Counting food stamps, she had actually been receiving $265 a month in public assistance, not $67 as she had thought. She wasn't going to put up with that for one more day. If the sheriff couldn't find David, she would. And when she did, she'd turn him in faster than he could say "run."

Recalling that David had said he was working for a finance company, Pat drafted her friend Lorraine, whose voice David would not recognize. She flipped through the *Yellow Pages* to "Finance Companies." "You might as well start at the top of the list," she told Lorraine. "Ask to speak to David. If it's him on the line, hang up. If it's not, wait and see if he works there."

Pleased that Pat was looking for David not to get back together with him but to make him pay, Lorraine was glad to play sleuth. And it didn't take her long to score. When she called Credit Recovery and asked for David by name, the receptionist said, "One moment please." Lorraine slammed down the receiver, grinning. "Nothing to it," she said.

Now that Pat knew where David worked, she called Bill Daniels to ask where David lived. Bill had always been a friend she could count on. Since David had left, she spoke to him nearly every night for emotional support. Warm and understanding, he listened without telling her, as everyone else did, to forget about David.

It wasn't just revenge she wanted, Pat told Bill. It was important for her dignity that David pay child support. She knew where he was working. Did Bill know where he was staying?

Pat could tell from the sheepish, almost guilty tone in Bill's voice that he knew, but his loyalty toward David was standing in the way. Sensing that if she got mad, Bill might clam up completely, she played a game she was very good at. "Please, Bill," she said in her best little-girl voice. "It's important."

Bill wavered, then compromised. He said he and David had had dinner recently in a Mexican restaurant near David's apartment, but he would say no more. If he thought he was protecting David while pacifying Pat, Bill had miscalculated. He had offered her a challenge, and she grabbed it. Knowing which bus Bill took to work each day, Pat borrowed a car and drove the entire route looking for a Mexican restaurant. She eventually found one not far from a bus stop and two apartment buildings. Not wanting to meet David in an apartment lobby or risk having the desk clerk say a blonde woman was looking for him, she called Bill back.

"I know where David is staying," she bluffed.

"You do? How did you—Where?"

Choosing the apartment building that looked like it would suit David best, she said, "In the Duchess Gardens."

"Well, I'll be damned." Bill was impressed. First, Pat had chased a lead and found out where David was working. Now she had followed a hint and traced him to his apartment. "What are you going to do now?"

"Call Phil Brophy."

Brophy told the court where David was working and living. It issued another subpoena for him to appear before the bench on April 14 and show cause why he should not be punished for failing to pay the more than one thousand dollars in support he owed his children. The sheriff went to Credit Recovery to serve him. David wasn't there. The sheriff said he'd be back later that day. When the sheriff returned, David was gone again. Not surprisingly, no one at Credit Recovery could say where he had gone or when he might be back. Later that night, the sheriff rapped on David's door in the Duchess Gardens apartments, but David's roommate said he had just moved out. No forwarding address.

When David failed to show up in court on April 14, the judge issued a warrant for his arrest. Pat did not take the news calmly. She was convinced the sheriff had allowed David to slip away, and she couldn't understand why. Deserting one's children was a crime in Virginia. Yet the sheriff, who had taken an oath to uphold the law, had done everything but make an appointment for David's arrest. Having pinned her hopes for justice on the court and the law, Pat was devastated.

Although her parents and friends were convinced that David was finally gone for good and glad of it, Pat was not. She gave the law one more chance and reported David as a missing person to the Fairfax County Police, which sent an officer to interview her. While she told her story and answered his questions, the officer took notes. She gave him a picture of David, and he promised to file a missing-person report and send out an alert. Pat grew uneasy, however, when the same officer came back to her apartment several times to ask the same questions. After he made a pass at her, she gave up on the Fairfax County Police. The officer had not filed a single report, she learned later.

About a month after David had disappeared, Pat got a phone call from one of his friends, who had received a postcard from David from somewhere in the Midwest, saying he was on his way to California. Pat finally admitted to herself that David would not be coming back for a long time, if ever, and that she had better do what everyone had been advising—plan a life without him.

The first step, she knew, was to figure out a way to get off welfare. Although she didn't consider herself poor, she knew she ran the risk of becoming permanently dependent. She had read somewhere that poverty is an acid that eats away pride until all pride is gone. She believed that. Welfare was only a fragile lifejacket. She either had to use it to help herself swim to shore or spend her life bobbing in the sea, looking for rescuers who would never come. The longer she waited to swim, the weaker she would become.

The first step was to break David's hold on her life. Although he had apparently run so far away that she doubted she would ever see him again, he still controlled her feelings and, in some vague way, cast a shadow on her future. Having abandoned his children, he nevertheless continued to sap vital energy that she and they needed to survive. The only way to deal with him was to bury her anger and her ache for justice as deep as she could under her determination to make it on her own. The pain of those feelings stood in the way of her future. She couldn't afford to use up any energy now on David.

It also became clear to Pat that as long as Marcia and Andrea were babies, she'd never get a job that paid more than welfare paid. And once the children started school, Pat knew, her expenses would go up. That meant she would need an even better paying job to support them without public assistance. The best, and maybe the only, way to ensure a decent job with a future was more education—her ticket out of the welfare ghetto. While her children were growing up, she could go back to school and take courses in business, maybe finish her second year of college. That ought to give her an edge in the job market.

Instead of encouraging and supporting her, Pat's welfare case officer all but killed her enthusiasm. None of the mothers he counseled had ever asked to go to college, he told her. He wasn't sure his supervisor would approve it. All he could promise was to pitch it as hard as he could.

Pat was stunned. She had come up with a way to get off welfare permanently, to save the taxpayers money while regaining her pride and dignity, and her counselor wasn't sure his supervisor would allow it. She could have wept with frustration. Having three young children limited where, when, and how long she could work. This in turn meant she was confined to a childlike dependence on her own parents. Was there anything about her life she could still control?

The social worker returned the following week with a grin.

No one in the welfare department, he said, knew of any recipient in the state who had asked to go to college; therefore, there was no policy. But the department had decided to make hers a test case. Although it would not raise her monthly allowance to help her, it would permit her to go to school as long as she did not use welfare money for books or tuition. She'd have to get a full scholarship and student aid through the normal channels. If he could help her with references, of course, he'd be happy to.

Pat was too pleased to be discouraged. Welfare's permission to go to school was the first positive thing that had happened to her since David walked out. Wasting no time, she targeted George Mason University, part of Virginia's state college system. It was close to Fairmont Gardens and it was new, so it was still trying to build its student body. Pat applied for a scholarship to cover tuition for the first five-week session of summer school and financial aid to help with books and gas. Intrigued by the idea of setting a precedent for welfare recipients, the university granted the scholarship and helped her get a federal student-poverty grant. The school further recognized most of her credits from Immaculata and East Carolina, which amounted to more than one and a half years of college. Pat's father bought her an old Dodge Dart. She hired her sister, Maureen, who was still in high school, to babysit for fifteen dollars a week, with payments spread over twelve months.

Pat's routine was punishing. Up at six each morning to feed and dress Christine, Andrea, and Marcia, she would leave for school by half past seven for an eight o'clock class. At half past twelve she would get home in time to join the other mothers and kids out front for a half hour. Then there was a midafternoon nap with the children, a visit on the stoop, and another meal for the kids at six. She would begin studying at eight, put the girls to bed at nine, and study until midnight. Often she would wake up in the middle of the night to Marcia's crying. Then she would rock her back to sleep, worried about how her youngest would survive knowing her father had abandoned her. If she was lucky, she would catch a few hours' sleep before she was up again at six.

Sometimes Lorraine would watch the children after dinner

so Pat could have an extra hour with the books and get to bed earlier. But long before the summer session was over, Pat had ugly bags under her eyes. She was convinced she would flunk out. David's walkout had destroyed her confidence on every level. She felt stupid, unattractive, and worthless. And she began to doubt that she was a good mother. School was stealing time from her daughters. Smart enough to recognize their competition, the girls would sit on her books to get more attention.

Pat was torn. She felt guilty, especially about Marcia who was only five months old. She had held and rocked both Christine and Andrea a lot when they were small, but as a student she had less time for Marcia. On the other hand, more study and better grades would lead to a better job, which would help her and her daughters in the long run. Caught between guilt and her determination to get off welfare, she found herself snapping and yelling at the girls and relieved when Lorraine would take them off her hands.

Sometimes the gnawings of guilt almost drove her to quit school. All she had ever wanted was to be a good wife and mother. She had already failed at the one and was beginning to fail at the other. Was she just being selfish? Was she merely using school to distract her from her problems and give her a sense of control over her life? Then Pat would remember standing in the supermarket line with food stamps; she would remember waiting for her number to come up in the welfare office; she would remember the handouts from her parents. Better the guilt than the shame. At least the guilt would buy a future for her children. The shame was worthless.

If the routine was killing and the guilt painful, school itself was confusing. She couldn't shake thinking of herself as a loser: a college dropout, a wife without a husband, a mother with three fatherless children, a medical secretary without a job, a ward of the county. She was afraid of failing again. What would happen to her plan for independence if she flunked? How could she face the future if she lost her one hope?

Pat also discovered she was angry at men, and George Mason was full of them. They were the enemy she couldn't trust, each a potential David. Equating closeness with dependency, she didn't want to risk getting involved. Never again

would she give a man control over the tiniest piece of her life—
she would support herself and her children alone. At the same
time, however, Pat felt lonely and hungered for sharing and
tenderness.

Moreover, Pat was different from her classmates. Most of
them had either just graduated from high school or were just
back from Vietnam. She felt like a curiosity item. A mother on
welfare going to college? Some students and teachers resented
her. She was abusing the taxpayers' money, they told her to
her face. If she could find time to go to school, she could find
time to work. Why wasn't she home taking care of her kids?
What kind of mother was she?

She felt isolated and confused. Although she didn't wear
rags or panhandle on street corners, she knew she could easily
slide into permanent poverty and degradation. That fear
haunted her. She was certain her classmates were aware she
had only three outfits, which she carefully rotated. She quickly
learned to skip meals; she couldn't afford them. Saying she
wasn't hungry, she'd have only a cup of coffee or a piece of
pie. A few friendly classmates encouraged her not to give up,
helped her with homework, loaned her books, even teased her
until she blushed. She was afraid to let them become real
friends, however, because she had no time to socialize. School
and children were all she could manage.

Back at Fairmont Gardens, Pat often felt sad. School had
changed her relationship with the women there. Before, her
apartment had been a neighborhood social center. She had
organized an informal morning exercise class for three or four
women in her living room. In the evenings, one or two women
would stop in to chat. But once Pat started school, the exercise
classes ended and she told her friends not to visit at night
because she had to study.

When her grades came in the mail, Pat was afraid to look,
certain she had failed. Her classmates were brighter and had
more time to study. They would push her to the bottom of the
grading curve. When she finally ripped open the envelope, the
two Bs shocked her. Maybe she wasn't as stupid as she thought.
Maybe she should take a second summer session while she still
had the courage. It would only be for five weeks.

By the time she finished summer school, Pat was exhausted.

But it had been worth it. She had gained confidence and felt ready to try the job market once again. Employers should find it harder to turn her down, given her two years of college. Even if she did have three children.

Before she could fill out her first job application and get on with her life, however, Pat got news of David.

6

>>>>>>>>>>>>>> Pat and Lorraine had just finished putting the girls to bed and cleaning up after Christine's third birthday party. Christine in particular had been flushed with excitement and difficult to get in bed, so when the phone rang, Pat grabbed it before it could wake anybody up. The call was from David's foster mother. In tears she told Pat she had just gotten a call from a man in Atlanta. She didn't know who he was and hadn't thought to ask his name. He said David had been killed in a plane crash.

It had been five months since David had disappeared, and in spite of her demanding schedule and her resolve to erase him from her mind, Pat still thought of him often. Where was he? What was he doing? How did he feel? Did he ever think about her and his daughters? She thought she still loved him, even though she knew he had fled the state. She had received two Mobil credit card receipts—one from Gainesville, Virginia, the "gateway west," issued the day the sheriff had tried to arrest him, and one from Kansas.

By the time she hung up the receiver, Pat was shaking. Then she began to cry uncontrollably. "He's dead," she kept telling Lorraine. "He's dead. All those rotten things I said about him. Now he's—"

Once she calmed down, Pat began calling every airport in and around Atlanta. That he might have been in a fatal plane crash didn't strike her as odd. Maybe he had finally passed his flight test in the Midwest and had gotten a job as a pilot. But when no one, including the Federal Aviation Administration, could tell her anything, Pat concluded that the phone call to David's foster mother had been a hoax. She felt relieved, for as long as David was alive, he might come back. She still could not accept the fact that he would abandon her and his children forever. Nor could she admit that David might have perpetrated the hoax himself. He would never be so cruel as to fake his own death on Christine's birthday.

Faced with an unrelated but important decision in her own life, Pat soon stopped worrying about the bogus plane crash. One of her George Mason classmates had suggested that she try school full-time in the fall, just for one semester to see what it was like.

After a good start, Pat was torn. Her summer grades had only been average. However, they proved that she could at least pass and meet the demands of single motherhood at the same time. But she was also sure that she had managed to limp through summer school only because she could tell herself the session would be over after five weeks. But five courses for five months? Now that her sister was back in high school, Pat couldn't afford a sitter. And if she managed to hire one and the welfare department found out, it could cut her off. No welfare money for school—that was the deal.

On the other hand, Pat knew she had to begin living her own life and preparing for an independent future. As long as she was on welfare, every monthly check would have David's face printed on it. She knew she'd find a job if she looked for one, but she wanted more than a job—she wanted a real life for herself and her children, not just existence without welfare. She wanted a career.

Pat's next-door neighbor Joan made up her mind for her. Joan had four children and worked from four until midnight. She agreed to watch Andrea and Marcia from eight in the morning until three in the afternoon. In turn, Pat agreed to sit Joan's children from three until ten at night, when Joan's husband would pick them up. That meant minding and feeding seven kids after class for seven hours every day while still trying to find time to study. It also meant finding a place during the day for Christine, who was so active that no one wanted to sit her. If Pat was going to attend school, she would have to send Christine to a day-care center.

Too ashamed to ask her parents for more help, Pat called her parish priest, Father Finley, who had been supportive ever since David left. She needed seventy-five dollars to send Christine to nursery school for one semester, she said. Could Saint

Michael's parish help? Her parents had been contributing to the church weekly for more than fifteen years, and she'd pay the money back someday.

Although Father Finley was eager to help, the pastor was not. He called Pat's mother. "Why should the church pay?" he scolded her. "Can't you take care of your own daughter?" Reluctantly, Pat accepted another loan from her parents for Christine's day-care. George Mason awarded her a scholarship and a student loan and secured another federal grant.

Pat decided to major in business and planned to look for a job in hospital administration after semester exams in January. The semester turned out to be even more difficult than she had anticipated. She left for school before eight and returned home at three. When she wasn't in class, she was studying in the library. To concentrate on her books at home, she taught herself to tune the children out. But when she did, she felt she was neglecting them. Between these emotions and the seven kids for seven hours every day, she was drained to the point of exhaustion.

When her grades came in the mail in January 1970, however, Pat knew she could do it. She had passed all five courses, even though there had been days when she couldn't find time to study for tests she was not prepared to take. Although she still didn't feel as bright as her classmates, she felt for the first time that it might be *possible* to graduate. She signed up for another semester—then for both summer sessions. By the end of the summer of 1970, a year and a half after David had run away, she had completed her third year of college. Graduation was no longer just a dream.

Although still distrustful of men, Pat felt the edges of her anger blunted. Men were flirting with her, and she began to think of herself as attractive. When a fellow student asked her for a date, she was surprised—and thrilled. It was her first night out in almost a year. Her date brought her home, ripped her blouse, and tried to rape her. Shocked and mortified, she cried for days. Then she began feeling guilty, as if the attack was her fault, just like David's leaving.

Months passed before Pat could bring herself to date again. The second time, the man was gentle and loving. He and Pat began seeing more and more of each other until he suggested serious involvement. Pat balked. She could manage her family and school, she told him, but nothing more for the time being. He stopped calling.

Her responsibilities were not the only reason Pat refused to get involved after David ran away. She was afraid that a serious relationship would make her dependent again. With three children to support, she wanted to become so self-reliant that she would never have to trust a man with her life again. She was determined to allow nothing to stand in the way of her education and her independence—not even loneliness. If it meant living like a nun until she graduated and got a job, then that's what she would do.

The only way Pat could go back for her final year of college, in the fall of 1970, was to find a better babysitting arrangement. The thought of another year of coming home from school and caring for seven children was overwhelming. Fortunately, the Welfare Department softened and agreed to give her the same day-care assistance it offered working mothers. Her happiness lasted until she visited the center chosen for Christine, Andrea, and Marcia. It was in an airless church basement—a smelly place, ugly and depressing. It offered no classes and no playground. What's more, almost every child in the cramped school was a welfare kid. She had worked hard to protect her children from the indignities of a monthly welfare check and food stamps, and subjecting them to the "welfare brat" label was something she would not tolerate.

Pat began visiting nearby day-care centers until she found Annandale Springfield Country Day School, a real school with real teachers. The children there wore clean, attractive uniforms; they sang, studied French, danced, looked healthy. Pat told Welfare she wanted her daughters to go there. When the department refused, she recruited the school's director, Jinks Roach, to help her. They pleaded, argued, and won.

Soon a school bus was picking up the girls each morning before Pat left for her first class; they returned at five-thirty in the evening, an arrangement that gave her two whole hours of uninterrupted study after classes. To her surprise, she was feeling no guilt at leaving them. Christine, no longer the cheerful, smiling child she had been before her father ran away, had become a withdrawn and moody four-year-old at home and around adults. At school with children her own age, she seemed happier. In fact, she liked Annandale Springfield so much that she bounced up the bus steps each morning and didn't want to come home in the evening. Christine's aloofness with adults seemed to be her way of saying, "I don't trust grown-ups. I loved my father and look what happened."

Three-year-old Andrea, on the other hand, didn't want to leave her mother or the apartment, the only place she seemed to feel safe. She would cry when Pat put her on the bus, but once at school she created few problems and played quietly— mostly alone. It was as if Andrea were saying, "The only person I can count on is me."

Marcia, almost two, also fought school. She didn't want to get up on school mornings, resisted getting dressed, and began crying even before Pat put her on the bus. As soon as she got to school, she would roll down her gray knee socks, pull her blouse out of her skirt, and muss up her hair. She spent most of the day playing with boys. Marcia didn't seem to like who she was. At times Pat even felt that Marcia wished she were a boy.

One of Pat's courses at George Mason that fall of 1970 was federal taxation. Her teacher invited an Internal Revenue Service recruiter to speak to the class. The IRS sounded so exciting that Pat applied for a job as either a grade-five tax auditor, which paid just under seven thousand dollars a year or, if she was lucky, a grade-seven revenue agent, at just over nine thousand dollars. The IRS seemed ideal. It was as stable as the government itself and offered an almost unlimited opportunity for growth. A grade seven would get her off welfare immediately and for good. Besides, she liked people; accounting was her favorite subject; and she had a natural aptitude for investigative work. She went in for an interview dressed in a new brown suit her mother had bought her, then waited anxiously to hear the results.

Pat's goals for her final semester of college that began in February 1971 were ambitious, even for her. She planned to take the CPA exam immediately after graduation in June. The certificate would help her advance more quickly at the IRS, if they hired her, and she was certain they would. To qualify for the exam, however, she needed three more credits in accounting. Since George Mason didn't have the course she needed, she decided to enroll at the University of Virginia extension in her area. That meant taking eighteen credits instead of the usual fifteen. Pat was sure she could handle the work—after all, it was only for one semester. She would simply make herself do it because the CPA certificate would guarantee her daughters and her a better future.

To take the extra course, however, Pat needed permission from her accounting professor at George Mason. On a cold, icy February day, Pat made her way to his office to explain how important the CPA certificate was for her.

"Plain stupid," the professor said, refusing permission. "A full load here is more than you can handle."

The refusal meant that, to qualify for the exam, Pat would have to go to night school after graduation while holding a full-time job and caring for three children. She seriously doubted that she and her daughters could take that much punishment. But the harder she pleaded, the more stupid she felt and the more her self-confidence began to waver. By the time she left his office, she was quaking with anger and doubt. The man had no right to say that, she told herself. And he called himself a teacher. He was supposed to encourage her dreams, not kill them. "Stupid" was what David had called her.

"If that ignorant man thinks he can get away with this, he's in for one hell of a surprise. I'll go over his head—I'll fight him all the way to the top if I have to. I'm not going to let a sparrow-brained professor tucked away in the business department of some little school stop me!"

Pat was in tears as she drove to her parents' home to pick up the children. As she turned off the busy road into her parents' driveway, still furious at her humiliation, a tractor trailer behind her skidded on a patch of ice, and slammed her car into the front yard. While Christine, Andrea, and Marcia watched from their grandparents' window, paramedics arrived, lifted Pat into an ambulance and drove off, red lights flashing and sirens screaming.

7

>>>>>>>>>>>>>> Pat was bedridden for three weeks, in constant pain, and on medication. Fortunately, her mother was able to help with the children. When she finally returned to school, she was behind in all her courses and still in a great deal of pain. Four of her five professors allowed her to make up homework and tests, but her accounting teacher refused, giving her an F for whatever she had missed. Mixed with the bitter, however, was a sweet piece of news. The IRS had hired her as a tax auditor, grade five. Her salary would be less than seven thousand dollars a year and she would still need some public assistance until she got a promotion, but at least she had a career waiting as soon as she finished school.

Graduation on June 6, 1971, offered no special thrill. Pat was too exhausted to feel proud. Still disappointed that she hadn't made grade-seven revenue agent, she began work the next day without even a weekend to rest. She was anxious about her new job and wondered how much time and energy she'd have left for the girls after a full day in the office.

But Pat could be happy about one thing: she was beginning her new life debt-free. At six dollars a month, she had finally paid Dr. May and Phil Brophy. And her four thousand dollars of insurance money from the truck accident had repaid her parents, cleaned up a backlog of small bills, and bought some new clothes for work. Now, at the age of twenty-five, she was ready to begin a new life, a little over two years after David had walked out. The final step was to get off welfare completely.

The day after graduation Pat began a six-week IRS training course in Baltimore. The service arranged for all students to stay in a motel near the school, but Pat decided to commute so she wouldn't be away from the children. The routine was worse than school had ever been. Up at four-thirty or five each morning, she would drive an hour to suburban Maryland to catch the train to Baltimore, get home by seven-thirty or eight, and play with the children until bedtime. Her friend Vi usually brought over some dinner. "Just a few leftovers," she'd say.

Pat discovered that her course in taxation law at George Mason had pushed her ahead of most of her IRS classmates. It was fortunate, for she slept through a good part of those six weeks. The teachers, who knew her circumstances, were firm but understanding. When they awakened her with a question, she would ask them to repeat it. They would do so with patience and a suppressed smile, but she had enough correct answers to get her through the course comfortably.

Pat's grade-five take-home pay was $315.46 every month, or 46 cents more than she was getting from Fairfax County. The Welfare Department decided that since her expenses had increased now that she was working, it would supplement her IRS income by $58.50 a month. It also continued to pay for day-care for Christine, Andrea, and Marcia. Pat's first welfare check in July after she had received her IRS paycheck was $157 too much. With a great sense of satisfaction, she returned the money. She didn't want one penny more than she needed; what she wanted was the raise that would get her off the dole forever.

As an IRS auditor, Pat interviewed taxpayers to see if they owed the government money. It was a stressful position and the attrition rate was high. Still shy, at first she had so little confidence and blushed so easily that red blotches appeared on her neck. To cover them, she usually wore high-necked blouses. Exemption cases for women became her favorites. Having lived on welfare and stretched dollars herself, she had a special understanding of poor women. When a single mother said she had spent nothing on clothes all year, Pat knew she was probably telling the truth.

Eight months after Pat started working for the IRS, the service promoted her to revenue agent. Four months after that, she advanced to grade seven. Although she was still eligible for some public assistance after her two-thousand-dollar-a-year raise, she asked to be removed from the welfare

rolls. It was one of the proudest days of her life. She had made
it. She was free.

Finally independent and with a promising future, Pat felt
she was now ready for a relationship. In 1972, one year after
she began working for the IRS and three years after David
had disappeared, Pat divorced David and married an IRS
attorney, Eugene Bennett. She changed her children's names
to his. Twelve years older than she and with a son from a
previous marriage, Gene Bennett had what she wanted most
from a mate at that point in her life—stability and a sense of
responsibility. Soon after her wedding, however, Pat began to
realize that her strongest motive in marrying Gene was to
provide a father for her girls.

As hard as she tried to keep David pinned in the past, he
kept intruding on her marriage. Besides the bogus airplane
crash, she had heard about him again in 1970 while she was
still in school. She and the girls were visiting David's foster
mother as they frequently did. Even though Pat hadn't quite
forgiven the woman for shielding David, she knew that David's
running away without a word had hurt her deeply. Besides,
she was still the girls' grandmother and they loved visiting her.

The phone rang while they were sitting in the living room
sipping coffee. David's foster mother went into the bedroom
to answer it. When she returned, her face was white and she
was shaking. "Patsy, Patsy," she said, "pick up the phone.
There's someone who says she knows David."

Her name was Lenora Parker. She was calling from Dallas
and spoke with a lilting Southern accent. The woman told Pat
she was married to a Jim Parker, whom she believed to be
David. She said she had married him in November of the
previous year—seven months after he had abandoned Pat and
his children.

Jim Parker had walked out on her two weeks ago, she said.
It was a total shock. While poring over the papers he left
behind, she had found the name of his sister in Miami who,
she knew, had married a doctor. She located the doctor through
directory assistance. He had given her the phone number of
David's foster parents.

Pat was trembling. When she steadied herself enough to

speak, she and Lenora compared notes—height, weight, face, appendix scar, bridgework, voice, habits. There was no doubt that David and Jim Parker were the same person. Since David was still married to Pat, he was a bigamist.

Pat and Lenora both started crying. Pat felt sorry for the woman and so angry at David she wanted to kick him again. Knowing exactly what Lenora was going through, she tried to console the woman as best she could. After promising to send Pat a copy of her marriage certificate, Lenora hung up.

The next few weeks were traumatic for Pat. Her conversation with Lenora Parker had opened old wounds and revived both good and bad memories. She couldn't help but wonder again where David was, what he was doing, and why he had left the way he did. She called the FBI, hoping it would be able to find him. She explained to an FBI agent who interviewed her that David was a runaway father and a bigamist, wanted for contempt of a court order to pay child support. She asked the agent to file a missing-persons report. She was convinced that he was hiding in another city, probably married to another woman. Personally sympathetic but professionally uninterested, the agent told her that David would be on the bureau's active list of missing persons for four years. If his fingerprints turned up anywhere, the bureau would notify her.

To Pat, it sounded like a bureaucratic brush-off. Maybe the FBI would find him, probably not. If it did, she would deal with David then. In the meantime, she was not about to spend another dime or expend another ounce of energy looking for him. Pat assumed David had adopted a new identity and moved to yet another city, and she returned her attention to her children, school, and career.

But David still lurked in the shadows of Pat's life. She sought his face in every crowd, scanning the streets for a tall man with David's distinctive gait. And she would turn her head as cars passed, looking for a tall man behind the wheel. Despite years of intense, repressed anger, she found herself confused, with tender feelings and gentle memories welling within her.

Eight years passed. In 1978 the FBI was still insisting that David's name had never flashed up on its missing-persons computer. And in all that time his foster mother—once very close to him—heard nothing. Like everyone else, Pat now concluded David was dead. On that presumption, she applied to the Social Security Administration for death benefits for Christine, Andrea, and Marcia. As far as Pat could calculate, those benefits would amount to nearly seventy thousand dollars by the time Marcia turned eighteen.

When it comes to presumption of death, however, Pat found the Social Security Administration as cautious as the Kremlin. The SSA denied her request, arguing that before it would pay, Pat would have to prove David was "unexplainably unheard of" for seven years. From six sworn statements, a Social Security claims representative concluded that David had good reason to disappear and then hide: he didn't want to pay child support, and since he had changed his name and committed bigamy, he was afraid of arrest.

Her request denied, Pat asked for a reconsideration. Two years after she had first applied and without any further investigation, a second claims representative reviewed her case and upheld the denial. Pat then requested a hearing before an administrative law judge. While preparing for the hearing, she studied decisions on similar presumption-of-death cases and could not find a single instance in which an original decision, reconsidered and upheld, had been reversed by an administrative law judge. Concluding that it would be wiser to leave her file open, in case incontrovertible proof of David's death was found, Pat withdrew her request for a hearing.

Initially, Pat felt somewhat at peace because at least she had done everything she could to settle David's official and legal status.

But far from laying David to rest, she had created a new uncertainty and ambivalence that began troubling her sleep in a recurring dream: There'd be a knock at the door. She'd open it dressed in an evening gown. It would be David. She'd invite him inside and they'd sit at the kitchen table. She had been four months pregnant when he ran away, and her hair had lost its sheen. But in her dream she'd be slim, her hair full and shiny. When he ran away, a baby was crying and there were toys, diapers, and baby bottles all over the small apartment. In her dream, the large house would be empty, spotless, and quiet. He would seem surprised, as if he expected a bedraggled woman in a tiny cluttered place.

"Where have you been?" she'd ask without bitterness or anger.

"I can't tell you," he'd say.

"What have you been doing all these years?" she'd ask.

"I can't tell you."

He'd try to hide how impressed he was by her looks and the elegance of her house, but she'd know he was thinking, How did I ever leave her?

In her dream she'd feel his desertion had been her fault— that he had run away because she wasn't perfect, hoping to prove that she'd never make it without him. So she'd feel a sense of forgiveness toward him. But she'd also be firm, silently telling him with her eyes, "Yes, I know, but you can't have what you see. I don't need you anymore. I'm happy now and I want you to know it."

She'd wake from the dream feeling somewhat satisfied; she had shown him how well she had done without him, and he had understood. But ultimately the dream raised more questions for Pat than it resolved. Why did she feel forgiving and not consumed with anger? What *was* he doing all those years? Why wouldn't he tell her?

The longer Pat was married to Gene Bennett, the longer David's shadow became. Her relationship to Gene, they both recognized, rested in part on an unreasonable but very real fear of abandonment and an exaggerated need for independence and control. Woven into the fabric of their commitment was a foreboding that Gene might run away as David had. As a protection, Pat always held back a piece of herself. She decided to continue working just in case Gene left. And when she finally talked herself into quitting her job so she could spend more time with her daughters, it didn't last. A year later, she was back at work. She felt too dependent and insecure without a job.

Gene was quick to recognize how destructively David haunted his marriage. "I'm not going to pay for *his* sins," he'd tell Pat. After ten years of marriage and two years of counseling, they separated by mutual agreement. They remained friends.

The year after the separation Pat received a master's degree in business administration from Marymount College in suburban Washington and was promoted to grade thirteen at the IRS. Pat at last felt free of fear. But a sense of sadness pervaded her freedom. Her daughters had learned to love Gene as a father, and now, thirteen years after their abandonment, they were fatherless once more.

Part Two

>>>>>>>>>>>>>>>>>>>>

The Search

8

>>>>>>>>>>>>> The summer of 1984 began with promise. The scars of Pat's separation from Gene had healed and David's memory faded like an almost-forgotten nightmare. But beneath the welcome peace, Pat felt a vague, persistent tug to face and resolve her past. Perhaps some people could live comfortably surrounded by questions and doubts. She could not. As an accountant, she liked tidy ledgers.

Pat knew part of the problem was David. Although she did not allow herself to feel angry at him and never talked about the abandonment, she was still stung by curiosity. She had heard nothing from or about him for fourteen years. Was he dead or alive? Was he hiding under another assumed name in another city, married to still another woman?

The state of Virginia had officially declared David dead at the request of his foster mother, and his insurance company had paid the woman over eleven thousand dollars in death benefits without even challenging the state. Hoping to lay her own doubts to rest, Pat refiled her petition with the Social Security Administration. If the FBI couldn't solve the dead-or-alive question once and for all, maybe SSA would.

For a second time the Social Security Administration denied both her request and reconsideration. As far as it was concerned, Pat decided, David was alive until she mailed in his jawbone. She appealed the decision again on the slim hope that an impartial hearing judge would give more weight to the new facts than the claims representatives had. In many ways, the hearing had become a symbol, the last step in her journey to bury David emotionally and psychologically. If she lost the appeal that summer as she expected, then so be it. She could at least officially declare David dead in her own mind.

Three weeks before the hearing, the IRS sent Pat to San

Francisco to help the Western Regional Office evaluate its accounting procedures. She planned her free time carefully. While in San Francisco, she would look up her cousin Joe, whose whereabouts she had discovered only recently after twenty-three years, and Cheryl, an old classmate from Immaculata College. On the way home and at her own expense, she would stop in Salt Lake City to see Vi, an old friend from Fairmont Gardens, and then touch down in Denver to visit Arlene, her closest friend during her difficult year in Miami.

Even though she had seen her older cousin Joe only one week each summer during the family's annual vacation in Indianapolis, he had been tremendously important to her. Unlike her teachers and classmates, Joe had always accepted her as an equal and a friend, caring enough to listen as she chattered about her feelings and dreams. He didn't seem to think she was unattractive even though she did, and he seemed to like her just as she was. The week with Joe during summer vacations loomed so large that for the first six months after she returned from Indianapolis each year, she'd replay it in bed each night. Come January, she'd begin spinning dreams for the summer ahead.

After the death of Pat's grandparents, her aunt stopped speaking to her mother and the visits with her cousin suddenly ended. She never heard from or saw Joe again. The petty behavior of grown-ups contesting her grandfather's will had driven a wedge between them. As she grew older and discovered how rare were friendships such as Joe's and hers, Pat buried her loss deep inside. Now, after twenty-three years, Joe was a piece of unfinished business, another man who had meant a great deal to Pat and then suddenly disappeared.

With an irrational fear gnawing at her, she dialed Joe's home from her hotel room in San Francisco. His wife answered. "He'll be so pleased to hear from you, Pat," she said. "Call him at the office. Here's the number."

"Would you warn him I'll be calling?" Pat asked. In spite of the reassurance, she was afraid that he might hang up on her, or pause in embarrassment because he couldn't remember her, or tell her he was too busy to talk. This way, if he didn't want to see her, he could let her down easily. She didn't think she could bear rejection from the man who, in her mind, was still the boy who had accepted her, listened to her, and cared about her.

She recognized his voice immediately. "Did your wife tell you I was going to call?"

"Yes, she did, Patsy. Where are you? It's so *good* to hear from you again."

She didn't try to stop the tears of relief. "In San Francisco . . . Do you really remember me, Joe?"

"Of course I remember you. The last I heard, you were married to a Marine."

Joe called her back so she wouldn't run up a huge phone bill. They talked for over an hour with Pat doing most of the talking. Feelings and stories poured out as if it were another summer visit. "I needed to talk to you so much over those years," she said.

"Well, I'm here now and we'll never be separated again," he said. She could tell he meant it.

That evening, Pat rode the subway down the bay to Daly City and climbed the escalator, looking for gray slacks and a blue blazer. Joe was standing at the top—she could have picked him out anywhere. He hugged her and she said through her tears, "It wasn't fair. It just wasn't fair."

They talked through most of the night, long after Joe's wife went to bed, bringing each other up to date about family and children. Talking to him still gave Pat a deep feeling of calm: the twenty-three years fell away easily. As she said good-bye the next morning, she felt like the child who left Indianapolis each summer. She clung to Joe and the security he represented, as if she had a premonition that a storm lay ahead.

The night before she left San Francisco, Pat did the town with Cheryl. Back at Pat's hotel later that night, the conversation drifted to Immaculata and to how devastated Pat had been when the college expelled her for marrying David and demanded that she return her class ring. Pat told Cheryl she had finally figured out why the school had punished her. The nuns assumed she had married David during the Christmas break because she was pregnant, and they didn't want the evidence of her sin showing in their school. Recently, Pat had written the new president of Immaculata explaining what had hap-

pened and why. The nun wrote her a touching letter of apology
and enclosed a new black onyx school ring engraved with her
initials. The return of her ring dissolved the last traces of
bitterness toward the school.

"Remember," Cheryl asked, "when I stopped you after class
and asked what it felt like to lose your virginity? And your face
turned as red as the Sacred Heart?" They both laughed.

"What ever happened to David?" Cheryl asked.

Pat told her how he had changed his name to Jim Parker
after he abandoned her and her daughters and how he had
married Lenora. She hadn't heard a whisper about him in
fourteen years, she said, and had concluded he was dead. The
state of Virginia had declared him dead and she was asking
the Social Security Administration to do the same.

"Well, I don't think he's dead," Cheryl said.

Her reply left Pat shaken. Everyone she had talked to about
David so far had agreed he must be dead. But Cheryl argued
like an SSA claims representative, and coming from her friend,
the logic was more convincing.

The way Cheryl saw it, David had a good reason to run
and an even better one to hide once he had. Why should he
risk everything by calling or writing his foster mother, who
had already collected life insurance money? Wouldn't it be to
his advantage if everyone, especially the woman who raised
him, actually believed he was really dead?

"You just may be right," Pat finally admitted. And with her
admission, her old doubts returned like a toothache.

Pat left San Francisco for Utah, her link with Immaculata
renewed and the twenty-three-year-old silence between her
and Joe finally broken. But the fourteen-year-old problem of
David festered unresolved.

Pat's old friend Vi was waiting for her at the airport in Salt
Lake City. Along with Lorraine, Vi had watched the girls at
night so that Pat could study for her courses at George Mason.
Pat and Vi lunched at the Snow Bird ski resort above the city
and talked and laughed about the old days in Fairmont
Gardens. It was Vi who had first advised Pat to apply to the
Social Security Administration for death benefits for her daughters. To the practical Vi, it was immaterial whether David was
actually dead or alive. No one had heard from him for fourteen

years, so in all the important ways, he *was* dead. Let the
bureaucrats take it from there.

Meeting Vi and remembering, even laughing about, those
nightmarish years reminded Pat of something she tended to
forget: if pressed, she could be tough, and when the time came
to fight or bear pain, she always managed to find inner
resources. She left Salt Lake City for Denver, and Arlene,
asking herself, "Does it really make any difference whether
David is dead or alive? Shouldn't I just take the money and
run if I can get it? Shouldn't I, in effect, bury David alive?"

Arlene had never liked David and couldn't understand why
Pat put up with him. Like Lorraine, she believed David had
done his wife a favor when he ran away. And like Cheryl, she
was convinced that David was still alive, probably doing to
another woman what he had done to Pat.

Yet in spite of her dislike for David, which she did not try
to hide, Arlene stirred up emotions and memories Pat did not
want to face: all those happy times before there was any hint
of trouble. The tiny apartment in Lejeune, studying history
together then making love, her long-awaited pregnancy, the
birth of Christine—tender feelings washed over Pat. She had
loved David so much and still loved him the day he walked
out. How could she reconcile her feelings when the man who
had given her so much happiness was the same man who had
abandoned her? Love and anger wrestled, but neither won.

On the flight from Denver back to Washington, exhausted
from emotion and from lack of sleep, Pat was overwhelmed
by what had happened in four short days. For years she had
been afraid to face the past and suffer again, but on this trip
she had found that pain remembered is often a healing salve.

Pat came home determined to face it all—herself, her
feelings toward David, and her anger at what he had done to
her and her daughters. Legally defining him—dead or alive—
was the first simple step, and her Social Security Administration
hearing suddenly took on new meaning.

9

>>>>>>>>>>>>> Back in Washington it took Pat only a few minutes from her lunch hour to photocopy the seventy-one pages in David's Social Security Administration file. As she fed the copier, she glanced at each page. Along with the documents she herself had submitted, there were five affidavits, including the one that she was itching to read—Bill's. From what she had already learned, Bill's sworn statement more than anything had convinced the claims representatives that David was probably still alive.

Her curiosity smoldering, Pat fidgeted throughout the IRS reception she had to attend that afternoon. When the speeches began, she slipped back to her office. She had half an hour to read the affidavits before the rest of the staff returned. Pat barely glanced at her mother's; she already knew what was in it: a statement claiming David had to be dead because he had made no attempt to contact those closest to him, his foster parents. David's foster mother's affidavit did not surprise Pat either: he must be dead because normally, he either came home once a month or wrote or called when he couldn't. His sister's statement held no revelations: if David was alive, he would have no reason to hide from his family.

But the affidavit of David's *real* mother was as puzzling as the others had been predictable. She had a "feeling" he wasn't dead, his real mother wrote, and no idea why he wouldn't reveal his whereabouts. He was an insurance salesman, and she had not seen or heard from him since July 1968, when he had run away.

What puzzled Pat was that David had never sold insurance before or during their marriage. Was his real mother confused, or did she know something she didn't want to talk about? The more Pat studied the standard two-page form, sloppily written and filled with minor inaccuracies, the more she questioned it. Maybe David's real mother hadn't heard *from* her son after he ran away, but it sure sounded as if she might have heard *about* him.

Pat saved Bill's affidavit until last. If the sworn statement of David's real mother puzzled her, Bill's angered her. David was dead, Bill had written, but if he wasn't, he was hiding to "avoid child support and alimony."

Why the hell didn't Bill just argue one way or the other? Either he thought David was dead or he thought he was alive—not both at the same time. No wonder the Social Security Administration had denied the claim. If David's closest friend had agreed with everyone else that David must be dead because he hadn't tried to contact family or friends, the issue would have been settled years ago. Bill was taking David's side again. The good old boy network was still alive and well.

Pat found it difficult to concentrate on IRS business that afternoon; new questions arose and her anger toward Bill simmered. Where did David's mother get that insurance sales- man idea, and why was she so convinced her son wasn't dead? What would Pat find in David's file if she began looking for clues suggesting he was *alive* instead of dead?

Too curious even to change her clothes when she got home that evening, Pat kicked off her shoes and spread the file out on the kitchen table. Trying to be the objective IRS revenue agent, she began analyzing the SSA summary reports.

Evidence in support of the "dead" theory: David's foster parents had not heard from him since he disappeared. But of course, they stood to gain over eleven thousand dollars in insurance money if he was declared dead. Also, David's fin- gerprints had not turned up on the FBI computer, meaning he had not been arrested and police had not found his prints at the scene of a serious crime.

Evidence in support of the "alive" theory: It would be in David's best interest to hide. As Bill had pointed out, David was anxious to avoid child support. His only reasons for surfacing would be to meet his daughters, to talk to his foster parents, or to stop running.

Next, Pat studied the affidavits. Everyone, including her, agreed on two key points—David had had no previous history of disappearing, and he had always kept in touch with his family. That the family had not heard from him in sixteen years seemed to suggest he was dead. But there was a huge hole in that argument. If David hadn't felt the need to contact family or friends between 1968, when he ran away, and 1970, when Lenora had called and confirmed David was alive, why would he do so later on? He had changed his name and covered his trail like an escaped convict. Would loneliness or guilt or curiosity be strong enough motives to drive him above ground? Or was it more logical to assume that his behavior had remained consistent and that he was still hiding somewhere with a new name and a new wife?

Included in the Social Security investigative file was a copy of Lenora's marriage certificate to James Clinton Parker, which Pat had already seen. Lenora had sent her a copy fourteen years ago and she hadn't really looked at it since. The SSA file document was in fact a copy Pat had submitted when she first applied for death benefits.

As she studied the certificate, it struck her as odd that Social Security had never bothered to ask Lenora for a sworn statement. After all, she was David's "wife" and the last person known to have seen him alive. Pat had assumed that SSA claims representatives or FBI agents had interviewed the woman. She had always felt that if David was still alive, his real mother and Lenora would be the two people to know, not his foster mother, who saw her granddaughters regularly and could let slip that she had heard from their father.

Pat also found it strange that there was nothing in the file to suggest that SSA had searched for James Clinton Parker on its computer. If he wasn't currently listed as a Social Security contributor, wouldn't that be an important fact to note? And if he was in their computer, couldn't a claims representative easily determine if he was the same man Lenora had married?

The last line on Lenora's marriage license suddenly leapt out at Pat. She could not believe she had never noticed it before: Place of birth of female—Mamou, Louisiana. She ran to get her road atlas. Lenora's maiden name was not a common one, she reasoned, and Mamou couldn't be very big. Lenora must have family there. She thumbed through the atlas to

Louisiana, then down the alphabetical list of towns to Mamou—population 3,275.

It was Thursday, and her hearing was scheduled for the following Wednesday, June 20. If anyone could confirm that David was dead or have any leads if he was alive, it would be Lenora. Should Pat do what the Social Security Administration had failed to do—call the woman?

Pat hesitated for a moment. If Lenora had any leads for her, Pat knew she would *have* to pursue them, no matter how long it took or where they might end. If she didn't, they'd gnaw at her forever. Pat grabbed the phone and called the Louisiana operator. She had no choice: there was an odor clinging to those affidavits and she had to find out where it came from and why.

"Which city?" a woman drawled.

"Mamou," Pat said. She gave the operator Lenora's maiden name and waited.

"There are several listed," the operator said. "But no Lenora."

"The names and numbers, please." Pat tingled, knowing somebody on that list would lead her to David's "wife."

"I can't do that," the operator said. "I can give you two numbers. Which ones do you want?" She recited the list.

Pat took the first two names and dialed one quickly before she could lose her nerve. She didn't like the idea of intruding on Lenora's life again. Like Pat, the woman wouldn't be happy about someone prying into her past.

"I'm looking for Lenora," she told the woman who answered the phone. "I wonder if you know how I can—"

"Why, yes. She's outside next door mowin' the lawn." The woman's voice was soft and lilting. Pat placed her in her late fifties. "I'm her cousin. You want me ta yell for her?"

"Could you give me her number?" Pat asked. "I'll call her later."

"She should be in the house in about five minutes," she said. "I'll tell her ta expect a call."

After she hung up, Pat paced the floor, replaying in her mind the day Lenora had called fourteen years earlier. In spite of her own shock, she had felt sorry for the woman who sounded so sweet and innocent. The last Pat had heard, Lenora was trying to get her marriage annulled.

Pat waited ten minutes, then dialed the number. From the first gentle, cautious hello, Pat knew it was Lenora. Afraid to alarm her, Pat spoke calmly and slowly as she tried to hide the tremor in her own voice. She wanted the woman to feel she was not out to hurt her; she only wanted information about David.

"Lenora? This is Pat," she said. "Do you remember me?

"Yes, I do. How could I forget?" Lenora said. She seemed surprised.

Pat was nervous. For Lenora to hear her voice after all this time, she knew, was painful, and what Lenora might tell her about David could hurt even more.

"I thought about you all these years, Lenora, and I wondered what happened to you," Pat said. "I'm trying to get Social Security benefits for my three daughters and I'll be going to a hearing next week. David was declared legally dead in Virginia last year. Even so, I don't want to go to the hearing if there's a chance he is still alive."

Pat paused to let the shock wear off and the message sink in. "I need to ask you a couple of questions," she continued. "Anything you might know could really help me settle this thing once and for all."

It worked. Lenora began to tell her story, slowly, quietly, and without further coaxing. After talking to Pat in 1970, she said, she had her marriage to Jim annulled. A few months later, in January 1971, Jim came to her door. He was out of work, he said, the bank had repossessed his car in Houston, where he had been living, and he wanted to move back in with her. Would she take him? She was leery, but he charmed his way back into her home. It worked out fine. Hoping to start fresh, they moved to Jacksonville, Florida, where Jim managed a men's clothing store. Then they moved to Tampa, where he walked out on her for the second time, in 1975. They had no children.

The more Pat heard, the angrier she became. She had asked Lenora in 1970 to call her if she ever heard from David again. She had told her then that she had three babies to support, was on welfare, and needed help badly. Lenora had promised she would call. Now Pat knew Lenora not only hadn't contacted her, but had moved right back in with the runaway father of her children. Pat tried not to let her emotions show in her voice.

"He left you in 1975?" Pat asked, with an appropriate note of surprise.

"Yes. And he kept in contact with me until 1976."

Now Pat was overwhelmed with anger and confusion. She needed time to sort through what she had just heard and to get her feelings under control. If she showed hostility, Lenora would snap a double bolt over the past.

"Can I call you back?" Pat asked. "I have to take Marcia to diving practice at the pool. She's my youngest."

Lenora hesitated as if to say, What else can I tell you? When she finally said yes, it was almost a sigh.

Pat drove Marcia to the pool, careful not to let her daughter suspect whom she had been talking to, or why. Marcia had grown into a sensitive fifteen-year-old with reddish brown hair and dark brown eyes that mirrored her every feeling. She spoke in rapid fire as if unable to express her thoughts fast enough to suit her, and she said exactly what was on her mind.

Although each of her daughters had been hurt by David, Marcia's pain was special. When the truck had rammed Pat's car in front of her mother's house that winter afternoon in 1971, Marcia, who was two years old at the time, had seen the paramedics lift her mother into an ambulance and drive off. Although she knew better from discussions around the house in later years, Marcia had talked herself into believing that her father had been killed in that terrible scene. She couldn't accept the fact that he had abandoned her before she was born, and Pat did not discourage the accident story because for all she knew David *was* dead.

By the time she was ten, Marcia finally accepted the fact that her father didn't die in that car accident but had run away from her and her sisters. For the next few years, she'd creep into Pat's bed at night to cry and be cuddled. "If only I could hear Daddy's voice," she'd say. "I wish I knew what he sounded like." Then her guilt feelings would pour out. "If only you didn't have *me*," she'd whimper. "You'd still have Daddy, and so would Christine and Andrea. Why was I ever born?" There was little Pat could do but hold her daughter tightly to make her feel wanted and secure and to encourage the tears to flow.

By the time Marcia was fourteen, anger had replaced feelings of guilt, even though she did not understand the roots of her anger. With a hostility that went well beyond the usual teenage rebellion, Marcia began needling Pat about the smallest thing as if to punish her because she couldn't punish her father. There were temper tantrums and outbursts for almost no reason, and her school grades began to slip.

Now, at fifteen, Marcia was beginning to snap out of her angry phase and settle down. She still flew into rages, but they didn't last as long and they were tempered by other admirable qualities. Marcia was a leader in sports, which she loved, and in organizing activities. She stood up for her rights fiercely. And most important as far as Pat was concerned, she chose her friends carefully, and once she did, she committed herself to them tenaciously. When a friendship broke up, which was rare, she mourned its loss as if it were a death. Marcia seemed to be trying to be as loyal and caring as her father had been disloyal and uncaring.

Pat also watched Marcia become more and more domestic. She made dinner for her mother every night. She baked and made cookies for parties and for her friends, just as Pat had done in her apartment after David had run away. Coupled with her domesticity, Pat noted with concern, was a dependency on her mother, a kind of clinging that Marcia didn't seem to be outgrowing. It was almost as if her daughter was telling her, "I want to stay close to you so you won't leave me too."

With this puzzling dependency and the smoldering anger she was still working through, how would her youngest daughter react if she found out the object of her anger was still alive?

Yes, Pat concluded as she dropped Marcia off at the pool, it was best to wait until the last minute to tell her.

On the way home, her feelings somewhat under control, Pat mulled over what Lenora had said. The whole picture had changed completely with one phone call. She had phoned Lenora expecting to dig up facts to support presumption of death and had found instead evidence pointing to presumption of life.

Pat rehearsed the additional questions she wanted to ask Lenora, then dialed Mamou again with a vague sense that she was about to set out on another journey. She thought of her cousin Joe and felt a renewed strength. She would listen, probe, and then weigh what she learned before deciding what to do next. One thing was already clear: in spite of her shock and anger, she would cancel the SSA hearing if she seriously doubted David was dead—even though she wanted and needed the death benefits for her daughters.

Pat began with chitchat, then said, "Lenora, he left you in 1975 in Tampa—why?"

"Well, you know how he was." Lenora sounded defensive and embarrassed. "I lived from day to day not knowing whether he would come home. Then one evening, he said, 'I have other plans for my life and they don't include you.' "

"Weren't you upset?" Pat asked, trying to keep Lenora talking.

"Yes, but what was I to do?"

"Didn't you try to stop him?"

"No," Lenora said. "I even helped him move his furniture. I stayed in Tampa for a while, then came back home."

"Then what?"

"Jim went to Baton Rouge for a while, then moved on to San Antonio. That's the last I heard of him."

"Do you have his address in San Antonio?"

Lenora gave her a number on Gardendale Drive, then said, "I've often wondered myself whether he's dead or alive. There isn't a day I don't think about him."

"Lenora, are you still in love with him?" Pat asked gently.

"Well, I do think about him a lot."

The realization that Lenora still loved James Parker helped Pat frame her next questions. Like an attorney probing a hostile witness, she began picking the story apart, looking for details, clues, leads, all the while taking notes furiously. When she sensed that Lenora was being evasive, she didn't press the point. Slowly the facts began to pile up:

The name of the shop in Jacksonville where David had

worked was the Suburban Men's Store. When its owners decided to move to South Carolina, David stayed in Florida. He took a job with the Safeco Insurance Company's branch office in Jacksonville. In 1973 Safeco transferred him to Sarasota, then to Tampa, in 1974. In March 1975 he left Lenora for good.

Although there was no reason to disbelieve what Lenora told her, Pat sensed there was a lot she had left out. Did Lenora know he was alive and was she protecting him? Or did she really lose track of David after 1975?

Pat probed a few more times, and when she felt resistance she asked the question she had been saving for last. "Lenora, please believe me when I say that all I want to do is find out if David's dead or alive. If he's dead, I'll go through with my hearing for death benefits for his children. If he's alive, I'll ask the child-support office to help me. Is there anything else you can tell me?"

"No," she said. "I told you all there is."

"Can you give me his Social Security number?" Pat asked. That alone would solve the mystery quickly and easily.

"I don't have that," Lenora said. But from the way she said it, Pat knew Lenora would not tell her, even if she did have it.

Nonetheless, Pat asked again in a pleading voice. When Lenora began crying, Pat thanked her and hung up, still not sure what the woman was hiding.

Pat found it hard to sort out how she felt. She was sorry she had made Lenora cry. Yet she was angry at her for going back to David after learning he had abandoned a young wife and three children. She also felt pity for the woman; obviously Lenora was still in love with David and hadn't gotten over the pain after ten years. And, of course, she was angry at herself for her own anger. Above all, Pat was afraid of what she had to do next.

David's trail was only eight years old now, and she had two good leads—an address in San Antonio and the name of an employer. And she had every reason to believe David was alive. She would cancel the hearing in the morning and then try to find him. She didn't want to think about what she'd do if she actually did.

That night, when she wasn't staring at the ceiling, she tossed and turned. The next morning, her thoughts were clearer, even if her feelings weren't. Shortly after nine, when the Social Security Administration offices opened, she canceled the hearing. All afternoon she chafed to get home and take the next fateful step.

10

>>>>>>>>>>>>> Pat burst through the kitchen door that evening. It was only four-thirty in Texas, so she had half an hour to dig around before the work week ended. She didn't think she could stand the tension of waiting until Monday.

Pat called the operator in San Antonio and asked for the listing for James C. Parker who lived on Gardendale. No one by that name. Disappointed but not surprised, she redialed and asked another San Antonio operator for the phone number of the Safeco Insurance Company. Quickly she called that number.

"May I speak to James Parker, please?" she asked the receptionist.

"There is no James Parker here," the woman said. "But there is one in our Dallas office. Would you like that number?"

Bingo, Pat thought, her heart thumping. She couldn't believe how easy it was. She called Dallas. "One moment, please," a cool voice said. Pat held her breath. A man came on the line. "This is James Parker," he said. "Can I help you?"

Pat felt relieved. It was the voice of a young black man. Drained from the emotional stress, she hung up and sat down to catch her breath. When she felt calm again, she took stock. One of her clues—David's last known address—was a blind alley. But given the number of moves he had made between 1970, when he had married Lenora, and 1976, when Lenora had last talked to him, it was unlikely he'd lived at the same address for eight years. And that he wasn't working for Safeco in San Antonio or Dallas didn't surprise her either. He still could be living in San Antonio at another address and no longer working for Safeco. Or he could still be with Safeco— there might be more than one James Parker in a big company—

and they had transferred him. Hadn't they moved him from Jacksonville to Sarasota to Baton Rouge to San Antonio like a piece on a Monopoly board?

It was after five o'clock in Texas. Before searching any further, Pat decided to tell her daughter, Christine. She felt the need to share her secret and wanted someone to confide in. Christine was the oldest, and Pat knew it would please the eighteen-year-old that her mother trusted her not to leak a word to her younger sisters.

Tall and striking, Christine had long auburn hair and freckles. Her brown eyes, shaded by thick brows, had a tentative, sad look. But when she smiled, they became suddenly warm and friendly. Like her father, she had large hands and a gait so distinctive that Pat could pick her out of any crowd.

Unlike her sisters, Christine remembered her father. Abandonment had hurt her deeply even though she was only two years old at the time. Today, reserved and introspective, Christine held everything inside, seldom expressing her true feelings, especially her anger. While Marcia was impulsive and challenging, Christine thought before she spoke. A peacemaker, she looked for everyone's best side and was almost always warm and considerate, if somewhat naïve.

All through high school, Christine worked hard at her grades and at part-time jobs, but she seldom dated. At five feet ten, she felt different. And like her mother at that age, she was so shy and insecure that she seemed surprised when boys showed interest. Although she wanted to be noticed, she didn't like dealing with the attention. As a compromise she took up dancing; on stage she could have it both ways—be seen but at a safe distance.

When she started to date seriously after graduating from high school, Christine developed an interesting pattern. If she cared about a young man, she clung to him and wanted to be with him constantly. But she only managed to develop relationships with men who lived in cities far from home, making intimacy possible only on the phone and in letters. She sensed that her habit of long-distance loving had something to do with her father and it bothered her, but she wasn't sure how the pieces fit together.

When Pat told Christine that her father might still be alive,

Christine was neither surprised nor curious. If he showed up after sixteen years, he couldn't undo what he had done, and she didn't want to pick up their relationship where he had left off. Finding and meeting her father would only bring more disappointment, so why get excited?

Given Christine's tendency to bury tough issues, Pat was not surprised at her lack of emotion. She merely noted it and went on to explain that she didn't want David's foster mother to find out about the lead because she might know where he was and alert him. Then he'd burrow so deep they'd never find him.

"Well, what do you think?" Pat asked finally, trying to get her daughter to share some of her thoughts, if not her feelings. But Christine's brown eyes, so expressive when she wanted them to be, showed nothing.

She said only, "Mom, you better not tell Marcia; she'll freak out. And don't tell Andrea or she'll say something to Grandma."

Nevertheless, Christine was flattered by her mother's confidence, and like co-conspirators, they set up Pat's bedroom as a command post where they would plan the search and share the news. Then, nervous and excited, Pat continued the chase.

Hoping David was still in San Antonio, Pat made several phone calls to the operator and put together a list of all the James, Jim, Jimmy, and J. Parkers in the city. She ended up with twenty-eight. Dallas was worse, with sixty-four. Pat concocted a cover story. Using the name of a girlfriend, she would ask to speak to Mr. Parker. She would say she was looking for a James Parker who worked for an insurance company, then explain she was with the Executive Research Corporation in Andover, Massachusetts, a recruiting agency with several management jobs open in the insurance field. If Mr. Parker was interested in applying, she would send him a questionnaire. In the event she actually located David, she would have special stationery and a questionnaire printed and ask a friend who did not live in the Washington area to mail it to him.

After three San Antonio blanks, she hit a live one.

"In insurance? How long ago?" a Mrs. Parker asked.

"I'm not sure," Pat said. "We have a list of people who used to work for insurance companies. And we have an old San Antonio address for a James Parker." Nervously, Pat fed the woman details about her "company" in hopes of wheedling more information.

"The reason I ask," the woman said, "is that my husband did work in insurance several years ago—like eight or nine years ago."

"It's been that long?" Pat was disappointed. "Well, it's still possible he's our man."

"He's not here right now," the woman said. "He's due back in about thirty minutes."

"Do you think he would be interested in talking?"

"I don't know because I don't have any idea what you have in mind."

"Well, if he's interested, I can't guarantee anything because we don't guarantee jobs. But—" Pat fumbled to explain precisely what the Executive Research Corporation of Andover would do for James Parker.

"Is this strictly door-to-door sales?" the woman asked. She sounded suspicious.

"No, no, these are *executive* positions. We have an application—"

"Is this a full-time job?"

Pat's heart was pounding so fast and her voice became so breathy she hardly heard the woman's questions. More out of nervousness than anything else, she began running through the "history" of the company, how it recruited and for whom, making it up as fast as she could. "We've been very successful with people who have left the business," she explained. "I can't say I have a particular job in mind for your husband. He'd have to fill out our application and tell us where he wants to work and we'll try to match him with an executive job on our list."

"Well, my husband is retiring soon," the woman said. "And he's thinking of doing something on the side."

Retiring! Pat's heart began to sink. "Just how old *is* he?"

"Sixty-five. You might give him a call."

Pat suddenly felt exhausted.

"Generally, we are interested in people under thirty-five," she said lamely.

"Well, if you can't find anyone," the woman volunteered, "give him a call."

Not sure she could take any more false alarms, Pat never-theless forced herself to phone the other Parkers on her San Antonio list just to get them out of the way. She got nowhere. It was nine o'clock on Friday night when she finished. It didn't seem worthwhile even to try the Parkers on her Dallas list, for she had no evidence that David worked there.

Drained but not completely discouraged, Pat called Richard Froemming, a private investigator she had met a few months earlier at Boomerangs, a singles watering hole where young professionals gathered. Richard was a former D.C. cop who had quit the force and started his own company, Shamus, Inc. He and Pat had dated a few times and frequently chatted on the phone. Richard already knew the story of Pat's former husband.

When Pat called on Friday night and told him about her San Antonio phone calls the day before and why she thought David was still alive, Richard was amazed at how far she had come in just a few days.

"Will you find him for me?" she asked.

As an investigator, Richard worked on the principle that as long as there are leads, there's hope. Pat had at least one good lead, and she was bright and determined. "Why pay me?" he said. "You're doing just fine."

"But I'm stuck," she complained. "I don't know what to do next."

"Begin with Safeco," he suggested. "Find out where its headquarters are. Call Personnel and take it from there."

It would be a long wait until Monday, Pat thought.

11

>>>>>>>>>>>>> Pat waited until after work on Monday to call
Safeco's corporate offices in Seattle. Deciding to play it straight,
she asked to speak to the personnel director. When he came
on the line, she told him she was looking for her husband, who
had disappeared twice, the second time eight years ago. "At
that time," she said, "he was working for you in San Antonio.
I'd appreciate any information you can give me."

"I'll help as much as I can," the personnel director promised.
"But privacy laws are pretty strict. About all I can do is confirm
or deny. What's his name? I'll see if we have his file."

"James Clinton Parker."

"Hold on a minute," he said.

To Pat, it seemed like a long wait. The man was cautious
and if he felt sorry for her, his voice didn't show it. Pat wasn't
used to that. Most people went out of their way to help once
they understood what she was after and why.

"Yes, we have a file for a James C. Parker," he said finally.
Again Pat tried to read something in his voice, but it was flat
and businesslike. "Do you have an address?"

She read him the San Antonio address on Gardendale.

"That's the address we have in his file. He left Safeco in
1976. Do you have his Social Security number?"

"No," she said, thinking of Lenora who might have been
able to give it to her. How easy it would have been if she had.

"Date of birth?"

She gave him the one on the marriage certificate Lenora
had sent. It was not David's real date of birth but it was close.

"It's not the same," he said.

"What do you have?" she asked. It looked as if David was
trying to cover his trail again. If he had changed his date of

birth a second time, she thought, he had probably taken a different Social Security number as well.

"I'm sorry, but I can't give you that," the Safeco man said. "Describe him to me."

Pat went into detail.

"The height and weight match," he said.

Without saying as much, they both concluded that Safeco's James C. Parker was Lenora's Jim and Pat's David. She tried to coax more information out of the personnel director, but he showed no sign of weakening. Finally, she thanked him and hung up. Except for the different date of birth, a minor discrepancy, all the pieces fit.

Pat called Richard. She told him what she had learned and how frustrating it was to be so close yet so far. Richard encouraged her. That was an important call, he said. It confirmed that David had worked for Safeco and had been an insurance man for six years. And if he had *been* in insurance, Richard pointed out, he was probably still in insurance.

Pat was not impressed. "There must be ten thousand insurance companies," she said.

"Probably . . . but only fifty state licensing offices."

The insurance business was tightly controlled, Richard explained, and every legitimate insurance agent had to be licensed in the state or states where he or she sold insurance. Licenses had to be renewed periodically—the information was public.

Now Pat's strategy became clear. Fifty phone calls at most. If David was still in insurance and still using the name James C. Parker—two very big *ifs*—she'd find him. If not—well, she'd face that when she got there.

Pat made a list of the state capitals she wanted to call. She knew David had worked for Safeco in Texas, Louisiana, and Florida. So she would call the insurance licensing offices in Austin, Baton Rouge, and Tallahassee. Then, figuring that if she couldn't find him there, he would probably still be working in the South, she added Montgomery, Little Rock, Jackson, and Atlanta to the list.

Before calling it a night, she decided to lean on Safeco once more. This time she explained to the personnel director that when her husband had deserted her sixteen years ago he had left her with three babies. She had thought he was dead, she said, but now, there was every reason to believe that the James C. Parker in Safeco's files was her former husband. She and her children needed to be certain for their peace of mind.

"Has anyone requested employment references for James C. Parker?" she asked. Surely someone had, and the information would be a fresh lead.

"I can't give you that information," the Safeco man said. "You'll need a court order for his personnel file."

Frustrated, she tried a few more questions and once again asked for Parker's Social Security number. From his voice, the hemming and hawing, and the shuffling of papers, she got the impression that Safeco knew where David was. His refusal to help her only confirmed that she was on the right trail. If Safeco knew, others must know as well.

Pat took leave on Tuesday so she could call the state capitals on her list. It was not a difficult job, but there was always a bureaucracy to cut through, going from one clerk to another until she found the right person, and long waits on the phone while files were checked. She drew blanks in Texas and Louisiana.

When she got to Florida, Pat changed her tactic. Instead of going directly to the central office in the capital, she decided to try the regional office in Jacksonville, where James C. Parker had once worked. "Yes, we show a James C. Parker licensed . . . but in Tampa," the Jacksonville clerk said. "I suggest you call our Tampa office."

When Pat hung up she was trembling. She knew she had found David even though there was no reason to be so sure. She paced the kitchen floor, trying to summon enough courage to get back on the phone. Then she dialed the Tampa number. "You'll have to call the central office in Tallahassee," another clerk said. "We don't keep licenses here."

The Tallahassee clerk was very helpful. She pulled James C. Parker's file and read Pat the information on his license application that she was permitted by law to reveal: the date on which James C. Parker's license had been renewed, his Tampa address, and his date and place of birth. The birth date and place were different from David's real ones and different from the information on Lenora's marriage certificate, but again they were close enough to convince Pat she might have found the right man.

She was now in mild shock. If she had just found David, she had found a piece of herself as well. Her feelings were so confused that she didn't even try to sort them out. What should she do now? Tell Andrea and Marcia? Or wait until she was sure?

Reason prevailed, and she called the clerk in the insurance licensing office in Tallahassee once more. Woman to woman, she explained that David had deserted his babies sixteen years ago and that Virginia had declared him dead. She said she was convinced that James C. Parker was her former husband, but she needed to be absolutely certain before she could tell her teenage daughters that she had found their father.

"Can't you give me any more information?" she pleaded. The clerk had told her she was permitted to reveal only public information. That meant there *was* private information.

There was a long pause. Pat could hear the clerk draw a deep breath. "I could lose my job for this," came the voice finally.

"Don't worry. I don't even know your name," Pat said.

"Hang on."

A moment later, the clerk returned with Parker's file and began reading it almost in a whisper. Every detail matched: James C. Parker had spent four years in the Marine Corps as David had, but the service dates, like his birthdates, didn't quite match. He had worked at Suburban's Men's Store in Jacksonville in 1971, as Lenora had said, and he had begun working for the Safeco Insurance Company in 1972, as both Lenora and Safeco had agreed.

There was no doubt in Pat's mind now that James C. Parker was the man who had married Lenora. And the man who had married Lenora was the father of her children. She was amazed at how easy it had been to find him, after all those years when she had been wondering whether he was dead or alive, whether she hated or loved him.

As soon as Pat hung up, however, she felt sick to her stomach. She began pacing the floor and hyperventilating. She found herself saying over and over, "What am I going to do? What am I going to do?" She struggled with an urge to call the licensing clerk back and make her prove that she had made a mistake, that the James C. Parker in her file was not David. But it was too late. She knew she had found him.

Pat called Richard instead. "You won't believe this," she said. Words began spilling out.

"Calm down," Richard ordered. "Slow down and begin again."

Pat told him what she had learned and how. "I want to hire you," she said, placing the responsibility for the next step on his shoulders.

"You don't need me, Pat," Richard said. "You've already found him."

"Well, I want you to *prove* it's him," she said. "Go down there and tail him. Follow him into a restaurant. Get him to touch a glass and then take it and dust it for prints. Maybe you can—"

Richard laughed. "You watch too many movies," he said. "What would I do with fingerprints? I'll send someone down there to get pictures of him and his house, and they can poke around in the court records. If it's him, you'll know when you see the pictures."

Richard asked his partner, Rick Hager, who was finishing a surveillance job in Miami, to stop in Tampa on his way home. It was a breeze assignment: find Parker's house and snap pictures, get the make and tag number of his car, check the courthouse for anything on Parker in the public domain, and get pictures of the man himself. Not a boring assignment, and not interesting either. One day's work, then a day or two on the beach.

A former police officer like Richard, Hager was used to the methodical background checking that makes up a large part of any investigation. He rented a car in Tampa and bought a local street map, but Foxwood Drive, where James Clinton Parker lived, wasn't on it. And Parker's company, Frontier Adjusters, was just a number in the Tampa phone directory. No help there. Next, Hager checked at the post office and found out there was no Foxwood Drive inside the Tampa city limits. Figuring it must be in a nearby suburb, Hager walked over to the Hillsborough County Sheriff's office, where he discovered two Foxwood Drives in two different towns outside

Tampa. He chose one and found the street without much trouble, but there was no house with Parker's number. By that time, it was almost dark.

The next morning, Hager drove out to the second Foxwood Drive in the suburb of Lutz, about a half hour from downtown Tampa. He found James Parker's house in the Cypress Cove development, a typical single-family home sitting on a corner lot: blue with white trim, a chalet roof with two dormers, and an attached garage. A grove of cypress trees shaded the rear of the house. There was a swing and slide set in the backyard. Parked in the driveway were a blue Chevy Camaro, a red Dodge Diplomat, a blue Honda, and a Chevy truck. Hager guessed that Parker worked out of his home, as most insurance adjusters do, and that was why there was no address in the phone book for Frontier Adjusters.

Hager also concluded that Cypress Cove was not the place to play photographer. The houses were nestled close together, separated only by small patches of green; with no cars parked on the street, someone was sure to get suspicious of a stranger watching and waiting. Besides, Hager found it almost impossible to cover both exits from Cypress Cove. He couldn't be sure of catching sight of James Parker, much less of freezing him on film. So he copied down the license numbers of all the cars in the driveway and left.

Hager checked into a Holiday Inn down the road and then drove over to the Pasco County Courthouse nearby to find out who owned the house and whether James C. Parker had a criminal record. He learned that Parker was renting and was clean. Next, Hager drove back to Tampa to check the Department of Motor Vehicles. The red Dodge was registered to James C. Parker, he found out, and the truck to Frontier Adjusters. Neither had a lien on it. The other two cars were registered in the name of Parker's business partner.

Finally, Hager visited the bureau of marriage licenses and found out that James C. Parker had married a nineteen-year-old woman in January 1979. Noting she was sixteen years younger than Parker, Hager bought a certified copy of the marriage license. He could forget that day in the sun.

That night Hager began to plan his sting. That was the fun part of being a private eye, outsmarting the mark. Betting that the best way to reach Parker would be through his pocketbook, Hager worked on a hook until it was fish-bone sharp: "My name is Bill Henderson and I'm a businessman from Philadelphia. Someone rear-ended my new Cadillac Seville. How much would you charge to take pictures of the damage and do an adjustment? I have to drive back home today and I'm worried. If I get into another accident, I won't be able to figure out which one caused which dents."

Hager smiled in satisfaction. It was a good hook and he knew it would take. The first thing the next morning, he called Frontier Adjusters. A man answered. Hager tossed the bait.

"Why don't you take your car into a local Cadillac dealer," the man said after he heard Hager out. "They'll do it for nothing."

Hager was staggered. He never figured Parker would follow the bait so closely but refuse to take it. Had he misjudged the man? Thanking him for the suggestion, he asked, "By the way, who am I speaking to?"

"Jim Parker."

Hager hung up. Over a cup of coffee, he tied a second barb on his hook and called Parker back. "I'm in a hurry to get back to Philadelphia and I don't have time to check in with a Cadillac dealer. How much will you charge to look at the car, take pictures, then drive out to the scene of the accident to photograph that too? I'll pay cash."

Hager didn't think Parker would pass up tax-free money.

"At least fifty," Parker said.

"Fine. Come on over. I'm at the Holiday Inn in Lutz and I'm getting ready to check out. I'll be waiting for you in the lobby."

Hager gave Parker a phony description of himself. Parker said he'd be there in ten minutes. He was six foot one, he said, and would be wearing a tan shirt and tan slacks and driving a red Dodge Diplomat.

Hager picked up his camera bag and rushed out to his white compact car parked about twenty-five yards from the motel's front entrance. He selected a 200-mm lens and waited. Less than ten minutes later, Parker rolled into the lot and slowly drove around the motel looking for a black Cadillac. Then he went around a second time. When he started his third loop, Hager was afraid he might drive right out of the lot and go home. He sighed in relief when the Diplomat turned the corner again and slipped into a parking place out front. Hager fired a series of clean shots—Parker getting out of his car under a "Prime Rib $10.95 All You Can Eat" sign, Parker walking toward the lobby, and Parker returning to his car.

Hager pulled out of the lot before Parker had climbed back into his car, and tooled over to the house on Foxwood Drive, where he snapped another series. On the way back to the motel, he passed Parker, jaw set and hands tightly gripping the wheel. Hager sensed that Parker wasn't the least bit suspicious, just mad as hell that fifty bucks had slipped through his fingers.

Hager smiled to himself. He had pulled it off neatly, cleanly, and with no fuss. Tidy investigations always gave him a great sense of accomplishment and pride. He couldn't wait to call Richard, who had been following the Parker case as it unfolded.

Back in Washington, Pat worked in a daze. She'd call Richard during her lunch hour and from home at night. When he was on a stakeout, she'd reach him on his van telephone. Hungry for details, she grilled the investigator: "Describe the house! What did his voice sound like? What did he look like? What did he say—exactly? Tell me again."

The more Pat heard, the more she felt her emotional tension mount. She was surprised that David lived in a nice house, even if he didn't own it, for she could only remember him the way he was when he left her—barely scraping along. She was shocked to hear that he had married a woman just a few years older than Christine and that he had said on his license application that he had never been married before. The wife complicated matters for Pat. Hadn't enough people been hurt already? Did she want a broken marriage on her conscience?

When some of the shock and numbness wore off, she made a decision. Why shouldn't she finish what she had begun? Her first obligation was toward her daughters and herself. Besides, she argued, she'd be doing the woman a favor if she ripped the mask off James C. Parker. If David had walked out on her and on Lenora, he would probably abandon his present wife too. Better for her to find out now, while she's young.

But it was the slide and swing set that really took the wind out of Pat. Although it had crossed her mind when she first began looking for David that he might be married, she never allowed herself to think that he could have more children as well. Richard tried to reassure her. Other than the swing and slide behind the house, he explained, there was no evidence that Parker had children. And since he was renting, the backyard set was probably not his.

Pat fretted for two days. If Hager proved Richard wrong, she had decided she would let go of the whole thing. To embarrass David and shock his wife who apparently didn't know his background was one thing. They were adults and could cope. But to hurt children? Who would protect them? Christine, Andrea, and Marcia were three casualties too many. Pat didn't think she could add any more to the list.

Looking for legal advice about what to do next, Pat called an attorney friend, Victoria Gordon. Go to the Juvenile and Domestic Relations Court, Victoria advised, and ask the clerk for a certified copy of the sixteen-year-old court order telling David he had to pay $99.11 every two weeks. Then call back.

What Victoria didn't tell Pat was that without a certified copy of the original order she could never prove to the court that David owed her daughters sixteen years of back child support. The best she could hope for then would be a new judgment ordering David to begin paying for Marcia, who was fifteen, and Andrea, who was seventeen. Christine would turn eighteen in three months, at which time she would cease to be David's responsibility. And Victoria also didn't tell Pat that the chances of finding the original court order after sixteen years were slim indeed.

12

>>>>>>>>>>>>> The Fairfax County Juvenile and Domestic Relations Court was housed in an old two-story brick building in downtown Fairfax. It had been the hub of the county's entire judicial system until the commonwealth attorney, his staff of prosecutors, and their judges had moved down the street to a new glass high-rise befitting one of the richest counties in the nation. As for the old, asbestos-ridden building, Fairfax had given it to its women and children and the professionals who try to help them.

The Juvenile and Domestic Relations Court intake office, where all the court's paperwork began and ended, was located in an airless beige corridor that desperately needed a new coat of paint. A few hard chairs and benches lined one wall for the hard-luck cases who came for help. Taped on the wall next to the intake desk was a list of phone numbers for treatment centers. Most of the court's domestic relations counselors worked in tiny basement offices with unfinished walls of painted brick and exposed pipes.

A door from the back parking lot of the old building led into the juvenile holding tank. Its reception area, where prisoners were logged in, and where the guards sat around chatting on slow days, was dirty; cigarette butts littered the floor. Behind the reception area were the cells where juveniles waited to be called into the courtrooms upstairs. The two rows of cubicles, one for boys and one for girls, were stuffy, dreary, and smelled of urine. Near the cells was a counseling cubbyhole with paint peeling from the walls and asbestos flaking from the pipes. A bare bulb dangled from the ceiling. Under it stood a small table on which the initials of half the teenagers in the county seemed to have been carved.

When Pat walked into the intake office late in the afternoon, the day after she had talked to Victoria, Linda Schnatterly was working at her station behind a counter. On her desk sat a typewriter so old that county services had condemned it, promising her a new one within twelve months. For four years, Linda had been supervising the clerical staff of six women who processed the papers for all child custody and support cases, disputes over visitation rights, and domestic criminal activity. The clerks also scheduled the twenty to thirty daily counseling appointments with the professional staff, tried to help the ten or so walk-ins that showed up each day, and handled 150 to 200 phone calls daily. A single file clerk maintained the center's 128,000 records. Linda, who had been working for Fairfax County for fifteen years, also drove eighteen-wheel semis part-time; she had to supplement her income to support herself and her two children.

After one quick look, Linda knew Pat was in a highly emotional state. She seemed confused and her face was ashen and drawn. Linda listened as a garbled story began to tumble out. She tried to slow Pat down, for part of her job was to pinpoint the problem so she could direct her clients to the right help quickly. After a few questions and some jumbled answers, she concluded she was dealing with a child-support case.

"Where's the father?" Linda asked.

"In Florida," Pat said. "I finally found him."

Good luck, lady, Linda thought. You'll have to file an interstate court action and by the time it's settled, if it ever is, your kids will be grandmothers. And Florida of all places.

Linda told Pat that she would have to file for child support for her children under eighteen. If Pat wanted to do that, Linda said, she would make an appointment for her with a counselor.

"That won't work," Pat said. "He doesn't know I've found him and if he hears I have, he'll run again."

You're right on that score, Linda agreed silently. Deadbeat dads and runaway fathers got so much advance notice from legal filings that they could easily keep a step ahead of the lead-footed law.

"I have a child-support order and an arrest warrant," Pat said. "But they're sixteen years old and I don't have certified copies."

Linda shook her head as she fired up her computer. She would have liked to believe that the 128,000 names and case numbers in the computer were complete and accurate, but she knew they weren't. Some files had been lost; others never got on the list because a clerk had misplaced them or a tired keyboard operator had overlooked them or entered them incorrectly. If a woman's husband wasn't on the computer correctly, she'd never find his file.

Linda keyed in David's name and hit the search code. His case number flashed on the screen—15-292. "You're in luck," she told Pat. "It's stored in the basement. But don't hold your breath while I'm gone."

Linda figured that after sixteen years and frequent reorganizations, there was about a fifty-fifty chance that file 15-292 would be collecting dust where it was supposed to be. If it was filed out of sequence, it was probably lost forever. Even if it *was* sitting between 15-291 and 15-293, there was no guarantee that the court order and arrest warrant would be in the file. And if they were, would the papers and the judge's signature still be legible after sixteen years?

Linda walked down two flights of stairs to the basement and into the brightly lit file room lined with rows of identical folders on gray steel shelves. She went over to the 15-200s— and there it was. She couldn't believe it. She opened file 15-292 and began flipping through the twenty pages inside. Each was as crisp and clear as if it had been typed the day before. God must be with you, lady, Linda thought as she carried the file back upstairs.

Pat sat on a wooden bench in the intake corridor. Her stomach began to knot as she read the file Linda had given her—the court order of October 7, 1968, signed by Judge Frank Deierhoi; a second support order for fifty dollars a week signed by Judge Richard Jamborsky four months later; and the arrest warrant of April 1, 1969. The file tapped a deep well of sadness, like a death remembered. When Pat returned the file to Linda, she was crying quietly. They were the first tears she had shed over David in more than ten years, and in

spite of the pain they brought, they felt good. Following
Victoria's advice, still not sure why, she asked for certified
copies of the support order and arrest warrant.

"Now, let's just go over this again," Linda suggested.

Pat started once more from the beginning, coherently this
time, and it became clear to Linda that David had been missing
for sixteen years, living under an assumed identity, and that
Pat had actually gone out and found him. She had never heard
this sort of child-support case before. By the time Pat finished
her story, the other clerks and women waiting for intake
services had gathered around her in disbelief.

Linda studied the old child-support order for a minute.
"At fifty dollars a week, that's twenty-six hundred dollars a
year. . . . My God, that's almost forty-two thousand dollars in
back child support. He owes you forty-two thousand dollars!"

Linda began to boil as her thoughts turned inward. Her
own father had left her and her three younger brothers for
several years. They were nightmarish years for the family, and
Linda never forgot what it was like to be a fatherless child.
Besides her own two children, she always seemed to have a
stray or two around the house—scared, battered, abandoned
kids, unwanted and in trouble with nowhere to go. Over the
years she had sheltered more than fifty of them, some just
overnight or for a weekend until they could get professional
help; others for as long as two years. One of the saddest cases
had been the twelve-year-old she accepted for a weekend.

Late one Friday as she sat at home recovering from surgery,
Linda had gotten a call from a probation officer she knew. The
officer had a twelve-year-old on his hands and needed a place
for him until Monday morning, when the court convened.
Would Linda take him for the weekend?

She agreed, and the probation officer dropped the boy off
at her doorstep early Friday evening. From the start, Linda
knew the child was deeply disturbed. He acted like a wild
animal. He didn't talk, he looked at her and her two boys with
strange wariness, and he crept about the house staring as if he
had never seen one before. At mealtimes he didn't know how
to eat at the table, and he couldn't seem to get enough food
into his stomach.

It was only after a social worker picked the boy up Monday

morning that she got the full story. He and his younger brother, who had spent the weekend at another foster home, had been abandoned by their parents. To survive, they had dug a hole in a field and made a roof over it out of old boards and tin. They stole clothes off clotheslines, raided garbage cans, fought dogs for scraps, and broke into houses for food and blankets. They scrounged for a year before someone finally spotted them and called the Fairfax County Police. No one knew where the parents were or why they had left. The court issued a warrant for their arrest, but the police never found them.

Linda still had nightmares about that boy ten years later. She was less angry at runaway parents than at the thoughtless system that let them get away with it. They have their fun, make their babies, walk out when the going gets tough, and nothing ever happens to them. But not Pat's husband. Pat was special. After sixteen years, she'd actually found the son of a bitch. Good for you, lady, Linda thought. Go for him. Even if all you get out of it is a fistful of money. Send a message to other runaway fathers: "Hey, Dad, if we can get you in Florida, we can nail you anyplace."

Although she was neither an attorney nor a counselor, Linda understood how badly the system was stacked against women and children. Fail to pay your income taxes, and you commit a felony. The IRS doesn't let up even if it costs them two hundred thousand dollars to collect ten thousand dollars in back taxes. Imagine what would happen if word leaked that the IRS wasn't bothering with delinquent taxpayers anymore. Fail to pay your bill at Sears, and the company hires bill collectors or takes you to court even if it loses money. Imagine what would happen if word got around that Sears wasn't bothering to collect unpaid bills. Fail to pay your tag fee, and the county tows your car away or refuses to renew your license. But steal forty-two thousand dollars from your kids, and the system looks the other way or slaps your wrist. Runaway dads were giving the court the finger, and the system was winking at them.

Although she felt sorry for Pat, Linda's heart went out most of all to Pat's daughters. Mothers could usually survive; they could wait on tables if they had to, seek counseling, even find a new husband or lover. But what about the kids? They didn't choose their parents. They weren't responsible for the failure. And they weren't mature enough to understand or handle it. It wasn't easy to grow up an abandoned child. Linda knew that.

Convinced that the case was important and unusual, Linda introduced Pat to Kathleen Meredith, supervisor of Domestic Relations. Meredith was just as impressed, but for a different reason. She couldn't believe that Pat would still be fighting after sixteen years. Most women simply didn't have the mental and physical stamina, professional guidance, and money to do what Pat had done. And few, if any, would unearth a sixteen-year-old child-support order in perfect condition. Her case was, to put it mildly, intriguing.

Assuming Pat wanted to do something about the unpaid child support, Meredith quickly calculated the options: file for criminal prosecution on the grounds of desertion and non-support; seek a civil judgment for back child support based on the sixteen-year-old court order and then try to collect the money; or try both. None of the choices was simple.

Leading Pat from the intake office on the second floor to her own basement office, where they could explore the alternatives, Meredith bumped into a judge in the Juvenile and Domestic Relations Court, Michael Valentine. Meredith knew Pat could find no better court ally than Judge Valentine. She would also be willing to bet a week's salary on what Judge Valentine would advise her to do.

"This lady's husband has been missing for sixteen years and she just found him," Meredith explained to Judge Valentine. "He's never paid child support. Linda has the file upstairs. Will you listen to her story and see if there's anything you can do?"

Soft-spoken and friendly, with sympathetic brown eyes that couldn't hide his underlying moral toughness, Judge Michael Valentine seemed born to sit on the bench of the Juvenile and Domestic Relations Court. With degrees in both foreign service and law, he had interned in Fairfax County's legal-aid program for the poor. After passing the bar, he slipped easily into a general practice centered around juvenile and domestic relations cases. In 1980, after ten years as an attorney, he was named to the bench in the court where he now practiced.

Married and the father of two, Judge Valentine believed children deserved a lot more than their parents, the county, and its prosecutors were giving them. He had appointed himself their spokesman. Surrounded by clerks, bailiffs, counselors, and child-support case files stuffed in tomato boxes, he had a reputation for dispensing as much justice as the law allowed, as patiently and as quickly as he could.

On child-support day, Judge Valentine saw them all: Men arguing they weren't the fathers of children even though court-ordered blood tests showed a 99.8-percent probability they were. Women who had finally found their former husbands and were asking for court orders to attach their wages. Mothers seeking child support for the first time, and fathers saying they'd pay but not that much and only if the court guaranteed that the mothers wouldn't spend the money on themselves. Women making false charges out of spite. Mothers in tears, clutching unpaid bills, begging the court to make the fathers of their children pay the back child support they owed even if it was only twenty-five dollars a month.

Through it all, case after sad case of broken relationships, anger and mistrust, selfishness and poverty, Judge Valentine never seemed to lose sight of the absent children. "Do you have health insurance for your daughter?" he'd ask a mother with concern. Then, hoping to reach a settlement, he'd tell a father, "She's only asking for two hundred twenty-five dollars a month. Don't you know a good deal when you see one?"

A sense of urgency and fairness seemed to hang over his court. "Just tell me what you want me to do for you," he'd say to a woman who couldn't make up her mind how much child support she needed. "Turn around and look at all those people out there waiting for me to do something for them." He'd order a blood test in a paternity case and tell the couple to pay half of the fee each. "If the child turns out to be yours," he'd tell the man, "you'll reimburse her. If it doesn't, she'll reimburse you."

If Judge Valentine had learned anything in his years on the bench, it was that delinquent fathers who didn't understand words like "justice" and "duty" knew the meaning of the word "jail." Threaten them with it and they mysteriously found money to feed their kids. If they didn't have it, their girlfriends, buddies, or new wives waiting outside the courtroom did. Valentine used that fear of the jail cell on fathers in contempt of court for not paying. "But Judge," they'd say like tape recordings, "I don't have four hundred dollars. And how am I going to get it if I'm in jail?"

Valentine showed no sympathy. After cheating their children and insulting his court, they deserved to be paid in kind. "I'm here to enforce the law," he'd lecture. "You were warned. You had a chance to appeal. Now you have only two choices— pay or lose your freedom. Do you have the four hundred dollars?" He'd pause. "You don't have it?" His face would redden and his voice turn to granite. "Then I sentence you to ten days in the county jail." Out would come the bailiff with handcuffs. Next case! The courtroom hum would break into ripples of excitement, and word would trickle back to Linda and the staff that Mike had just nailed another bastard.

Valentine was proud of his record. His jail sentences had scared as much as nine thousand dollars out of fathers who claimed to be broke, and he wished the law were even tougher. He had sent half a dozen outrageously delinquent fathers to jail for up to a year for criminal desertion and nonsupport. And even though other judges had commuted those sentences under appeal, he had made his point: Give the law the finger in my court, and it's jail time.

Judge Valentine was not without critics, many of them judges and prosecutors. They'd tell him, "It's not fair to put a father in jail just for not paying child support." He'd argue back: "We'd toss him in jail for drunk driving because he has endangered society, wouldn't we? Well, for him to neglect his children is far worse. They'll be deprived of a good education and be emotionally scarred. We'll see a lot of them right back here in juvenile court someday."

As he listened to Pat's story, Judge Valentine's face turned a delicate pink. In his fifteen years in juvenile and domestic relations work, he had rarely seen such blatant criminal desertion. Although he had sat on cases where a father had burrowed somewhere in Virginia for a few years before being caught, he had seldom dealt with a father who had skipped the state and assumed a new identity to avoid paying, or who had been found after sixteen years. He wanted James Parker before his bench. If Pat's facts were correct, he'd throw the book at him; the man had committed a crime for which he deserved to be punished. By listening to Pat Bennett, however, Valentine knew he had prejudiced himself. Should Parker come to Fairfax, some other judge would get him.

"This guy's a criminal," Valentine told Pat, who didn't know yet that he was a judge. "You can't let him get away with it. You *have* to do something. I suggest you file a petition for criminal desertion and nonsupport."

"Nothing will happen to him," Pat said. "The judge'll just slap his wrist and let him go."

"Oh no, he won't," Valentine said. "We'll extradite him back to Virginia to stand trial. He'll go to jail and still have to pay what he owes." He explained the system step by step:

Pat would first meet with a counselor who would help her fill out a petition to prosecute for criminal desertion and nonsupport. As soon as the petition came to the judge's desk, a warrant for Parker's arrest would be issued. The common-wealth attorney would recommend extradition to Virginia's governor, who would ask Florida's governor to send Parker back. The sheriff in Tampa would arrest him, and Fairfax County Police officers would fly down to get him and bring him back to face charges. Criminal desertion and nonsupport in Virginia carried a maximum penalty of one year in jail and a fine of one thousand dollars.

Judge Valentine promised Pat he'd do everything he could to speed the case up. He didn't tell her that, to his knowledge, the state of Virginia had never requested another state to extradite a runaway father for criminal desertion and non-support.

Still not realizing that Valentine was a judge, but encouraged by his confidence, Pat agreed to file. But first, she said, she wanted to see pictures of James C. Parker to make sure he was really David.

"When you need me," Valentine said. "I'll be here."

Linda was standing nearby listening. "Who is that man?" Pat asked her.

"That's Judge Michael Valentine," Linda said.

"Oh, my God!" Pat said. "And I told him that the judge wouldn't do anything to David even if he ever appeared in court."

"Don't worry," Linda laughed. "He's the best . . . and he's heard worse."

Pat left the Juvenile and Domestic Relations Court that afternoon with her mind made up. Finding the sixteen-year-old child-support order and talking to Judge Valentine had cleared her head. She wasn't going to let David get away with what he had done to her and her daughters. He had been summoned before the judge sixteen years ago to explain why he wasn't paying the fifty-dollar-a-week child support the court had ordered, but he had never kept that date. For all those years, she had been powerless to make him do so. No more. With the support of people who cared, like Linda, Kitty Meredith, and Judge Valentine, she'd have him brought back to face the same court. She'd listen to a judge shame and sentence him, and then enter the punishment into the record. Until she did that, David would still have some control over her life. Even if her daughters never received the forty-two thousand dollars their father owed them, it was important to set the record straight. It was time to tell them.

13

>>>>>>>>>>>>> Andrea and Marcia were in their rooms when Pat got home. With no easy way to begin, she called them both into the hallway and simply said, "I've got some news for you. It's about your father . . . I'm almost certain he's still alive and I think I've found him in Florida." Then she waited.

"Oh, my God, my God!" Marcia screamed. "He's still alive!" She put her hands over her face and began to cry hysterically. "I want to see him . . . I want to see him. Where is he? Give me his phone number. I have to call him—now!"

Trying to calm Marcia down, Pat explained that she couldn't phone her father because if she did, he'd probably run away again and they would never find him. But Marcia's feelings were deaf to logic, and when Pat refused to give her the phone number, she turned on her mother: "Why can't I call him?" she demanded. He's *my* father. You have no right to keep his phone number to yourself. . . . Please, Mom!"

Andrea listened to her sister with disdain as if to say, "When are you going to grow up, Marcia?" Pat wasn't surprised. Now a cool, pencil-thin seventeen-year-old with dark brown hair, Andrea was conscious of her good looks and how to use them, and she had a sharp mind and a tongue to match. She received the news that her father was still alive with icy coldness, then anger.

"The asshole," she said. "He didn't stay around to raise me. He's not my father, and I don't care if he's dead or alive."

Pat knew Andrea meant every word, and allowed her to vent her feelings, wishing Christine could do the same.

"Put his ass in jail, Mom," Andrea said. "How can he get away with this? Can't you do something?"

"I'm working on it."

Pat explained Judge Valentine's recommendation. She'd

probably go to Florida to identify their father for the sheriff, she said. The girls would see him when the police brought him back to Fairfax.

"No way!" Andrea exploded. "You're not going down there without me. And how come you told Christine first? That wasn't fair. I had a *right* to know."

The tense day ended with Marcia pestering her mother for her father's phone number, with Andrea threatening to tell his foster mother, and with more crying and silence and anger. If it's this bad now, Pat thought, what's it going to be like when they actually *see* him?

Private investigator Richard Froemming sat watching for Pat from inside his surveillance van parked in the lot of the Landmark Shopping Mall in Alexandria. It was early evening and he was waiting to give her the Parker pictures before going to work on another case.

Knowing how deeply David had hurt Pat, Richard admired her fierce determination to face her old feelings. He knew she had been in love with David the day he left her, and that the image of her former husband she had been carrying in her mind for sixteen years was of a young and handsome man who had silently taken his clothes out to his car and driven off. Richard knew the photographs of James Parker he had sitting on his dashboard would shock her, and he wasn't looking forward to handing them over. Showing clients pictures of the man or woman they had hired him to watch was never fun. There was always anger or tears. He felt Pat Bennett would be no exception. The photos would be her first undeniable evidence that David was really alive. All the facts she had unearthed so far were only pieces of an intellectual puzzle that happened to fit perfectly. But the pictures were real. They would hurt.

Richard watched Pat park her blue Oldsmobile and get out. In the spill of parking-lot lights, her face looked pale and drawn. She barely said hello as she climbed into the van and sat beside him. He gave her three clearly labeled manila envelopes—one with pictures of James C. Parker, one with photos of his house, and one with all the negatives. Her hands trembled slightly, Richard noted, as she opened the first

envelope slowly, gingerly, as if it would break. The pack of
photos slid out. She turned over each one in silence. Her face
wrinkled in puzzlement as she studied the middle-aged man
with a dark beard, sunglasses, the hint of a paunch, and a
balding head. Reading disappointment and shock, Richard
almost expected Pat to say, "Hey, Richard, Hager got the wrong
man." Each time she leafed through the pictures, she'd stop at
the shot of James Parker walking toward the entrance of the
Holiday Inn in a long, sure stride, his head bent forward
slightly, his arms swinging, and his shoulders back. But there
were no tears or labored breathing, no "I finally caught you,
you son of a bitch!" A kind of softness seemed to light her
face. A youthfulness, Richard thought, as if she were reliving
moments of happiness and feeling their loss.

"It's him," she finally said. "I'd know his walk anywhere."

When he was a Marine, she used to pick him out of a crowd
of a hundred uniforms, so distinctive was his gait and bearing.
Christine had inherited some of those same features. Pat's
voice was sad, almost tender, as if she was giving up something
precious.

"He's lost his hair," she said. "He's aged. He's forty years
old."

Richard could feel Pat trying to bridge sixteen years in ten
minutes. It was too much, too fast.

Thanking Richard quietly, Pat climbed back into her own
car. She was numb. She felt no anger or hatred. No love or
warmth. Just an indefinable sadness and shock. For sixteen
years she had been scanning crowds, looking at faces in bus
windows and in passing cars, searching for a handsome twenty-
three-year-old former Marine who didn't exist anywhere but
in her mind. Beneath the painful sense of void there was a
great relief.

As she drove home, doubts began to return. Maybe Parker
wasn't David after all? Maybe she just wanted to believe he was
David, just as she wanted to believe David had no other
children? Torn with indecision, she stopped at her mother's
house and showed the photos to her mother and sister.

"That's him," her mother said.

"Definitely him," her sister echoed.

But Pat was still not satisfied; she wanted to show the photos to one more person before she filed a petition to prosecute David.

Bill Daniels had just moved up from Florida, and Pat was anxious to see him again for a lot of reasons. She would always remember how he had supported her emotionally during those hard months after David had run away. But she could neither forget nor forgive Bill for giving David a place to stay when he ran out and for keeping David's whereabouts a secret, all the while knowing how humiliating it was for her to be on welfare. Over the years, she and Bill had often discussed what might have happened to David, and Bill had always seemed curious. She called and told him she had found David and how.

"Well, I'll be damned," he said.

"I've got pictures of him, Bill," she said. "Wait till you see them. You won't believe it."

Pat was in Boomerangs with half a dozen of her friends when Bill walked in. Trim and self-assured, with a hint of gray in his curly blond hair and mustache, he was hands-down the most handsome man in the place that night, Pat thought, but she gave no sign she recognized him.

Bill ordered a drink and soon spotted Pat seated at the bar, as they'd arranged. Leaning over a railing that separated one part of the bar from another, he said to her, "Excuse me, don't I know you from somewhere?"

Barely giving him a glance, Pat said huffily, "I've never seen you before. You guys are all alike—you think you can just walk in and pick anybody up."

"All I did was say hello," Bill said. "What's your problem, lady?"

"Really," Pat sniffed, "just because you look like Paul Newman you think every woman is going to fall at your feet."

Pat's friends gaped. The act was a bit of fun she and Bill had cooked up on the phone. When the introductions were finally made, there was a gale of laughter.

Later, when the merriment died down, Pat excused herself. She and Bill found a quieter corner. After giving him a detailed account of her investigation, she handed Bill the package of photographs. "Tell me what you think."

Bill studied the pictures almost as intently as Pat had. Finally, he said, "It doesn't look like him, but it is."

"How do you know?" Pat asked. If she had any doubt, it was gone now.

"There"—Bill pointed—"look at the way he's standing. Look at how he's carrying his shoulders. I'd know that walk anywhere."

"You sure?" she asked.

"Positive."

It was the beard and the baldness that had made both of them hesitate. Pat fished out of her purse some old snapshots of David as well as the more recent pictures of Jim Parker that Lenora had sent her. Hunched over the photos spread out on the cocktail table and straining to see in the dim light, they compared noses and faces, noting that on Lenora's pictures, David's hair was already beginning to thin and his hairline had receded.

Bill turned serious. "Pat," he advised, "you better let sleeping dogs lie. You don't know what you're getting into. You don't know his frame of mind. You could answer a knock on the door and face a shotgun."

Bill wasn't trying to frighten her. His concern was genuine. The David who ran away, changed his name, and became a bigamist was not the David he grew up with. Bill felt he really didn't know the man in the photographs anymore. Weren't the newspapers full of stories about husbands and wives shooting each other in rages of anger or jealousy? He couldn't imagine that David would be pleased with Pat for having unmasked him. He was married. He had a business.

In fact, he was thinking that if she went down to Tampa, he wouldn't be surprised to get a call saying David had killed her and the girls and then committed suicide.

Misreading his concern, Pat thought Bill was feeling sorrier for David than for her and her daughters. Not about to back down, especially not because of anything Bill told her, she said she was going to Florida not only to identify David but to have him extradited to Virginia and hauled before a Fairfax judge for criminal desertion.

"Why mess up his life?" Bill argued. "Why not just call him

up? The kids want to meet their father. So set up a time and place."

"Because he'll disappear again."

"You don't know that. Why not give him a chance? For God's sake, Pat, you're going to ruin his life."

"You just don't understand, do you, Bill?" Pat was getting angry now. "What about what he did to me and the girls? Should I just let him walk away from that?"

"He probably doesn't even have any money," Bill said. He was getting upset, too. Money was no reason to crush a man and ruin his life. "You can't leave well enough alone, can you? You know he's alive. You know where he is. You know what he looks like. So just drop it. Aren't you going to feel rotten if he has to spend a year in jail?"

Same old Bill, Pat thought. Still taking David's side no matter what. When you nab a burglar, you don't decline to press charges because he and his family might find jail a hardship.

"Come on, Bill," Pat said. "You don't really believe he's going to jail for deserting his kids, do you? Nothing ever happens to guys like that and you know it. He'll just stand before the bench, the judge will say, 'naughty, naughty,' the girls will see him—end of story. I'm sure he doesn't have any money, either."

Pat unleashed her anger on Bill. "You were a wimp, Bill. You took his part sixteen years ago. You took him in when you knew I was looking for him. I was just a pregnant kid on welfare. But you couldn't stand up to David and tell him he was wrong, could you? You're still a wimp."

"Well, I was wrong back then and I regret it," Bill admitted to Pat for the first time. In fact, he had always felt guilty about taking rent money from David when David's children were getting nothing. "But this is now."

Pat left Boomerangs that night with a lot to think about. It had been only a week since she had phoned Lenora, but it seemed like a whole summer. In those seven days, she had found David, located a sixteen-year-old court order, had an audience with a judge, looked at photographs of a husband she barely recognized, and watched her daughters try to cope with the shock that their father was still alive. During that hectic week, she had never really asked herself what extradition would do to David. Would it really ruin his life?

Pat felt torn. Whose advice should she follow? Judge Valentine's or Bill's? Bill's solution seemed simpler and less painful. But she knew it was short-term and ultimately unacceptable. To jail or not to jail, to pay or not to pay, to destroy or not to destroy were red herrings. The real issue was—to resolve or not to resolve. Put that way, she knew she had no choice. David had robbed her of inner peace for sixteen years, and she would never get it back until she confronted him personally and legally and gave her daughters the chance to do the same.

She would request extradition the next day, Pat decided. But first, she'd show her daughters the pictures of their father. As Andrea would say, they had a right to see them.

Pat called the girls into the kitchen later that night and told them she had photos of their father. Marcia almost ripped them out of her hand. "Let me see," she cried. "Let me see!" Christine was tentative and silent. Andrea was hostile and indifferent, as if afraid to admit she was curious.

If Pat was shocked at seeing David, she knew her daughters would be, too. Like her, they had been carrying an image of him in their minds for years. For Christine and Marcia, at least, it was a romantic one. Tall and good looking. Someone to be proud of. They had fantasized about him coming to their graduations or escorting them to a school activity, impressing all their classmates and friends. "See, we told you he was handsome," they would say.

At first, Christine, Andrea, and Marcia all reacted the same way. After a moment of silence, they appeared let down and somehow cheated.

"That's *him?*" they asked with the general disdain of youth for middle age. "That's him? He's almost bald! He's so old. Yuk, he's ugly."

As she listened to them work through their initial disappointment, Pat noted subtle differences in her daughters' responses. Christine seemed almost relieved that her father wasn't mounted on a white charger. The ordinary forty-year-old man she saw only reassured her that there was no reason why she should care about him or go out of her way to meet him.

To Andrea, the pictures also came as a relief, and Pat could hear her sigh inwardly. It would have been more difficult for Andrea to be angry at a father who was dashing. To her, his looks reflected what she felt. "What a sleazebag," she said.

Marcia seemed genuinely disappointed. She kept looking at the pictures trying to find something she could relate to. Finally, she said, "Christine stands just like him."

Pat smiled to herself. She had asked Richard to get pictures of James Parker so she could make a positive identification. She always knew she'd show them to the girls if he turned out to be David, but she had never thought about how the first glimpse of their father might affect them. She couldn't have been more pleased, for the pictures forced her daughters to face their real father and to come to terms with their fantasy father. With "I wonder what he looks like" out of the way, maybe they could start dealing with the deeper questions she knew were troubling them.

14

>>>>>>>>>>>>>> No longer doubting that James Parker was
David, Pat went to see Nanette Hoback, an intake officer in the
Juvenile and Domestic Relations Court, after dinner the following night. At Hoback's office Pat signed a sworn affidavit
stating that David had failed to pay child support for sixteen
years, and that he had gone to extremes to hide his identity by
changing his name, Social Security number, and date and place
of birth, as well as inventing a fictitious background. She
requested in the affidavit that David, alias James C. Parker, be
ordered to show cause why he should not be held in contempt.

The court moved as swiftly as a greyhound. The next day,
Linda called Pat at work to say that a petition asking the court
to prosecute David for criminal desertion and nonsupport was
waiting in the intake office for her signature. Pat signed it that
night after work. The next morning Judge Valentine issued a
warrant for the arrest of David aka James C. Parker on the
grounds that he "as a spouse and without just cause, deserted
or willfully neglected, refused or failed to provide for the
support and maintenance of his children under the ages of 18
years." At the same time, Judge Valentine asked Fairfax
County's commonwealth attorney to recommend to the governor that Parker be extradited.

The Virginia code, like most state codes, provides for
extradition for criminal desertion and nonsupport, but prosecutors have rarely invoked that power—with good reason.
Whether a father owes his children one hundred dollars or
forty-two thousand dollars, the law defines the crime as only a
class-A misdemeanor. Criminal desertion is put on a par with
shoplifting. By relegating desertion and nonsupport to the
category of misdemeanor, lawmakers ensured that prosecutors
would not take it seriously. The state of Missouri is an exception.

There, nonsupport is a class-A misdemeanor "unless the actor leaves the state for the purpose of avoiding his obligations to support, in which case it is a class-D felony."

To Judge Valentine, the law was a sad commentary on how society values its children. He preferred a statute that made criminal desertion and nonsupport a felony once the amount a parent owed reached a certain limit. Valentine didn't care much whether lawmakers drew the line at one thousand or three thousand dollars, as long as there was a clearly defined line. Until then, runaway fathers would continue to ignore the toothless snarl of the law.

By sending his request for extradition to the commonwealth attorney, Judge Valentine was asking for an exception to Fairfax County practice, an exception he believed was justified by Parker's outrageous flouting of the law. Valentine knew that in Virginia petitioners like Pat Bennett had to exhaust all *civil* remedies in child-support cases before requesting extradition, unless civil proceedings "would be of no avail." Since Bennett's former husband had deserted her and their three daughters and had hidden under an assumed name for sixteen years, there was good reason to believe that civil action would be "of no avail" in her case.

Valentine had no illusions about how effective an out-of-state "civil proceeding" would be. James Parker would get a letter from the court, saying in effect: "Dear Sir: Your former wife has found you and wants you to appear in court so she can collect the forty-two thousand dollars you owe your children. She has a valid sixteen-year-old court order for the money, and there is a warrant for your arrest in Virginia should you decide to return. The warrant, however, is no good outside the state. If you appear and fail to pay, you can be prosecuted for criminal desertion and nonsupport, which carries a penalty in Virginia of up to one year in jail. The court is giving you thirty days to tell us what you intend to do."

Of course, Parker would just sit right down, pull out his checkbook, and write a check for forty-two thousand dollars.

The final decision on extradition rested with Fairfax's commonwealth attorney. If he recommended extradition to the governor, Valentine knew the governor would routinely sign the order. Otherwise, it was impossible. The whole matter simply boiled down to, Would the commonwealth attorney, an elected official, be willing to set a county precedent in desertion and nonsupport cases?

As Fairfax County's commonwealth attorney for twenty years, Robert Horan was a powerful man, and not simply by virtue of his office. Over the years, the rotating crop of assistant prosecutors who had served under him had matured into an influential and loyal network of lawyers, judges, business executives, and politicians throughout the state. Horan loved big cases and headlines and had few critics in the media, in part because he was one of the finest prosecutors in Virginia. The prosecutor had a mind like a steel trap and could argue with logic as hard and as cold. Not many people in the state wanted to challenge him or find themselves on his bad side.

An exception to that rule was Judge Valentine, who fought with Horan constantly in private and in the press over how poorly the Commonwealth Attorney's Office treated the Juvenile and Domestic Relations Court. At the heart of the squabble was the role of the county prosecutors. Valentine wanted Horan to assign full-time assistant commonwealth attorneys to his court. Horan always refused. Across the Potomac, in Washington, there were twenty-seven full-time prosecutors in the family division, serving a population of 650,000. Serving just as many people, Fairfax County did not have a single full-time prosecutor in its family division. Although Valentine yelled and screamed, he got nowhere. If Horan didn't have enough assistants, Valentine would argue, he should hire more. After all, wasn't Fairfax the fifth-richest county in the nation? But Horan was as stubborn as he was bright. Sometimes the situation got so ridiculous that Valentine was forced to throw cases out of court because there simply weren't any prosecutors to try them, which left the judge angry, the police bewildered, and the victims wondering where they'd have to go to get justice.

If Judge Valentine was hard on Horan, child-support specialists were even tougher. They had learned that the Commonwealth Attorney's Office held a rigid party line: child support was a civil matter, not a criminal one; it was the job of Juvenile and Domestic Relations Court counselors to investigate all child-support cases and prepare all paperwork; if a prosecutor was eventually needed, he or she was not obligated to study the case file before entering the courtroom; prosecutors were not to get involved with collection or enforcement.

In following that line of legal and administrative thinking, the Fairfax County Commonwealth Attorney's Office was, like James Parker, thumbing its nose at the law, which mandates that each state prosecute *diligently* and represent its clients at *all* hearings. In Fairfax County, despite the law, mothers routinely stood before the bench without legal counsel. And should the Commonwealth Attorney's Office manage to send a prosecutor to handle a case, the lawyer was generally one of the least experienced on the staff, someone profoundly ignorant of the complex and fluid body of child-support law. To compound that ignorance, the assigned prosecutor rarely reviewed the case file until a few minutes before entering the hearing and facing an experienced defense attorney. Unembarrassed by his lack of preparation—especially since most hearings involving children were private and thus closed to peers and the press—the prosecutor then proceeded to anger by his incompetence the judge who sat on the case.

Through bitter experience, Fairfax child-support experts had learned to expect the Commonwealth Attorney's Office to push child support to the bottom of its list of concerns: chasing delinquent fathers reaped few if any political benefits.

As he signed his letter requesting extradition, Judge Valentine wasn't sure how Horan would handle the Bennett case, which required his personal signature. To make sure his letter would not end up in a slush pile, Valentine called Horan's righthand man, Assistant Commonwealth Attorney Britt Richardson. After summarizing the Bennett story, he told Richardson that he knew Horan did not recommend extradition in desertion and nonsupport cases on principle, but that Bennett was a clear exception. "A perfect case," he said.

To Judge Valentine's delighted surprise, Richardson agreed. "It seems to me that this is the kind of case we ought to do something about," he told the judge. "I'll take care of it."

When she got home after signing her petition to prosecute David, Pat called Beth, an old friend who had also been abandoned with an infant son by her husband. Like David, her husband had vanished, and Beth had not heard from him for more than ten years. Pat and Beth had become like sisters in spirit.

"Beth, I found David," Pat blurted.

"But why?" Beth was genuinely confused, for she knew Pat had asked the Social Security Administration for a death-benefits hearing. "I don't understand what in the hell you're doing. First, you want him declared dead. Now you're telling me you found him."

"I'm going to have him arrested for desertion," Pat said.

"I can't believe you're doing this," Beth said. There was a touch of panic in her voice. "For the first time in your life, everything is going well. Now you're going to— This makes me sick to my stomach. I can't talk about it. I don't even want to hear about it."

"But you don't understand—"

"I can't talk about it!"

Beth hung up, leaving Pat shaken. Her closest friend, who knew what it was like to be deserted and to bring up a child without knowing where the father was, wouldn't even hear her out. Feeling abandoned herself, she called Beth back, but her friend refused to talk and hung up a second time.

Realizing that Beth's rejection must have something to do with her own former husband, Pat called a third time. "I've *got* to talk to you," she said. "Don't hang up on me, Beth. Why are you acting this way?"

"I simply don't want to talk about it," Beth said.

"Well, I think I'm hitting close to home. You don't want to face your own past, and you're angry at me because I'm facing mine!"

Pat waited for Beth to slam the receiver down again. She knew she was on the right track, and she sensed she had just hit a nerve. There was a long silence, then Beth said quietly, "There's more to it than that."

What was really bothering her was that her son, who was Marcia's age, was begging her to find his father so he could meet him for the first time. But Beth kept putting him off because she didn't think she could go through with it. Then Pat called to say she had just done for her daughters what Beth's son was asking her to do.

"I can't," Beth said. "I just can't. Please don't call anymore."

Pat was crying when she hung up. Both for herself and for Beth. She realized that the shared experience that had formed the foundation of their friendship had just shattered it.

Beth was the first woman Pat had met who seemed threatened by her refusal to let runaway fathers hide, but she knew there would be others, and she had begun to understand why. Before Pat had decided to look for David, she had been a victim with whom most women could identify—dumped on, wronged, and hurt by a husband, and abused by a legal system created and run by men. But by challenging David and the system, she became a threat to those women who wouldn't, or couldn't, do the same. To them she was a victimizer not a victim. A cold, castrating, greedy bitch.

Although saddened and shaken by Beth's rejection, Pat was not about to call Judge Valentine and say she wanted to back out. Instead, over the weekend, she sketched out a plan.

Monday morning, she would call the Tampa sheriff to let him know she was coming and why, and to ask his full cooperation. She knew this would be dangerous because Florida sheriffs and their deputies had earned a reputation for helping runaway and delinquent fathers escape. But she felt she had little choice. With the help of Judge Valentine, she would make sure the warrant for Parker's arrest would not be on the national computer listing lest someone see it and alert David.

A week later, July 2, she would fly to Tampa with Victoria in tow as her attorney in case David fought extradition and her friend Stewart, a former Washington Redskin, as her bodyguard. Extradition order in hand, she would ask the sheriff to arrest Parker that night. The next day, July 3, she'd attend the extradition hearing and identify James Parker as David. Then she'd bask on the beach over the Fourth of July and return to Washington on the fifth in time for David's hearing in Juvenile and Domestic Relations Court on Friday, July 6. Christine, Andrea, and Marcia would see their father when he arrived in Fairfax, in a private conference room she hoped, instead of in court or in jail. But if they had to meet him for the first time in handcuffs, or behind bars, or facing a judge, then that's the way it would have to be.

The plan was clean, simple, and fast. It would all be over in just seven more days.

Pat made reservations on Piedmont Airlines for herself, Victoria, and Stewart. On Monday she called the sheriff in Tampa. He listened to her story and promised to be ready and waiting with cuffs. "It's very important that nothing go wrong or he'll disappear again," Pat said.

"Don't worry, I won't say a word," the sheriff promised.

All Pat needed now was the extradition order. A preprinted form. Just fill in the blanks, Mr. Horan, and ask the governor to sign.

If Pat was comfortable with her plan, the six counselors at the Juvenile and Domestic Relations Court were not. The male counselors tended to agree with Pat's decision to sic the law on David. The women, especially Kitty Meredith, were cautious, more concerned about how justice would affect Pat and her daughters than about justice itself. Meredith recognized that Pat craved satisfaction and resolution more than money, and she respected those deep needs. She felt Pat had a right to see her former husband stand before the bench, watch the court peel away the layers of lies, and hear a judge say he was a criminal and had to pay. The troubling question was, In this case, was justice worth the risk?

Meredith was worried. It was possible that prosecuting her former husband might resolve nothing for Pat. In fact, it might awaken in her a bitterness and thirst for revenge that could dog her for the rest of her life. In the end, she might have less peace than she had before. Meredith had watched that happen to other women. Just seeing their former husbands and listening to them make excuses for their criminal neglect often turned them into bitter women, thirsting for legal and financial blood.

Kitty Meredith was worried even more about Christine, Andrea, and Marcia. They had adjusted to being abandoned sixteen years ago and had learned to live without a father. True, they would be scarred for life and might always feel a sense of loss, hurt, and self-doubt. But each had probably created a fantasy father all her own. What would it do to them if they met their father for the first time in jail, in handcuffs, or standing before the court like a criminal? Was Pat taking pleasure in turning her daughters against David, using them to punish him? As volatile teenagers, they were quite capable of turning against Pat at any point, accusing her of a vendetta. They could even end up taking their father's side against her saying, "Now we know why he abandoned us. You drove him away."

Or it could go the other way. Meredith knew that if Pat could become bitter and angry in her search for justice, her children could too. If they did, any hope of a relationship with the only father they had, no matter how bad they might think he was, could be dashed. They could even go through a period of hating all men.

Then again, it could all turn out well. In Meredith's business, not everyone who skated on thin ice fell through. In the end, all she could do was encourage people to test the ice before they put their skates on. She was prepared to explore the risks with Pat if she wanted to talk about them, but Pat never opened up. All she had said was, "Kitty, do you think I should do this?" Sensing that Pat's mind was already made up and that she was just looking for support, Kitty replied, "Pat, you'll have to decide this one for yourself."

Pat took leave on Monday, July 2. Everything was ready but Robert Horan's signature on the request to extradite. Her plane left for Tampa at 5:45 that evening. Victoria was on hold. Stewart was ready to go. Her bags were packed and sitting by the kitchen door next to the carport. She was keyed up and kept calling Linda every hour to see if Horan had signed yet. One moment, she was pleased that it would soon be over. The next, she was afraid something might go wrong. Afraid of David. Afraid of herself.

At four o'clock, Linda finally called with news. "Horan has a problem with the papers," she said. "He won't sign."

Pat was crushed. She had always assumed that if she ever found David, Virginia would see to it that he faced the judge. She never believed he'd really be punished, but she never doubted she'd have her day in court.

Pat called Piedmont and canceled her reservations. Then she hung up the phone and cried. "Nobody cares," she sobbed. "Nobody cares!"

15

>>>>>>>>>>>>>>> Pat broke the news to Victoria Gordon, who was home in bed recuperating from a jaw operation and bored to distraction. Although she was in pain, her doctor couldn't find wires and screws strong enough to stop her from talking.

An independent woman, Victoria graduated from law school in Fairfax and hung out her own shingle. She didn't want to spend years doing someone else's research at a lawyer factory in Washington. Finding corporate law cold and remote from life, she easily slipped into the practice of family law. A high-energy person who lived on adrenaline, Victoria didn't have the patience to wait her turn in court. Born for the stage or the soapbox, front and center and before the bench was where she wanted to be.

It came as no surprise to Victoria that Horan had refused to sign the extradition papers. She had called him earlier in the day to say that Pat had airline reservations that evening for Tampa, where the sheriff was waiting. Horan spouted like a sperm whale because Pat had dared to assume he would sign. Victoria tossed all the arguments in her arsenal at him:

Pat would lose months if she sought civil redress as Horan demanded, instead of criminal sanctions as Judge Valentine suggested. James Parker might flee, and if Pat Bennett ever found him again, Marcia would probably have turned eighteen, making it even more difficult to seek justice. Even if Parker didn't flee, the Florida judge might reduce the amount of unpaid child support. Finally Victoria assured him that if the cost of extradition posed a problem for the county, Pat Bennett had volunteered to pay the cost herself.

Horan wouldn't budge.

In one sense, Victoria was relieved. She thought that Pat's game plan was unrealistic and made no legal sense. Ninety percent emotion and 10 percent strategy. For one thing, it was unlikely that Parker would be arrested one day and face an extradition hearing the next. If by some judicial witchcraft he did, Victoria felt she didn't have enough documentation to prove David's identity absolutely if James Parker contested it. Besides, her jaw was so sore that the only tempting thing about Tampa was the beach.

Victoria's alternate plan was, she thought, much more practical: get Horan to sign the extradition request as soon as possible; have Parker arrested immediately; then, after a preliminary bond hearing, put off the extradition fight for thirty days to give her time to prepare her case.

Pat sounded so disappointed and angry after Horan's resounding "No" that Victoria put in an immediate conference call to Judge Valentine so they could assess the damage and discuss what to do next. Valentine and Victoria did all the talking.

Like Victoria, Judge Valentine was angry with Horan's decision, but not shocked. As far as he was concerned, the commonwealth attorney had just kicked the state of Virginia in the legal groin. When Victoria told Valentine she had tried to lean on Horan earlier that day, he was frankly annoyed.

"Why did you do that?" he scolded.

"I wanted to make sure the request was signed," Victoria explained.

"Well, he might have signed it without noticing whom it was for," Valentine said. "But you just called his attention to it."

Valentine told Victoria that as far as extradition was concerned, he had done everything he could without jeopardizing his position. The rest was up to her and Pat. He'd always be there if they needed him.

Too angry and depressed to be alone, Pat drove over to Victoria's townhouse more as a friend than a client. Victoria switched on her new word processor, and she and Pat huddled in front of the screen, pouring out their frustration in a letter to Horan—nine single-spaced pages of angry words. Written in Pat's name, the letter ended: "I believe there is a difference between revenge and justice. I seek the latter. . . . The number [of men] who have fled to avoid child support is a disgrace in this country. I want to make a statement to all such men who believe that risking the penalties of the law is a better alternative to meeting their legal obligation to pay child support. Mr. Horan, I ask you, please give this request your utmost consideration." Although the letter made them both feel better, they didn't bother to revise or mail it because they knew it wouldn't help.

Since Victoria was in pain, Pat suggested that the attorney spend the night at her house. And since next to talking, eating was Victoria's favorite pastime, Pat ordered a giant pizza. Forced by her aching jaw to exercise some culinary imagination, Victoria scraped the topping off her half of the pizza, put it in a blender, and settled down to a serious evening of drinking pizza and looking for new ways to get Pat her day in court.

The next morning, Pat took Victoria out for a breakfast of blueberry pancakes floating in maple syrup. "I don't know any other attorney," Victoria said through slightly clenched teeth, "who'd work for pizza and blueberry pancakes."

Emotion caught up with Pat the following weekend at a pool party. Buoyed by a few drinks, the feelings she had been suppressing rose to the surface like bubbles and burst. Fortunately, Bill Daniels was there, and he did what he could to help her through it.

She was determined to be so tough, Pat told Bill. After David ran away, she had vowed never to depend on anyone again. Yet she felt like a little girl who needed her father's arms around her. She didn't think she could wear a brave face for even one more day. Her daughters and her friends thought she could handle anything, but she couldn't any longer. She was so tired—of carrying the whole burden alone, of always struggling, of fighting. And she was afraid too. Afraid of what she had found. Afraid of herself. Afraid of what she'd have to do next. Afraid of how it would all end. Now it was too late to turn back.

"I'm so scared," she sobbed as Bill held her. "Oh, my God, what have I done?"

But there was more to it than just being scared. Pat knew she should be angry at David. She should want him to suffer, go to jail, pay in pain and in kind. Instead, she found herself feeling sorry for him, and that made her mad at herself. She didn't want to feel anything *for* David, only something *at* him. Why did everything have to be so emotionally complicated when it was all so logical and simple?

Bill was touched. In the twenty years he had known Pat, he had never seen her afraid before. And although he had watched her cry many times, it was never the kind of weeping that grabs the body and doesn't want to stop. For a moment, she was the young Pat he had known when she was dating David. The little girl without pretense, unsure of herself, vulnerable.

After he had seen Pat's pictures of Jim Parker, Bill had had a long talk with his mother and she had taken Pat's side. She made Bill change his mind—to a point. David should be caught and punished, he concluded, but Pat was going about it the wrong way. What she was feeling now was just a taste of what was to come. Bill thought that she was obsessed with confronting David and bringing him to justice even though she was confused about how she felt toward him. Since she wasn't about to give up, the best thing he could do would be to support her.

Bill held her until the last sob ended, then said, "I understand, Pat. I was wrong to try and put you off. Go through with it. I knew from the moment you told me you found David that you wouldn't give up."

For the next two months, Pat called the Commonwealth Attorney's Office almost every day, asking to speak to Robert Horan. She never got through. Assistant Commonwealth Attorney Mindy Norton was assigned to return her calls. Although she was sympathetic, Norton firmly held to the party line. Pat sensed that Norton felt David ought to be extradited but couldn't say so because she had to be loyal to her boss. Pat was right in a way. Norton had told Judge Valentine that she would prosecute the case herself should Horan decide to recommend extradition.

Victoria also called Mindy Norton, whom she had known at law school. She had seen Norton work in court many times and found her a good, conscientious prosecutor, totally professional and cautiously friendly. Norton told Victoria that Pat had sent so many mixed signals that Norton was no longer sure why Pat wanted the county to extradite her former husband. First it sounded as if she had a personal vendetta against the man, Norton said. Then it seemed as if she might drop the charges against him if she ever got him into court. One minute it sounded as if all she wanted was justice; the next, as if she was merely using the state to get the man back to Virginia so her children could see him.

Victoria tried to convince Norton that Pat was balanced and serious, and that her motives, although complex, were honest.

"Well, I'll have to talk to Bob," Norton said. But she didn't sound as if she'd be talking very loudly.

Pat dug in for a long siege. She eventually got through to Britt Richardson, who was just as firm as Norton but not as sympathetic. After listening to her and explaining Horan's position, he finally said, "We've already spent too much time on this case. We have rapes, murders, and burglaries to deal with."

"What about the taxpayers?" Pat argued. "Doesn't the state want its money back?"

Pat had been on welfare for two years because David had refused to support his children. In effect, he had pocketed more than ten thousand dollars of the taxpayers' money. If she could collect the forty-two thousand dollars David owed his children, the state would be first in line for its share.

Richardson was annoyed. "Mr. Horan asked me to call you and to say *for* him that he will not see you and that his decision is final. He thought you understood that from previous conversations."

Pat would not let Richardson off that easily. "It makes no sense for me to file for civil action. My former husband has fled before and he'll run again. Virginia law covers situations like that. I've drafted a letter to the state attorney general and—"

"We're independent here and can't be swayed by the attorney general's office. It's the policy of the governor that all other means have to be exhausted before he'll agree to extradition."

"The IRS prosecutes tax cheaters to keep the rest of the country honest," Pat continued. "Can't you use this case as an example for others?"

"We don't make an example of one person!" Richardson's voice was getting louder, higher, and more emphatic.

"You sound angry and defensive," Pat said.

"Well, I'm not," he said and hung up.

Not convinced that Robert Horan, an elected official, stood above political pressure, Pat decided to try a little muscle as a last resort. If logic and pleading wouldn't work, maybe power would. Both she and Victoria spoke to Tyke Miller in the attorney general's office in Richmond. He was anxious to extradite. Virginia had a good national reputation for collecting support for its children, and Miller wanted to protect it. "You have Horan call me," he told Pat. "I'll tell him that if he signs the request we will definitely recommend extradition to the governor."

Next, Pat leaned on State Senator Clive DuVal, one of the most powerful politicians in northern Virginia. If you want something done, the word went, go see Clive. They spoke for an hour. "How could anyone just walk out on those children like that?" DuVal kept saying. In the end, he promised to talk to Horan on her behalf.

Pat waited a few days, then called Horan again. This time she got through. "I told your attorney to exhaust all civil remedies," he told her. He spoke as if he were in court, loud, self-assured, and righteous. "You're making this whole thing more complicated than it really is."

"If I file civilly, it'll take a year if not longer," Pat pleaded. By that time, Marcia would be eighteen, and because Pat would no longer have any minors, Horan would not have to represent her by law.

"Well, then, you better get started," he said.

"If I do, they'll give him notice. They'll send him a letter. He'll just disappear again."

"There are ways to handle that," Horan said obliquely.

"I realize you know more than I do about these matters," Pat said, fanning his ego. "The attorney general's office said it would recommend extradition if you asked for it."

"I don't know how they can say that." Horan was getting impatient. "We don't extradite for this."

"But would you talk to Tyke Miller?"

Grudgingly, Horan agreed.

"If he says he'll recommend extradition to the governor, will you then sign off on it?"

Horan didn't answer. Pat asked the question two more times. Still no answer. "I'll talk to him," was all Horan would promise.

"Would it help if I got ten thousand signatures on a petition to the governor?" Pat pressed. She had already drafted a letter and was ready to go door-to-door to get signatures. Even if it took a month of evenings, she knew she could do it. But Horan wouldn't answer that question either.

"Mr. Horan, I am *not* going to go away!" Pat burst out in frustration. It was the only threat she had uttered. "This case is important. It will help other women. And I know it will get a lot of publicity—"

"This case isn't going to help anybody," Horan said and hung up sounding as angry and defensive as Richardson.

Although Horan talked to Miller, it made little difference; he wouldn't change his mind. Pat was left with no choice. It was the civil route or nothing. Where it would lead her, how long it would take, and what it would cost in emotion and money, she didn't know. One thing was certain—she was not about to let one commonwealth attorney stop her now.

16

>>>>>>>>>>>>   As she had done so often in the past when facing a crisis or in need of strength, Pat decided to visit the site of the old farmhouse that had been so special to her as a child. She needed to hear what the place had to say to her now more than ever before. As soon as she turned onto Robin Lane, Pat began to feel a gentle sadness. It was the ghost of her childhood drawing her back as it had so often done before.

Her blue Oldsmobile bounced over the potholes past the row of ugly brick houses built just before she had moved away, almost thirty years ago. When the blacktop took a sharp turn to the left, she kept straight ahead, edging the car slowly down the same dirt road she had walked as a child. She came out into an open field surrounded by woods. Behind the trees in the distance stretched a ribbon of fast-food places and gas pumps, and beyond them the beltway connecting Washington, Maryland, and Virginia.

The twin holly trees with ice-cream-cone crowns still stood side by side in the empty field, but the old house, no longer worth the cost of repairs, was long since gone. So were the small red barn where she had played and the pear tree she used to climb.

She got out of the car, stood in the tall grass where the vegetable garden had once been, and gazed slowly about her. Other than a thinning of the treeline and a new school which had gobbled up part of the woods, the old place looked the same.

She was in Camp Springs, Maryland, a few miles southeast of Washington. Her parents had moved there from Georgetown more than thirty years ago before Georgetown was an address to brag about. At thirty-five dollars a month, the farmhouse had been a bargain even then and a relief from an apartment too small for a family of five. Sitting on cinder blocks and covered with fake brick siding, it had a large living room and kitchen, and two bedrooms upstairs. Bare lead pipes ran across the ceilings and down the walls, and a single wood-coal stove in the kitchen had struggled to heat the upstairs in the winter and usually failed. Renting that place, half a century old, while her father worked as an auto-parts salesman by day and a government electrician on the four-to-midnight shift, was the only way her parents could provide space for their growing family and still save for a down payment on a proper house of their own.

Pat had shared a bedroom with her younger sister, while her older brother slept on the downstairs couch in the winter and, in the summer, on a daybed on the porch, which her father had closed in.

It hadn't taken Pat long to learn that in some ways her family was poor, for all her neighbors and classmates, it seemed, lived in nicer homes. And just a mile behind the woods lay Manchester Estates, a manicured reminder that not everyone's house sat on cinder blocks.

But in other ways, important to a child, she understood she was rich. A one-hundred-acre farm ringed her house, turning her backyard into a private park on the edge of a cramped and noisy city. In the fields all around grew grass so thick and tall that she could weave caves and tunnels to hide in. The oak and maple woods that filtered out the hum of nearby traffic were a magic forest through which trickled a dark and mysterious creek. There were frogs and turtles and crayfish. And in back of the woods to the south was White's Store, where a nickel bought the world.

Each spring her father had ploughed an acre next to the house with a cultivator rigged up to an old car motor, and the family pitched in, planting, hoeing, and picking. Her strawberry patch, her friends told her, was the biggest in all of Camp Springs and that made her feel proud. When the summer began to wane, there'd be days upon days of canning the fruit and vegetables and jams she'd eat all winter.

Standing there now in the summer of 1984, Pat was intensely aware that the field where the house had stood was not just a plot of ground where she had once lived, but the

place that had molded her into the woman she was. Her deepest
feelings she could trace back to the old farm. What she craved
most in life, she found there. And whatever drove her onward
had its roots in those five acres. It was as if she could read her
whole life there, where she had been, where she was going,
and why.

She remembered how she had prayed the rosary each night,
kneeling on the hard wooden floor next to her mother as vigil
lights cast spooky shadows on the walls. They had asked God
for another baby and a new house of their own, and to send
her father home safely from work. Far from comforting her,
the Hail Marys only reminded her each night that maybe her
father wouldn't be back, that maybe he'd get into an accident
and go to a hospital, that maybe he'd die. A nagging fear she
didn't understand as a child but understood now, tugged at
her. She remembered how sometimes, when her father was
late, she'd hear her mother crying in the next bedroom, how
she'd go to comfort her, and how together they'd drop to their
knees. Beads in hand, each with a different terror, they'd pray,
"Please, God, bring him home safely." God always heard that
prayer, but the fear of being left alone never went away.

For the first time, standing at the old place, Pat understood
that when David ran away, leaving her pregnant with two other
babies, he had made that childhood fear a reality.

Pat had cried when her family had moved twenty-five miles
around the beltway into Virginia to a real house on their own
suburban acre. For her parents, the move was a hard-earned
slice of the American dream; for Pat it was the greatest loss of
her young life, and even now, almost thirty years later, the
memory of it brought tears to her eyes.

Even as an eleven-year-old she had understood she was
losing a freedom she'd never find in her new home, and it
struck her as odd that one of the things they had been praying
the rosary for every night for five years, and which God had
finally given them, could cause so much pain. Her parents
thought the memory of the old place would fade for her as it
had for her sister, but it never did. She missed it so much that
when she got her driver's license at sixteen, she drove right
over to Robin Lane.

Now, with an extraordinary vividness, Pat remembered a

vacation in Indianapolis when she was four years old. Her grandparents had taken the children to the State Fair, and like kids everywhere, they had run straight for the ferris wheel, hoping to see the whole world from its top. But when it was time to sit in the wooden seat and let the attendant snap the holding bar in place, Pat had become too frightened to get on. Instead, she stood below holding her grandmother's hand while her brother, sister, and two cousins rode the giant circle round and round. She listened to them squeal and laugh and returned their waves feeling ashamed and jealous.

Those childhood emotions came back to her now as she stood where the old house used to be, wishing she could fly back in time to the State Fair and take that ride after all. She remembered how timid and shy she had remained for nearly twenty-five more years, still a "fraidy cat," until one day she recognized that the fear of the ferris wheel had run much of her life. It was then that she made up her mind never again to refuse a ride simply because she was afraid. From that point on, challenging the ferris wheel fear had meant meeting issues head on and refusing to let others control her life. And now that she had found David, she was not about to back off from the ride, whatever might happen.

But more than for herself, Pat was afraid for her daughters. Warnings from friends to the contrary, she felt she owed them the chance, if they wanted it, to talk to the father they never knew. But she sensed all too clearly that this would be a painful gift to them. They seemed almost too cavalier about it now, unaware of how angry and hurt they really were. Like her, they would have to face their feelings or bury them even deeper. Either way, there lay a very real danger.

She worried about Christine, who seemed to bottle up everything inside, to push away the memory of her father so that she wouldn't have to face the pain. Would meeting him finally resolve things for her or tear open old wounds that would never heal?

She worried about Andrea, who seemed angry at the whole world and wrapped herself in an armor of indifference toward her father. Would seeing him help her face that anger or encourage her to bury it beyond reach?

She worried about Marcia, so volatile and sensitive. Her

need for love and acceptance was as strong as Christine's withdrawal and Andrea's anger. How would she react if her father rejected her as a teenager the way he had rejected her as an unborn child?

It was just plain wrong, the old place was reminding her, for the world to be indifferent to the injustice done to her and her children, or to say by its silence, "It's okay, David, that you ran out on your daughters, reduced them to poverty, robbed them of opportunity, and covered them with layers of insecurity, guilt, and fear. It's okay."

It's *not* okay, the old place was telling her. Fathers couldn't just be allowed to desert helpless children. If love and responsibility wouldn't shame them into supporting their families, then fear of the law should. You owe that much to your daughters, the old place was saying, and you owe it to other abandoned and hurting children.

As she climbed back into her car, Pat was aware of a profound upheaval within her. The tears were coming again but under them she felt a new strength and wholeness. Part of it was the energy of this place that fused past, present, and future for her. But part, she knew, came from a new bond she felt with mothers and children everywhere who were abandoned and suffering and voiceless.

Pat drove slowly back down Robin Lane to the beltway. Facing David and demanding justice was her only real choice.

17

>>>>>>>>>>>>> Judge Valentine knew that if Pat Bennett tried to thread her way through civil court, she'd need more than Victoria Gordon to guide her. Child-support laws and procedures were not only complex and confusing; they varied so much from state to state that it was hard to find two people who'd agree on anything. And one small mistake could cost Bennett months.

Judge Valentine could think of no better guide than Betty Murphy, who had been wading through the legal swamp for years. She already knew more about the child-support tangle than most judges and attorneys, and he admired her dedication and guts. He frequently attended the meetings of the support group she had founded called VOICES—Virginians Organized to Insure Children's Entitlement to Support.

Valentine met Murphy in the courthouse one day not long after Horan had slammed the door on Pat's extradition request. "Betty, there's a case you ought to look at," he told her. "I can't give you the name of the woman, but I can tell you who her attorney is—Victoria Gordon."

Not one to sit back when she could help another deserted mother, Murphy found Victoria and through her, Pat. Over the next year, she shared what she knew, offered suggestions, and encouraged Pat—for free. The picture she drew was dismal but realistic.

If Pat wanted to collect and have David face a judge, she had two basic choices within the civil court system: hire an attorney to pursue David in Florida under the laws of that state, or ask the state of Virginia to help her collect. If she asked Virginia's assistance, she could do it through the counselors at the Fairfax County Juvenile and Domestic Relations Court, or through the Virginia State Child Support Office.

If Pat chose to get help from court counselors, as Betty Murphy had, Kitty Meredith would interview her, gather the necessary documents, and then set a hearing date.

If everything went well, Pat would be in court in two months.

After a brief hearing to review the validity of her facts and documents, the judge would order that a notice be sent to the circuit court in Pasco County, Florida, saying that Fairfax was requesting its assistance under the Uniform Reciprocal Enforcement Support Act (URESA), passed in 1958 and strengthened in 1968 and 1984. Fairfax would also send David a statement specifying that he owed more than forty-two thousand dollars and was still under court order to pay current child support.

If Pat was lucky, phase two would also take two months.

The circuit court clerk in the county where David lived would receive Fairfax's notice and send it to the prosecuting attorney. If Pat pestered the prosecutor's office during this critical phase, refused to be intimidated, threatened to call in the media, or was lucky enough to find at least one person who cared, she might get action in six months.

Even if the prosecutor decided to move on her case within a week, the nightmare was just beginning. Since David would be notified that Pat was after him, he could simply move out of the county that had subpoenaed him to appear in court. In that case, the prosecutor could either send the notice back to Fairfax saying David didn't live there any more, or could request the new county to take over. Since such transfers required time and paperwork and yielded few votes at the polls, most prosecutors refused. If the notice came back to Fairfax, the court would then have to redraft and resend papers to the court in the new county and to David. David could migrate across Florida until Pat and the court gave up. With each refiling, he would gain another six months to a year.

Even if David lived at the address Pat furnished to the court and made no attempt to move, Florida law required the sheriff or his deputy to personally serve the subpoena. Since

David would be given advance notice, he could elude them in a hundred different ways, enlisting the help of his friends, employer, or business associates. Mothers trying to subpoena delinquent dads faced this all the time.

If David was actually served, he wouldn't even have to appear in court. The prosecutor could negotiate with him or his attorney over the phone without notifying Pat. Then— again without notifying her—the prosecutor could settle with David the amount of arrearage he actually had to pay, and when and how he would pay it. David could end up paying as little as twenty dollars a month on the arrearage; at that rate, Marcia would be 187 years old when she got her last check. Because the prosecutor didn't have to notify her, Pat could lose her right to appeal the settlement. Thousands of women before her had been ill served by prosecutors who, anxious to get the cases settled without fuss, often bargained away essential support for children.

Finally, if Pat's case ever reached a courtroom, the prosecutor would not have to notify her of the time and place, even if she specifically asked to be told. And the hearing judge could make whatever demands he wanted from David, including cutting as much arrearage as he wished and lowering the amount of support to be paid in the future. It happened all the time.

Although Pat would have a constitutional right to appeal any judge's decision, she might never get the chance. There is a specified time within which she must appeal, even though there is no specified time within which Florida must inform her of the court's decision.

If Pat wanted the state of Virginia to help her collect, her other option involved the Virginia State Child Support Office. There the collection process would be essentially the same, except she'd have to pay a processing fee based on her income and assets, and it would take longer.

Collecting from Florida, moreover, might prove difficult. Florida had long been considered by child-support specialists to be one of the hardest states in which to collect child support. "Florida is a cesspool of runaway fathers and deadbeat dads from all over the country," as one expert put it. Florida laws sound good on paper, but the old-boy network among prosecutors, judges, clerks, sheriffs, and their deputies is stronger than the pull of justice. And the State Office of Child Support Enforcement charges children hefty fees.

After listening to everyone, Pat Bennett decided to hire her own attorneys to corral David into court, not just to keep control over her case, but to make sure her daughters got a chance to see him. It would not be easy. The entire legal deck was stacked against her. She would need one attorney in Virginia and another in Florida. With luck and a few sympathetic people in the right places, she just might be able to resolve her case within a year, while Marcia was still a minor.

18

>>>>>>>>>>>>>> Terry Kellogg, Pat's cousin, passed through
Washington at the end of September on his way to conduct a
family therapy workshop in Lancaster, Pennsylvania. Since Pat
had not seen him for more than twenty years, she was looking
forward to his visit. The timing was perfect for the Bennett
household was tense with growing doubts and fears.

A low-key, nontraditional family-systems therapist who
wasn't afraid to give advice, Terry was a good listener, and his
approach to what was happening to Pat and her daughters,
and why, was fresh. Terry disagreed with traditional Freudians,
who believe that the root of an individual's problem lies within
deeply buried conflicts of the person, and that these conflicts
are related to early experiences with one's parents. He believed
that problems were a symptom of a disturbance of emotional
forces deep within the family itself. If you wanted to know
why you were feeling or acting a certain way, family-systems
therapists advised, don't focus on yourself or your childhood,
or on your mother and father. Look at your whole family and
how each member in it acts and reacts.

After they had brought each other up to date on family
and careers, Pat told Terry how she had found David, what
she planned to do, and why. She had chatted with her cousin
off and on over the years, and he had always been easy to talk
to, understanding, and helpful. Now she poured out her doubts
and fears.

Her biggest concern, Pat told Terry, was her daughters.
Now that they were closer to a meeting with their father, she
could see they were beginning to feel anxious even if they
didn't admit it. Christine was expressing a greater than usual
indifference to her father, while accusing Pat of being obsessed
and vengeful. Christine's indifference disturbed Pat. She knew

her oldest daughter must be feeling some deep anger or hurt that she couldn't express. Christine's nonchalance even bothered her younger sisters, who had begun calling her a wimp.

Andrea's aggressive behavior and open hostility worried Pat almost as much, she told her cousin. So did Marcia's obvious confusion and extreme emotional response to anything connected with her father. The two younger girls were constantly needling their mother because the law, courts, and lawyers were moving so slowly. They couldn't understand how someone who had committed what seemed such a horrendous crime could be walking the streets. As if to prove a point, Andrea had gotten herself arrested for disturbing the peace. She had waited for the police to arrive and almost begged to be handcuffed. The arresting officers had wanted to let her go with a warning, but she put out her wrists and insisted on going to jail. "My father is Jim Parker," she told anyone who would listen. "He deserted me and is still free. I'm the one who's going to jail."

Pat admitted she was pushing her daughters to meet their father, and that in some ways, it was cruel because it was so painful for them. But she wanted her daughters to be independent and free of the emotional burden she had carried most of her adult life.

"Maybe I'm wrong," she told Terry. "Maybe they'll be so devastated by all this that they'll fall apart emotionally and never recover. Am I making a mistake? Should I go to Florida alone?"

There was no doubt in Terry's mind that not only was Pat doing the right thing by facing David and urging her daughters to do the same; she was being courageous. He knew she was hoping the media would pick up on her case and that somehow it might help others, and he approved. In fact, he believed that what she was trying to do for other abandoned wives and children by exposing the rotten child-support system bordered on heroic. She was using her anger to bring about change while at the same time carrying out an act of justice for her children. Nothing could be healthier. He was delighted to give her any advice and support he could.

"It can't backfire," Terry reassured Pat. "Facing the anger and pain is healthier than sitting on your emotions. And meeting their father can only bring some degree of resolution to the girls' lives. You are offering them a chance to recover, Pat. That's a wonderful gift for a mother to give. Few deserted wives have the courage and strength to do that."

Terry went on to explain that abandoned children repeated the past by either abandoning others or setting themselves up to be abandoned over and over. They could only break the cycle by facing their feelings of anger, guilt, worthlessness, shame, and fear. That was the first step to recovery.

"The girls were devastated a long time ago," he said, "and have been living with the pain ever since. Meeting their father can't make that pain any worse. It may bring their anger to the surface so it looks worse, but it won't be. That's healthy. Even though they may not have expressed the anger yet, they know there's plenty to go around. They've been feeling yours for years. Besides, they have a *right* to see who their father is and what he looks like."

Pat smiled: Terry sounded like Andrea.

Terry went on to share with Pat his insights about her daughters, based on what she had told him and on his experience with other abandoned children. As the firstborn and a child who actually remembered her father, Christine had, in many ways, been hurt the deepest, Terry explained. What she was feeling was closer to rage than anger. She didn't know she was angry because she'd always been that way. Anger was her natural state, and she didn't know what it would be like not to feel it. Her indifference toward her father was the ultimate expression of her rage. It was her way of killing him, of saying, "You don't exist." To Christine, her rage was so terrifying, she was afraid to face it lest it destroy her. Instead, she found little ways to sublimate it and get temporary relief. Only by facing her rage could Christine release it.

As the secondborn child, Andrea was closer to Pat than to her father. Because of that closeness, she was very sensitive to her mother's feelings and tended to be protective of her. Andrea had a tremendous fear of abandonment—even more than Christine or Marcia. All her life she had felt her own fear of it *and* her mother's as well. She carried a double load. Fear of abandonment had almost become an obsession with her, and she reenacted it in her relationships. What you didn't resolve, you tended to reenact. She denied it on one level, then acted it out on another. She constantly set herself up to be rejected. She picked relationships that were doomed. She didn't know how or when to let go. She entered where she wasn't wanted. Expressing her anger at her father was the first step to breaking the cycle.

Marcia, more than Christine or Andrea, felt responsible for the pain of her mother and sisters. She might say that she no longer felt guilty or that she had worked it through, but she hadn't. She had turned her shame on herself and reenacted her abandonment by wanting to be punished and treated as worthless. Many of her problems in school stemmed from this. She underachieved as if to prove to herself she was no good. She tended to be *too* loyal in her relationships and she set up expectations that couldn't be met. Her conflicting feelings confused her. Facing her guilt could only help her accept that her father's abandonment of her mother and sisters wasn't her fault.

Relieved that her instincts about her daughters and their needs had been sound, Pat wanted to be sure she was doing the right thing for herself. Dr. Charles Crotty, whom she had known for years and who was more like a friend than a therapist, had told her it was even more important to resolve her own conflict than to give her children a chance to meet their father. Was she obsessed, as Christine seemed to think? Was she really doing the right thing for herself by confronting David and her darkest feelings in the process?

Terry once again encouraged her. She had never had the chance to resolve her relationship with David in 1968, he said. His running away was like cutting off her oxygen. There had been no discussion, no argument, no explanation.

Pat began to cry. She told Terry that for sixteen years she couldn't talk about what had happened in 1968. She held it all in as if it had never occurred. When she finally began to face it, the feeling of panic at having two babies with another on the way, and no food or money, came back to haunt her. It was foolish, she knew. She had a good job now, but the fear of being abandoned and penniless was still there, as she put it, "like a knife running through me."

The more Pat brought up the past, the more tears poured

out. Terry told Pat that there was more than anger and fear behind her tears. She was a victim, he explained, and like most victims, she was tormented by guilt: Was she responsible for David running away from his children? Was she responsible for their pain? If she was, how could she live with herself? Like most victims, too, she felt worthless: Perhaps she deserved the treatment David had given her? If not, would he have done that to her? And like most victims, Terry continued, she felt a deep sense of shame about what had happened to her.

Pat was driven more by these feelings of guilt, shame, and worthlessness than by anger, Terry continued. Her tremendous drive to find David was her way of trying to resolve her feelings. She needed to hear a judge say that David had wronged her and must pay for his crime because—hard as it may be for others to understand—a jail sentence and reparations would finally confirm her value as a person and as a member of society.

"Going after David," Terry summed up, "is your way of finally telling yourself after all these years of guilt, 'I'm worth something.' "

It all made sense to Pat: For sixteen years she had had to steel herself against those powerful feelings so they wouldn't overwhelm her. But now it was time to resolve them. The more she faced her feelings, the less they would control her.

"In order to get on with your life," Terry advised, "you have to face David's rejection of you, and you can only do that by going back emotionally to 1968 in order to do now what you couldn't do then. You have to confront him and you have to do it face to face. When you do, the anger you repressed for sixteen years can begin to come out. Only then can you grow beyond it."

Terry added a word of caution: "Maybe you'll resolve this whole thing when you face David," he said. "Maybe not. But you'll never know until you take the risk. Look at it as part of growing up and taking control of your life."

Terry's words were like a balm. Ever since David had left, Pat's feelings toward men had been mixed. She wanted a committed, loving relationship, but she was afraid of being deserted once again. She wanted to share her life, but she could never allow anyone to have the power over her that David once had.

Encouraged by Terry's gentleness and understanding, Pat expressed a fear she found difficult to talk about. "What really bothers me," she said, "is that when I see David, I may feel sorry for him—even worse, I may find I still love him."

Terry minced no words. "Maybe you'll feel sorry for him," he said. "But it's unlikely you'll still love him. If you feel sympathy or affection, take it as a positive sign of your ability to love and care for people. But you won't know until you try. If you don't try, your doubt will never be resolved."

There was one more thing.

"What if my daughters meet David and turn against me?" Pat asked. She didn't think she could go on if they did. "What if they don't see him for what he is and put all the blame on me? What if they want to live with him instead of with me?"

Even though he recognized her terror as real, Terry knew that Pat didn't really believe she'd lose her daughters.

"If the girls really become angry and need to express it," Terry said, "they may direct it at you. If they do, ignore it. It'll pass. They will recognize that *you* were the one who stayed with them, cared for them, and loved them—not their father. He was the one who abandoned them. Believe me, Pat, it *can't* backfire and it won't. In the end, the girls may decide they want a relationship with their father. Fine. Then they can have one with both of you."

Pat asked Terry if he would talk to the girls alone. It was important, she said, that they have a chance to express how they felt about meeting their father. Also, it would be good for them to know Terry better so that if a problem came up later, they would feel comfortable talking to him on the phone. Terry agreed.

Terry and the three girls spent the evening sprawled in the rec room. The girls asked him about his teenage children and wanted to know if they had messy rooms, too. When he said they did, they asked him to look at theirs and judge whose was the messiest. They took him around and there were a lot of giggles and groans.

"It's a tie," Terry said when the tour was over. "Anything growing in there?"

The room inspection was a good icebreaker, almost a test in a way, and the girls felt Terry was open-minded enough to talk to. It didn't take them long to turn to the topic of their father. Marcia and Andrea did most of the talking, saying more about what they expected than how they felt. Marcia said she was excited and told Terry that finally seeing her father and hearing his voice would be terrific; she had so many questions to ask him. Andrea spoke with coolness and nonchalance. She seemed to be trying to deal with him from a safe distance— close enough to satisfy her curiosity but not close enough to really be touched. Terry didn't push. He heard them out, then gave them an informal but important lecture.

"I want you all to remember one thing," he said. It sounded more like an order than advice. "If you see or talk to your father, you are to say *anything* that comes to your mind. You are to say *every* single thing you ever wanted to say but never had the chance. Don't be concerned about your father or how he feels. You have the right to say what you want, and it's very important that you do just that. Even though you were too little to remember, you had feelings as babies. Those feelings stayed with you. Get them out in the open so you can look at them."

Terry's words got to Christine and she brought up an issue that had been troubling her for a long time. She had a boyfriend who lived in Mexico, she said, and her relationship with him was very dependent. Although she knew he loved her, she constantly wanted him to say it and prove it. When he did, she couldn't believe him. And as far as she was concerned, he couldn't ever love her enough. "All my friendships with boys seem to turn out that way," she said. Could being abandoned as a baby have something to do with it?

Terry encouraged Christine to talk about each of her serious relationships. Although she was reluctant to discuss her father, she liked talking about her boyfriends. As Terry picked and probed, Christine began to see that each of her relationships followed the same pattern—long-distance and overly dependent.

"You're deliberately choosing relationships that are doomed," Terry told Christine when he sensed she was ready to hear it. "You are setting them up so that the man *will* leave you. One of your strongest and earliest feelings is that of being abandoned. You're reenacting it with each relationship. Part of you wants to go back to those feelings. They hurt but they are safe because you know you can handle them. You have to break that cycle by facing up to what your father did to you."

Pat drove Terry to the airport the next morning. She felt that nothing could stop her from facing David now. She had her cousin Joe for strength, Judge Valentine for support, Betty Murphy for advice, and now Terry for understanding and reassurance on the deepest level.

As she drove back from the airport, Pat mulled over something that Terry had said when she asked if David ought to be punished. He had told her, "Being someone like that *is* punishment. He was always a runaway father about to happen."

Terry's remark reminded Pat of what Dr. Crotty had told her about abandonment being generational, and that it would be good therapy to dig into David's family history for clues to understanding why he would run away. Crotty had studied under Dr. Murray Bowen at Georgetown University, a pioneer in family-systems therapy. Dr. Bowen taught that a patient's problem is the product of imperfections in his or her parents, and the parents' imperfections are a product of imperfections in the grandparents, continuing back generation after generation. Each generation was probably doing the best it could considering its stresses and its resources.

Pat knew David's mother had given him to her sister to raise, but she didn't know why. Was that a form of abandonment? She had also heard that David's grandfather had abandoned his children and disappeared. Was that true? If it was, and if Dr. Bowen's theory was correct, why should *she* feel guilty because David ran away? Why should *she* accept responsibility for "a runaway father about to happen"?

19

>>>>>>>>>>>>>>> Although David had used the last name of his foster parents, Pat had heard him mention his real last name. Never having seen it written out, she assumed it was spelled T-A-L-B-O-T. She also remembered David telling her that his grandfather and grandmother had worked in cotton mills, but he had never said where. She recalled that David's real mother had stated in her sworn affidavit to the Social Security Administration that David's father, Oscar David, was from Morrisville, Pennsylvania.

The hunt was on.

This time Pat wasn't trying to discover *where* David was but *who* David was. She started with the telephone operator in Morrisville, Pennsylvania. Although there were no Talbots in the area, there were two mills. She called them and asked Personnel to check mill records to see if an Oscar David Talbot—or any other Talbot—ever worked for them. She drew blanks at both.

Pat knew that David's real mother and her sister (David's foster mother) had grown up in or around Concord, North Carolina. Hoping that Oscar David, or O.D., as everyone called him, had married David's mother in Concord, she asked the marriage license office there to run a check on him. She gave an approximate year of marriage. There was no record.

Next, Pat called every Talbot listed in the Concord and Charlotte phone books. No one had ever heard of an Oscar David. As a last resort, she called all the cemeteries in Concord. No luck.

By that time, Pat knew something was wrong. If she had been poking in the right places and asking the right questions, she would at least have found a clue. There was only one way for her to get back on track. She knew the name and address of David's real mother from her sworn affidavit. Pat got the woman's number from the operator and called. After a somewhat strained chat about how Christine, Andrea, and Marcia were doing, Pat told David's mother she was drawing a family tree and wanted to talk to David's father. Did she know where he was?

David's mother said she hadn't talked to her former husband in almost twenty years and wasn't even sure if he was still alive.

"How do you spell his last name?" Pat asked on a hunch.

"Why, T-A-L-B-E-R-T."

Pat almost jumped out of her skin and couldn't wait to hang up. On her first phone call back to Concord, she scored. The Talbert she had fished out of the phone book told her that although he didn't recall any Oscar David in the family, that didn't mean there wasn't any. The Talbert clan in North Carolina was old and big. He said his sister-in-law was also working on a family tree and gave Pat her number. "You might want to talk to the retired mailman, too," he added. "He knows everyone in town. Why, just the other day, he was asking about the Talberts in the grocery store." He gave Pat the man's name and number as well.

When she hung up, Pat knew it was just a matter of time. From now on, finding O.D. would be like tracking a deer in fresh snow.

The sister-in-law turned out to be a history book. There was an O.D. on her family tree, she said, but he wasn't closely related to her side of the Talbert family. Although she didn't know where O.D. was living, she filled Pat in on the family background:

No one knew for sure when the Talberts came to America or from where. But census records showed they lived in Pennsylvania in the mid-1700s. In the late 1700s, they moved to Chesterfield County, South Carolina, to farm. One part of the Talbert clan stayed in South Carolina; another part, including David's side, moved to North Carolina in 1845. David's great grandfather, William, and his grandfather, Oscar Duberry Talbert, were born there.

Pat thanked the woman and hung up. She knew she had the right limb on the Talbert tree because David, his father,

and his grandfather all had the same initials—O.D. She called
the retired mailman, who was said to collect bits and pieces of
information about old Concord families the way some people
collect stamps. Like most local historians, he was delighted and
proud to share what he knew.

He remembered the Oscar Duberry Talbert family well, he
said, because he went to school with one of the Talbert girls
and he later delivered mail to their small house near the train
station on Depot Street. The Cannon Mills Company, founded
in 1887, owned the house, which was a short walk from the
mill where Mrs. Talbert worked. "She had a mess of kids," the
mailman told Pat, "and there was never a man around."

"Do you know where any of them are living now?" Pat
asked.

As far as he could tell, he said, they all moved out of town
except the Talbert girl he went to school with. She married a
man from Concord, but he couldn't remember the man's name.

Pat called the marriage license office once again. With the
woman's first name and the correct spelling of her maiden
name, it was easy to find out whom she had married. Fortunately, the man still lived in Concord. Pat called him.

He had divorced his first wife many years ago, he said. He
thought her family was from Mooresville, down the road a
piece. Bingo! O.D. was from *Mooresville*, North Carolina, not
Morrisville, Pennsylvania. Several calls to Mooresville later, Pat
was speaking to O.D. himself. She traced him to The Corral,
a restaurant-bar he managed in nearby Charlotte. After making
sure he was Oscar David Talbert, she asked, "Do you have a
son named David and a daughter named Betty?"

"Why, yes," he said. He sounded more curious than
cautious.

"Well, let me tell you who I am—it will probably shock
you," Pat said. "I'm your son's first wife, Pat. And I have three
teenage daughters—your grandchildren."

"Well, great day in the mornin', honey!" O.D. sounded
genuinely excited. "I didn't know. I just didn't know!"

"I've spent days trying to track you down," Pat said. "No
one in the family would ever tell me anything about you. My
children want to meet their grandfather."

"I wanna meet the children too, baby," O.D. said. His voice

sounded sincere and much younger than it was. "I'd give my
life ta see you and the babies. No one ever told me. Honey, I
don't have any grandchildren—I—I do *now.*"

"They're sixteen, seventeen, and eighteen years old," Pat
explained. "I think it's a shame that no one ever told me about
you. . . . Your mother's dead?"

"Yes, in '81," he said. "She was a beautiful, beautiful—the
nicest person you'd ever wanta meet."

"She was my daughters' great grandmother," Pat said. "I'm
sad they never got to meet her. When was the last time you
talked to David?"

"When he was fixin' ta go into the Marine Corps," he said.
"He came to the plant and we talked. I heard from Betty he
disappeared some time ago."

"Well, I found him—"

"You did?" O.D. was very excited now. He hadn't talked to
his son for over twenty years. "Where is he?"

"In Florida. He changed his name and everything about
himself. He didn't want to be found."

"He's still my son," O.D. said. "It don't make any difference—I love him."

"David told me that your father had deserted you, too,"
Pat said. "Is it true?" She wasn't sure whether he'd want to talk
about his own father, but he was as open as the sky. It was a
sad, almost uncanny story.

As O.D. told it, David's great grandfather William was a horse
trader. He left Concord and moved to Texarkana, Texas.
There, he married a cousin, Lilly Polk (a relative, some say, of
President James Polk). The couple had five children, one of
whom was David's grandfather, Oscar Duberry Talbert. Some
Talberts say William murdered Lilly with a clothes iron and
buried her in the backyard; others say she died in Texarkana
of blackwater fever. Whatever the case, William packed his
children in a covered wagon and took them to Columbus,
South Carolina. There, he was eventually convicted of mur-
dering his cousin and sent to prison. After the governor
pardoned him (no one knows why), he moved to Concord,
North Carolina, where he remarried and had four more
children.

David's grandfather Oscar Duberry stayed in South Carolina and married Haley Dunman in 1905. She was just fifteen and he was a twenty-year-old tenant farmer. In the early 1920s, he got caught stealing cotton. While he was in jail, Haley relocated closer to her husband's family in Concord, North Carolina, where she got a job as a spinner in a Cannon mill. She eventually had nine children. David's father, O.D., born in 1925, was her eighth.

David's grandfather Oscar Duberry had the habit of running away for a time, then coming back home. Sometimes he'd be gone for as long as a year. Once he left with a woman called Blossom. Another time, he and three other men skipped town when a girl they all knew turned up pregnant. Once he bought a new Whippet coupe on credit and headed for Texas. When the car dealer couldn't collect from Haley, he dropped charges. David's grandfather returned. On August 17, 1928, when David's father, O.D., was three years old and the youngest child was nine months old, Oscar Duberry ran away for good.

Haley cried for six months. Her brother helped her get a better job and a mill house in Concord on Depot Street. The county wanted to put the children in an orphanage, but she insisted on keeping her family together. She worked ten hours a day, six days a week; her oldest sons helped with food and money; people left clothes on her porch when she was at work; and the Salvation Army gave her children hot lunches and shoes. But no matter how hard she tried, she couldn't control her younger sons. Several, including David's father, O.D., had to attend a correctional school—The Stonewall Jackson Manual Training and Industrial School for Boys. Haley never remarried or even divorced David's grandfather.

After he left Haley for good, Oscar Duberry changed his name to James Ellis Jordan and bought a farm outside Mobile, Alabama. He "remarried" and had one daughter. In 1957, twenty-nine years after he had run away, he wrote to his sister, asking for a copy of his birth certificate so he could start collecting Social Security. His sister told her nephews where he was. Two of David's uncles went down to see him, and found him in his yard. "Do you know me?" one asked him. "No," he said. "I don't reckin I do, but I'm scairt I might."

His sons brought him back to North Carolina for six weeks so the rest of his children could meet him. The sons were happy he was back, but his daughters refused to talk to him. So did Haley. During his visit, he never told his sons he was sorry for deserting them. He had run away, he said, because they were becoming too difficult to handle. Over the twenty-nine years he was gone, he said, he had returned many times, parked down the street, and watched his children play in the yard.

Two years after David's grandfather returned to Mobile, he died of heart failure. Haley outlived him by twenty-two years. She died at the ripe age of ninety in a house in Mooresville her children bought for her after she retired from the mill.

"We're goin' ta have ta meet," O.D. said after he finished his story, " 'cuz I wanna see you and my grandchildren. Tell the babies I love 'em and wanna see 'em just as soon as I can."

O.D. wasn't trying to be polite, and the sense of urgency he communicated was real. Although Pat didn't know it, he was dying of brown lung disease from all the cotton dust he had breathed over the years. He told her he'd fly up to Washington or pay for their trip down to North Carolina, and he begged her to send him pictures of herself and the girls as soon as she could.

Pat promised she would. When she hung up, she was in a mild state of shock. Both Dr. Crotty and Terry had told her that abandonment tends to be generational. The doctor had said that the only way to break the cycle was to face the issue and the feelings and emotions that surround it. He was right, and the parallels between David and his grandfather rocked her: Both had run away in the month of August and almost on the same day; both hid in the South, changed their names, and became bigamists; neither attempted to pay child support, even indirectly; both were assumed to be dead; and both were found years later by a family member.

Andrea and Marcia—Christine was out of town—knew Pat was looking for their real grandfather. When she told them that night that she had found him in North Carolina, they weren't interested in hearing what she had learned about him and the Talberts. They wanted to talk to him directly. Marcia was so excited she insisted on calling O.D. immediately and Pat agreed.

"Can I speak to O.D. Talbert?" Marcia asked the man who answered the phone at The Corral. She could hear the jukebox playing in the background. Pat stood by nervously, hoping O.D. would say the right things. She didn't think her daughters could handle another rejection.

"You got him, ma'am," O.D. said.

"This is Marcia Bennett." Her voice was unsteady. "I'm your granddaughter."

"I know," O.D. said. There was tenderness in his voice. He paused. He was evidently choked up and close to tears. "I know—and I can't wait ta see you and your sisters and your mother. You see, I have a family I didn't even know I had."

"Me too." Marcia began to cry.

"Oh God, I can hardly wait," O.D. said. "Tell your mother ta get pictures in the mail just as soon as she can so I kin show 'em off all around the joint here. I'll have some big ones made and put 'em right here on the wall."

O.D. began to brag to impress Marcia, almost as if he were afraid that she'd reject him if he didn't. "I got a home on the lake," he said. "A hunting lodge in Maine on Lake George. I run this lounge and I have another home in the Dominican Republic. I have my own company—a loom service. We over-haul and repair all kinds a looms. . . ." O.D. paused self-consciously, sensing he was building himself up larger than life. "When you see me, you may not like me," he added.

"Don't say that!" Marcia said.

"I weigh around two twenty," O.D. said. "Six two. Hair is thinnin' on the top. I got a gray mustache, curly on the ends."

"I'm five seven and a half," Marcia said. "I don't know how much I weigh. I have long hair and—You'll see pictures of us." She was crying so hard it was difficult for her to speak. "I don't know you, but I guess I love you."

"When you see this mug of mine," O.D. said, "you probably won't. I'm as ugly as a mud fence."

"I don't care," Marcia said.

"But I *am* your grandfather. There's no doubt about that."

"I was tickled ta death when your mother called me tonight."

"Were you?" It was as if Marcia couldn't believe it. "Were you really?"

"I sure was," O.D. said. "I've been telling everyone in the lounge I have three beautiful granddaughters. Don't you worry none. I know you're bound ta be a beautiful little lady."

"Thank you," Marcia said through her sobs. She sounded like a little girl.

"I wanna see you so bad I can hardly stand it," O.D. said.

"Please fly up here," she pleaded. "I want to see you. That would make me *so* happy."

Andrea grabbed the phone.

"Oh gracious," O.D. said. "I don't know what in the world ta say. I'm overwhelmed. I didn't know."

"Really?" Andrea said. "You didn't know about us. Oh my God!"

"I know you belong ta me now."

"Our dad really messed up," Andrea said. "But we're glad we found you."

"You better believe it."

"How old are you?"

"Sixty. I have emphysema," he lied, "but I git along just fine."

"I'm seventeen," Andrea said. She could hear Marcia hyperventilating in the background, sucking and gulping air as if she couldn't get enough.

"I've always wanted to know who my father is," Andrea said. There was no anger in her voice nor the touch of hardness she frequently used to protect herself. Like Marcia, she sounded like a child. "Ever since we were little, we would talk about him and blame him. . . . I'd like to send you a picture of me."

"And write me a long letter," O.D. said.

"Believe me, I will." She felt the emotion in his voice. A kind of long-distance caress. "Are we upsetting you?"

"Nope, I hope I'm not upsettin' you."

"I've been upset all my life," Andrea said. "But this is the best upset I've ever been."

O.D. laughed. "You found yourself a grandfather and I found what I know are three beautiful girls."

"I hope I look like you," Andrea said. "I look like David."

"Dark hair—"

"He had those thick eyebrows. I have those."

"I got pictures of him when he was a little feller," O.D. said. "I'll bring 'em."

"I have a boyfriend," Andrea said. She was trying to cram her whole life into five minutes. "I've been dating him for about a year."

"Well, honey, you tell him if he's not good to you, your grandfather will come up there and skin 'im like a cat."

"If I get married, and I walk down the aisle and stuff," Andrea said, "you can give me away, if you want to." Andrea was crying, too.

"I'd love it," O.D. said. "I'd love it."

"I'm really confused now," Andrea said. "Maybe when I straighten things out we can talk some more. I'm so confused."

Breathing normally again, Marcia took the phone and said, "Granddaddy? I don't know you, but I love you. I love your son in a way, too. And I hate him in a way, you know. We all have to forgive . . . You better come. I want to see you *so* bad. I'm glad my mom did this for us. I'm glad we found you. I'm glad we know who you are. Now you know, too. You have three granddaughters."

"You're mine," O.D. said. "You belong ta me."

"We're going to make it worth it," Marcia said and hung up.

Pat could feel how much Andrea and Marcia were reaching out for O.D.'s love. They were like starved, greedy kids, and they kept pressing her to invite him to Washington or take them to North Carolina. They kept wondering what their grandfather looked like, where he lived, if they looked like him.

In the end, Pat decided to drive the girls to North Carolina the following week so they could see the house where their great grandmother Haley had lived and the mill where she had worked, and meet as many aunts, uncles, nieces, and nephews as they could. But still worried that O.D. might reject her daughters, she wrote him a long letter in which she came close to pleading with him not to push her daughters away.

"When the girls talked to you they were very afraid and nervous," she wrote.

You couldn't tell, but they were crying. After they talked to you, we stayed up till after two, talking. Andrea said, "Mom, that is the first man that hasn't rejected us. And he told us he loved us." They thought you sounded very honest. They have heard so many lies all their lives that they couldn't believe someone would tell them the truth. . . .

It's all very sad for them—the years they did without a father. You must understand because your own father did the same thing. They do not forgive David—they are bitter toward him because he hurt them so much.

But now they have a chance to know you, their real grandfather, and they want to meet you. All they want is for someone to love them and not leave them. . . . They need a relationship with someone who won't disappoint them—that is all they want. My girls will give you back more love than you've ever had because they want to love you as their granddaddy. They called you "granddaddy" on the phone and they liked the way that sounded.

They left for North Carolina on Friday. When they arrived in Mooresville, O.D.'s brother was waiting. "O.D.'s scairt a meetin' you," he explained as he drove them out to O.D.'s modest home on Lake Norman. "But he's real excited. He's dyin' of brown lung, you know, but he's proud and don't want anyone to know it."

O.D. was sleeping when they pulled into his driveway, and it took his brother five minutes of knocking to awaken him. They sat in the living room and talked for an hour. O.D. looked weak and tired, and he found it difficult to breathe and talk. Every now and then he squirted medication into his mouth from a vaporizer to clear his lungs.

O.D. was overwhelmed. He hugged the girls, stroked their hair, and held their hands like a sponge soaking up every drop of affection they and Pat showed him. "My granddaughters," he kept saying. "My grandbabies. If only I'd known you sooner I'da taken walks with you, gone fishin' . . . Why didn't I know?"

The more he looked at his grandchildren and touched them, the angrier at David he became. "You let me know when that trial is," he ordered Pat. "I'm goin' down there with ya. I wanna sit in the front row with my arms around my grandbabies. No one can do this to 'em. I'll tell David what a louse he is. I'll never turn *my* back on my grandbabies. I swear. You promise me now, you'll tell me!"

Pat promised. Then O.D. hung his head in guilt and shame. "I wasn't around to raise 'im," he said softly. "I wasn't around to tell 'im right from wrong."

That night, Pat and the girls played cards with O.D.'s brother until two in the morning, sitting around the kitchen table in Haley Talbert's old white frame house. Haley's children had left it just the way it was when she died four years earlier. O.D.'s brother was as lively and talkative as O.D. was tired and quiet. All night long, he told funny stories about the Talbert family and about growing up in a mill town.

The next day, Pat and the girls met more aunts, uncles, nieces, and nephews. By the time they settled down with O.D. for a steak dinner that night, they had a good sense of who the Talberts were. O.D. was very quiet during dinner, exhausted and drained by all the emotions that had flowed so freely during the visit.

Although she was glad she and her daughters had come to Mooresville, Pat left for Washington the next morning with mixed emotions. It was clear that O.D. felt nothing but affection for her daughters—it shined in his eyes and she could hear it in his voice, and she was grateful for that. She had merely hoped that O.D. wouldn't reject them and would find that he really loved them. But he was so sick and exhausted that he didn't have the energy to demonstrate the love he felt. She sensed that her daughters ended up giving him more than they had received. And like O.D., she felt sad they had found him at the end of his life.

Pat was also pleased that she had learned so much about David's family. Who they were. How they lived. How they had felt about being abandoned by their father. She had uncovered a history of early marriages, divorces, and abandonment unlike anything on her side of the family. It helped her understand why David would think of running away. But she was also disappointed that, after talking to O.D. and his relatives, she had no clear answer as to why David's mother had given him away and why she had kept his sister, Betty.

All she learned was that O.D. was sixteen years old when he married David's mother, whose own father had deserted her and her five brothers and sisters, just as O.D.'s father had deserted him. O.D. admitted walking out on his wife and two children, when he was twenty. While he was gone, his wife gave David to her sister and brother-in-law, who were childless. When he returned after a year, O.D. sued his wife for divorce— the grounds for his suit were unclear. O.D. said he had such great respect for his brother-in-law that when the man asked if he could keep David, O.D. said yes. David's foster parents legally changed David's name to theirs.

Pat returned home, disturbed as well as pleased by the visit. O.D. looked just like David. He moved like David. Walked like him. Even shared some of David's speech patterns. She felt a deep surge of affection for him, not because he was a likable old man, or was dying, or was the grandfather of her children, but because he reminded her of David. She didn't want to feel any warmth for David, even if it was through his father. She wanted him out of her life for good. My God, she thought, if I feel loving toward O.D. because he reminds me of David, what will I feel for David himself when I meet him?

If that wasn't bad enough, Pat had begun to feel a sympathy for David. It wasn't that she was about to excuse David for what he had done to her and his daughters, just because abandonment seemed to run in his blood. But she felt sad because of what he had missed. "If only David had known all this," she said to herself. "He had a whole family—a real history. And he didn't even know his own father."

O.D. died eight months later, and Pat and Christine went to the funeral. David wasn't there and probably didn't even know his father was dead.

Part Three
>>>>>>>>>>>>>>>>>>>>>>
Confrontation

20

>>>>>>>>>>>>> October and November turned out to be so busy for Pat that she hardly had time to think about David. Swept up in a new IRS training program, she had few spare moments to search for the documents needed to prove that James Parker was really David. Although she could go to Florida in December, Christine, Andrea, and Marcia didn't want to see their father jailed until after Christmas. The girls still weren't sure whether he had any other children, and since Christmas was so special to them, they didn't want to destroy their own or anyone else's. Pat agreed to go down in early January 1985—six months after she had found David.

If October and November flew by, December crawled. Pat grew so anxious as her trip to Florida approached, she found it almost impossible to sleep. She'd get into bed at one o'clock, only to wake up at three, unable to drift off again. She became so exhausted, she couldn't work or give her daughters the attention they needed.

It wasn't just Pat who was anxious. With each passing week, the girls were getting more tense as they sensed their mother's fear and began facing their own. They argued more with her over trivial things, almost as if they were looking for an excuse to pick a fight, and they squabbled more and more among themselves. Their comments never changed: "When are we going? Why not now? I can't wait. Give me his phone number. Why is everyone so slow? Doesn't anyone care?"

Marcia in particular was frightened, and although she didn't say what bothered her the most, Pat knew. Marcia felt trapped between two painful alternatives. On the one hand, she feared her father might reject her a second time; on the other, she feared she might love her father and sensed that this would hurt her mother. Pat felt there was little she could do to help Marcia except be there if her youngest needed her.

One evening, as Pat and her daughters sat around the kitchen table reminiscing over the photos Pat was putting together, the girls decided to take an album to Florida to share pieces of their lives with their father. Since each was proud of her athletic achievements, they chose an album filled with sports pictures. Their unspoken motive was: See what you missed? See what you left behind? See how well we did without you?

The girls concocted a plan to meet their father at his home because they didn't want to see him for the first time in handcuffs or in jail. It was Andrea's idea and Pat welcomed it. They would rent an old car and fake a breakdown in front of his house. Pat and the sheriff would be in another car down the street. The girls would go to the door, using the names of their three best girlfriends for cover—Kim, Laura, and Sharon. Andrea would do all the talking. "Our car broke down," she would tell her father. "Can we use your phone?"

The plan was riddled with holes. "Andrea, you talk too much," Marcia said. "You'd blow it."

"What if he wants to come out and fix the car?" Christine said.

"Maybe we should tell him we ran out of gas," Andrea suggested.

Bill Daniels walked in during the discussion and killed the whole idea. "David will know," he said. "Three girls all about the ages of his daughters. And look at Andrea—she looks just like him!"

Even though she was taking a sedative, the tense weeks of waiting wore Pat down. She started to have bad dreams about the trip. In one of them, she found herself sitting in her Florida attorney's office waiting for him to finish a conversation with David's attorney. Then she went outside for some fresh air and a stroll. When she came back, she saw David's attorney getting into a car. She forced her way in beside him and asked what was going on. He smiled and said her own attorney would tell her; she would be very pleased. Realizing they had made a deal behind her back, she began crying. Then she screamed, "You don't understand, there's supposed to be a judge! Jim

Parker is supposed to be here!" David's attorney replied, "But he's going to pay all the money." She began to panic: "But the girls are supposed to see him!" She got out of the car and started running down the street. Then she woke up.

To help ease her tension, Pat wrote David a letter she planned to give him before his daughters could ask to see him. She would wait in her attorney's car down the street from David's house. As soon as the sheriff arrested him, she'd rush over and give him the letter, saying, "The children want to meet their father, David. It's important that you don't reject them. Read this and then read it again!"

The letter, a plea not to abandon the girls a second time, read:

Dear David,

I realize that my finding you after sixteen years must come as a great shock. I believe, however, that it is something you have anticipated, or you would not have gone to the extremes you have to avoid being discovered. I can only guess what you may have felt during those years. Maybe you even tried to put this day out of your mind, believing that your past did not exist. I would like to believe, however, that from time to time you thought of your three daughters and maybe wondered what they looked like or what kind of life they had. I cannot begin to recount what has happened to them. There have been times of joy—of sadness. They were sick, sometimes depressed. In the hospital after auto accidents. They've laughed. They've cried.

I'm very proud of them. They are three very beautiful daughters.

Since I told them where you were, it was all I could do to keep them from telephoning you. They wanted to call so badly, but I thought that might only frighten you into running again, so I would not let them. I knew the only chance they would have of seeing you was to arrive unexpectedly and hope that you would meet them. They were very upset before this trip and are having a hard time coping. Marcia has been very depressed.

I do not believe that you, yourself, have been without

pain, David. I know that this letter is a very emotional one for you as well as for me. Hopefully, you will understand its importance. If you do, you will bury your own fears and react in a manner that is best for the children.

Our daughters are here with me in Tampa, and I have gone to a great deal of effort and expense to get them here—not for myself, but for them. They desperately want to see who their father is. They have things they want to say to him—to you—things they have dreamed about for years, things they have practiced over and over. They all have their own individual feelings, but I can tell you, a visit with you is the most important thing in all their lives. They have spent their childhood and teenage years not knowing if you were dead or alive. They have been hurt deeply, and all have feelings of being abandoned. They often told me how they wanted to become famous so you would see them and get in touch with them. So many times, they came to me in the night crying for want of you. They would say to me, "If only I could see him *once* just to know what he looks like, what he sounds like." No matter how much consolation I gave them, the hurt remained.

You must understand their feelings, David, for you were abandoned, too. Perhaps that was the biggest hurt in your life and it caused you to run from those closest to you. You are forty—too old to keep running. Well, you can stop looking over your shoulder.

Now—you have an opportunity to do something for your daughters. You cannot erase the years. You cannot erase their hurt. But you can meet them and your responsibility to support them. It is so important for them to face you. When you see them, you will only realize what you've missed.

They deserved better than they got out of life, David. They have carried *your* guilt by believing it was somehow their fault that you abandoned them. Especially Marcia. She feels that if she had been a boy you would not have left. I've had to get them counseling to help them realize it wasn't their fault. I would not have brought them with me or put them through this if I did not believe it was important for them.

I don't know what the outcome will be. But I believe they cannot be hurt any more than they already have. They are very afraid right now, as I am sure you are, too. They don't know how to react, but I do know that if you reject them again, they will be devastated. How they will feel in the end depends on you.

Our daughters are beautiful young ladies, grown up in many respects, but they are hurting inside deeply. You've missed them growing up, and I am sure that's something you must think about. They went through everything without you there to share it with them. They were cheerleaders, played soccer, were on the diving and swimming teams. They each have dreams of going to college. Christine's a freshman now. But they must resolve their conflicts of who they are and who their father is before going on with their lives.

I am writing this letter so that you will realize the importance of this meeting, so that you will put aside your own fears and do what is right for them—not for me. The past cannot be undone, but I ask that you do not perpetuate the suffering of our daughters. It's up to you, David, to give your daughters a father.

21

>>>>>>>>>>>>>> Pat could see it now. He would walk into the courtroom and tell the judge, "I don't know what she's talking about. I don't know her, and I've never heard of any David. I'm Jim Parker and here's my birth certificate to prove it."

Pat wasn't about to risk that. To clear all doubt about James Parker's real identity, she called the FBI for a copy of David's fingerprints, which she knew were on file; but the bureau said the Privacy Act of 1974 prevented it from releasing them to her.

A small hurdle. By this time, Pat knew how to play the game. She simply asked Judge Valentine to issue a Subpoena Duces Tecum for them. That way, the prints would go directly to the court, not to her.

"Anything else you need?" Valentine asked after he signed the subpoena.

"Could you get David's personnel file from Safeco?" she asked. She really didn't need the file to prove his identity if she had the prints, but she wanted to document how hard he had tried to hide from the court and the law, just in case.

Somewhat skeptical whether Safeco would respond to an out-of-state subpoena in a juvenile and domestic relations case, Judge Valentine signed it anyway. Corporate attorneys frequently advised companies to ignore such requests, since they knew that, with few exceptions, J and D courts didn't have time to force them to comply.

While waiting for the FBI and Safeco to respond, Pat began studying the papers David left behind when he ran away. Among them, she found a twenty-year-old traffic ticket that he and a fellow Marine had picked up in North Carolina. The name of the other Marine was James Parker.

Safeco sent James Clinton Richard Parker's file the day

after it received Judge Valentine's express-mail subpoena. Pat devoured it. In his job application papers, Parker had claimed that he was born in New York on August 30, 1944 (David's real date of birth was July 17, 1944); that his father worked for the U.S. Foreign Service; that he attended primary and secondary schools in Fair Lawn, New Jersey; that he had graduated from Rutgers University in 1967 with a B.S. in Food Science; and that he had been in the Marines, Camp Lejeune, from 1967 to 1971 (these dates were not accurate) and had won a Bronze Star in Vietnam.

Of course, little in Parker's job application was true. David's father, O.D., was never in the Foreign Service; David was born in Virginia, not in New York; he had gone to primary and secondary schools in Virginia, not in New Jersey; he had never been to Vietnam or won a Bronze Star; and he had never gone to Rutgers.

The Rutgers connection intrigued Pat so much that she called the Rutgers University Alumni Association to see if a James Parker had actually graduated in 1967.

"Yes," a clerk told Pat after she checked the records. "There was a James R. Parker, born August 30, 1944, who graduated in 1967 with a B.S. in agriculture. He is listed as a food chemist and now lives in Oregon."

"Can you give me his address or phone number?" Pat asked.

"I'm sorry."

"Can you tell me anything else about him?"

"I'm sorry."

Pat asked Judge Valentine to subpoena James R. Parker's student file from the alumni association. While she was waiting for the reply, David's fingerprints arrived. "A name check of the files of the FBI Identification Division disclosed a United States Marine Corps enlistment fingerprint card," the bureau wrote Judge Valentine. "A copy of this fingerprint card is enclosed for your release to Ms. Patricia Ann Bennett."

Although she should have felt relieved at having David's prints, Pat was in such a state of anxiety that she feared the worst. The FBI wasn't perfect, was it? It had made mistakes before. What if it had sent the wrong card? David would walk out of the court laughing.

When the alumni association file arrived, Pat learned a few

more details: The middle name of the James Parker who had graduated in 1967 was Rothery, not Richard; he graduated from Fair Lawn primary and secondary schools; and his father had been in the Foreign Service.

During the first week of January 1985, Pat and Victoria Gordon met in Pat's home to piece together their identity case and to decide exactly what they hoped to accomplish in Florida the following week. Pat knew that David had assumed the name James Parker soon after he had run away, because he had used James Parker—without a middle initial—on his marriage certificate to Lenora the following year. Pat guessed that he took the middle name Clinton from Clinton, Maryland, where he had flunked his private pilot's exam after he had been discharged from the Marines. She assumed that he later found the name James R. Parker and added the name Richard to Clinton.

The more they talked that night, the clearer their Florida legal goals became: first, positively identify Parker as David; second, get the Florida court to accept the Virginia decree for over forty-two thousand dollars in arrearage and to enter it as a judgment; third, hold David in contempt of court for not having obeyed the Virginia court order for child support; and fourth, amend the order to cover Marcia, who wasn't born when Fairfax issued the order almost seventeen years ago.

Pat and Victoria both recognized that although their legal strategy sounded fine on paper, it failed to address the main reason why the Bennetts were going to Florida in the first place. The money was secondary at this point. Pat neither expected to get forty-two thousand dollars, nor would she insist on it. She would settle for ten thousand dollars—enough to cover the trip to Tampa and her legal expenses—provided she and her daughters had the chance to face David. And there was the rub: If Victoria filed any petition in Tampa, David would be duly notified. If he was notified, he could flee. And even if he didn't run, his attorneys could line up so many legal straw men that it might be months before he would have to stand before a judge—if he ever had to.

Pat's Florida attorney, Frank de la Grana, who had been looking for a way to have James Parker arrested long enough for Pat and her daughters to meet him, saved the day. Why not post a bond and ask the court for a Writ of Ne Exeat? he suggested. That would allow the sheriff to arrest James Parker without prior notice and hold him in jail until he paid in full the cash bond the judge set, or until he had a hearing. Even though it wasn't certain a judge would sign the writ, which was an extraordinary legal measure founded in old English law, it was worth trying. The writ was designed precisely for cases like Pat's—someone owes money and threatens to flee to avoid paying, or the petitioner has reason to believe the debtor might flee.

The problem with a Writ of Ne Exeat was that the burden of proof fell on Pat. She would have to convince the court that David might flee if he found out she was looking for him. If she drew a grumpy judge or one of those Florida good old boys, she might never get a signature. At best, it would be a legal lottery.

If Pat managed to secure the writ, however, the sheriff could arrest David at night, when he was sure to be home and when the banks were closed. If he couldn't raise the cash for bail immediately, he'd have to spend the night behind bars. Pat and his daughters could then try to see him.

The plan was set. Christine would leave Saturday, January 11, for her summer job in Orlando. She would meet her mother, her two sisters, and Victoria at the airport Sunday afternoon and drive them to Tampa in her 1978 Camaro so Pat would not have to rent a car. Richard Froemming, who was in Miami on a surveillance job, would join them in Tampa on Tuesday or Wednesday. Not only was Richard pleased to help, he had declined to charge for his services and insisted on paying his own expenses.

The legal drafts from de la Grana arrived by courier late Friday afternoon—thirty-six hours before Pat's plane was to take off. She and Victoria worked all day Saturday in Victoria's office in downtown Washington, sharpening the motion and petition on Victoria's word processor. After breaking for dinner around eight, they went back to the word processor until three o'clock Sunday morning. Neither had done any packing and their plane left at eight a.m. But at least they had the paperwork neatly tied up.

The legal motion argued that David had a history of

running and hiding to avoid his responsibility to pay child support, and that his pattern of behavior indicated a probability he might run again if notified. It asked the court to set cash bond at forty-two thousand dollars—the amount of arrearage.

The petition asked that the court recognize and enforce the sixteen-year-old Virginia child-support order as a Florida judgment and enter it against David in the amount of forty-two thousand dollars, find David in contempt of the court order and enforce the maximum penalty of the law, amend the Virginia order to include Marcia and raise the amount David had to pay from two hundred dollars to at least five hundred dollars a month, and order David to pay Pat's court and investigative costs as well as her attorneys' fees.

When Pat got home shortly before four that morning, tense and exhausted, Marcia was waiting in a state of near hysteria. She lit into Pat as soon as her mother walked through the door.

"Where were you?" she screamed. "Why did you leave me alone? I needed you. I'm so-o-o scared."

"We're leaving in a couple of hours," Pat said firmly. Emotionally drained and raw, she was angry that Marcia was needling her after she had worked all night. "I haven't packed. I'm exhausted. Why don't you go to sleep and leave me alone!"

Pat went into her bedroom and closed the door. After tossing a few clothes in a suitcase, she lay down on the bed for an hour or two of sleep. But before she could drift off, Marcia barged in crying and yelling. She grabbed Pat's favorite lamp and threw it on the floor, screaming that Pat had no right to leave her alone when she was so frightened. She made such a commotion that she woke her sister across the hall.

Andrea flew into the room. "Mom, you have to do something about Marcia," she yelled. "She's flipping out!"

Her nerves close to shattering, Pat couldn't think. She kept worrying about the hundred things that could go wrong. On top of all that, Marcia was now blaming her for not being there, and Andrea was blaming her for not keeping the lid on Marcia. What did they expect of her? She was only human, and as scared as they were.

"Look, I'm wiped out, Marcia," Pat yelled back. "Just be quiet, leave me alone, and go to bed."

Pat slid off the bed to nudge the girls out of the room and to close the door again. But Marcia was so out of control that she hit Pat on the shoulder and shoved her back toward the bed. Then Marcia drew back and slugged Andrea in the nose.

Pat pushed both daughters out the door and sat on the bed so tired she could barely grasp what was happening. Across the hallway, she could hear Marcia crying hysterically, "I hit my mom! I can't believe I hit my mom!"

The shock over what she had done brought Marcia to her senses like a splash of ice water, and she went back into Pat's room. "I'm so sorry, Mom," she said. She was crying softly now. "I didn't mean it. I don't want to go."

"You don't have to go," Pat said gently.

"Part of me wants to love him, Mom," she said. "Part of me wants to hate him. And I'm scared I will love him."

Pat put her arms around Marcia and hugged her tightly. They were both weeping now, more out of relief than hurt or anger.

"I'm scared, too," Pat said. "And for the same reason. I don't want to love him either."

"Well, what if I *do*?" Marcia seemed to feel less alone now that she knew her mother had the same hidden fear.

"I don't know," Pat said. "But I have to find out for myself; you don't. You don't have to come if you don't want to."

Andrea came back into the room and sat on the bed. My God, what have I done? Pat thought. What right do I have to put them through this? They'll never get over it. What a mistake! It's out of control, and it's all my fault.

They held each other. A mother and two daughters closer together than they had ever been.

"Can I call Victoria?" Marcia asked suddenly.

Pat told her it would be all right. She was convinced that Marcia wanted to tell Victoria she wasn't going, but she would deal with that later. Right now, it was four o'clock, time for at least one good hour of sleep and peace.

Marcia called, and Victoria's sleepy voice came on the line. "I'm so scared," Marcia began. A jumble of words and emotions spilled over the phone as she tried to explain to the older woman how she felt. "I love him even though I don't know him. I'm afraid that's going to hurt my mother. I hate him. I don't want to love him. I don't want to go. I don't know what's going to happen down there. I'm staying home. I'm angry at her. She left me alone. She won't talk to me."

"Honey, don't get mad at your mother," Victoria said gently. "She's very tired. It's four in the morning. She loves you and she's doing this for you too. Not just for herself."

"I know she's been working hard," Marcia said through her tears. "And I love her. But I feel left out."

It was plain to Victoria that the girls were hoping for too much from their father. They expected him to be as eager to meet them as they were to see him. In reality, he might refuse to talk to them. They expected him to say how sorry he was that he had deserted them, how pretty they were, how sad he was because of what he had missed, and that if he had a chance to do it all over again, he'd love them and never leave them. In reality, he might not be the least bit sorry, just embarrassed that he had got caught.

Victoria knew that whatever David said, did, or felt, he was not going to be the father they wanted. She chose her words with care.

"I can see how tough it's been growing up without a father. You have all those dreams of what he must be like. But listen, honey, maybe he's not like the dad in your dreams. Maybe he's different—maybe not as nice. Maybe he won't want to see you and that's what's scaring you."

Marcia thought it over for a second. "What's he going to be like, Victoria?" she asked. "Will he love me? I don't want to go."

"Don't worry, honey, Victoria will be there." She felt touched and overwhelmed by the depth of Marcia's feelings and how completely vulnerable the girl was. Although she wanted to hold and protect Marcia, she knew no one could shield her from what she had to face. "I won't leave you, honey," she said.

22

>>>>>>>>>>>>>> Christine was waiting in Orlando when her mother, her sisters, and Victoria landed at noon. Christine wasn't happy to be leaving, even for a short time. She felt that her mother was obsessed with David, and she didn't think any good would come out of the trip for anyone, including David— so why get excited? Besides, Christine resented being pushed and put under such pressure. But she had agreed to drive everyone to Tampa and see her father, rather than risk upsetting her mother and have her sisters call her a wimp.

When Victoria saw Christine's old Camaro, however, she had second thoughts about the travel plans. She rented her own car and the group split up. Marcia rode with Christine, since she got along better with her older sister than Andrea did. Pat and Andrea joined Victoria.

Traveling in convoy, they got lost in Tampa, and by the time they found Frank de la Grana's office, it was almost six. To help Pat trim expenses, Frank had arranged the free use of a condo belonging to an attorney in Frank's office, at Indian Rock Beach near Clearwater, about an hour's drive from downtown Tampa. Frank drove Pat, Andrea, and Victoria out to the beach house in his gray BMW while Christine and Marcia followed.

Soft-spoken, laid back, and with the pure bloodline of an old and respected Spanish family, Frank knew his way around Tampa's courts and judges as well as Victoria did around Fairfax's. But unlike Victoria's practice, Frank's was mostly criminal defense. Though criminal law paid the bills, family law was really Frank's first love, and he wished he could do more of it.

On the drive to the balmy gulf beach, Frank was stunned by Victoria's energy. If someone hadn't told him, he would never have believed she had had only a few hours of sleep the night before. Without pausing for breath, she chattered about the case, the motion, the petition, and the likelihood she'd get the Writ of Ne Exeat. Then she bombarded Frank with questions—what was the court system like in Tampa? Who were the good judges? How far was the courthouse from Frank's office? All the while, Pat sat exhausted in the back seat, depressed because she felt like a stranger to her own case. She didn't like not being in control, and it was clear that Victoria had appointed herself commander-in-chief.

The condominium where they would be staying, in a development called Pelican Pointe, was a two-story, two-bedroom home tastefully done in a nautical decor. Victoria hardly seemed to notice. Glancing around and nodding her approval, she spread out her papers on the table across from the bar while the girls checked out each room and argued about who was going to sleep where.

Frank listened patiently as he resigned himself to a Sunday evening lecture on the law. He had left a family gathering to meet the noisy two-car caravan in the street below his office, and he was eager to return home. Finally, at nine-thirty he got up to leave. Reminding Victoria that he was in the middle of a federal narcotics trial, Frank said he would not have much time to spare that week, but that he would make sure someone showed her the legal ropes around town.

By the time Frank left the condo, the girls were tired, hungry, and cranky. Like Pat, they felt left out, not sure what was going to happen, and uncertain where or when they would see their father. Eventually, they settled in front of the TV with a bucket of Southern Fried Chicken. It was a quiet but tense evening. With the sleeping arrangements finally negotiated, they all turned in.

Around noon the next day, Monday, Pat and Victoria drove to Frank's office on the thirtieth floor of the First Florida Tower, overlooking Tampa, the Hillsboro River, and Frank's new home—a gleaming white speck on the riverbank. They spent most of the afternoon holed up in the conference room working out procedures: where to go, whom to see, how to file. By the end of the day, they had agreed on a strategy.

At Frank's suggestion, they would make an appointment

the next day, Tuesday, to talk to a judge he knew, Julio Gonzalez. Like Judge Valentine, Judge Gonzalez would be sympathetic and in a good position to advise and guide them. Tuesday evening, they would meet with Richard Froemming to coordinate plans. Assuming Richard found Jim Parker in town Wednesday morning, they would file the papers and Victoria would plead for a Writ of Ne Exeat before a judge that day. Since judges on the Hillsborough County Circuit Court rotated their assignments, there was no predicting whom Victoria would draw. If the judge signed the writ, they would ask the sheriff to arrest Jim Parker Wednesday night. If he didn't sign . . . it was anyone's guess.

Back at the condo, the girls were in a dither. With no clues about what was happening, they sat by the phone all afternoon, waiting for a call from their mother saying that their father was arrested and wanted to meet them. When Pat returned early that evening, she explained that nothing was going to happen for a couple of days, so they might as well get used to the waiting. To appease them, she gave them enough money to buy dinner across the road at the Hungry Fisherman. Then she and Victoria drove back into town to a private club Frank had suggested, for dinner.

Pat and Victoria spent most of Tuesday in the county courthouse; while Victoria met with legal officials behind closed doors, Pat sat on benches outside, growing more anxious by the hour. Judge Gonzalez turned out to be as understanding and helpful as Frank had predicted. After listening to Victoria explain the case, he supported their decision to seek a Writ of Ne Exeat. And he became so intrigued by David's having assumed the identity and college credits of another person that the judge suggested Victoria march down the hall to the prosecutor's office. Maybe David had committed another crime besides desertion and nonsupport.

Equally curious, the prosecutor pulled down his Florida law books. He had never tried a false-identity case before and wasn't even sure if it was a crime. He found Florida law quite clear: to assume someone's identity to defraud that person of money or property was larceny; but there was no evidence that David had done that. To assume someone's identity to get a job or a credit rating was a misdemeanor of the first degree (like desertion and nonsupport was in Virginia). In Florida, this crime carried a maximum penalty of one year in jail and a fine of up to one thousand dollars. The Hillsborough County prosecutor was no more interested in collecting misdemeanor trophies than Fairfax County's Robert Horan had been, even assuming there was hard evidence that David had committed a false-identity crime in Florida.

However, the False Identification Crime Control Act of 1982 made it a federal crime to "possess an identification document that is or appears to be an identification document of the United States which is stolen or produced without authority, knowing that such document was stolen or produced without authority." That law listed "birth certificate" as a document of the United States. If David "produced" or fraudulently obtained the birth certificate of the real James R. Parker, he could be fined up to twenty-five thousand dollars and could spend up to five years in jail. But no one knew how David had gotten the birth certificate he had furnished Safeco, and there was no copy of it in his Safeco file. Furthermore, if a federal crime had been committed, Victoria was talking to the wrong prosecutor in the wrong court. She'd have to see the U.S. attorney for Tampa, and it would take a lot of talking, even for Victoria, to interest him in prosecuting a man who allegedly used a false birth certificate when bigger crooks were getting away because the U.S. attorney didn't have the investigators or money to catch them.

When Pat walked through the door that evening, it was Andrea, not Marcia, who was waiting to turn on her. "You didn't call all day long. What the hell is going on?" she shouted at her mother, who was feeling just as helpless as her daughters. "You don't understand. You just walk in and don't tell us a thing. I'm really pissed."

If Andrea was angry, Marcia was quite calm for a change. The crisis of the day had been what she was going to wear when she saw her father. It was an important question for all three girls because they wanted to look their best. Christine had little trouble picking an outfit, but Andrea and Marcia couldn't decide. Andrea ended up borrowing a beautiful red suit from Victoria. It fit her perfectly, and she knew she looked stunning in it. Pat had given Marcia money to go out and buy a new dress. Since she would be turning seventeen in less than a week, the clothes were an early birthday present.

Marcia had bought a bluish purple dress, which she really seemed to like. That was unusual, for Marcia seldom wore dresses and rarely found one that pleased her. As she modeled it for Pat and Victoria, she appeared light-hearted and excited. After getting the girls settled for the evening, Pat and Victoria drove down the beach to a French seafood restaurant to meet Richard, who had just flown in from Miami.

Richard did not share Pat's fears. He didn't think Parker was dangerous, because he had no history of violence. Nor was Richard concerned that someone might slip Parker a message that Pat was in town. But as a private detective, Richard believed in patterns, and he was convinced that Parker would run if he got wind of what was about to happen. The investigator had agreed to come to Tampa to make sure that this time Parker would find no place to hide.

One look at Pat and Victoria told the whole story. Pat would barely say a word; she seemed tense and drawn, almost numb. Richard had never seen her like that before. Victoria, on the other hand, was so pumped up that even food could not slow her talking.

"What do you want me to do?" Richard asked Pat, between courses.

"Follow him," Pat said.

"That's the worst thing," Richard said. "What if he spots me? He'll run for sure. . . . Here's what I'll do. I'll go out to his place first thing to make sure he's there. Then I'll call you. I'll hang around the pool at the Holiday Inn. When you get your paperwork tied up, page me. I'll see to it he's around for the arrest."

The job wasn't that simple, but Richard would never tell Pat that. Jim Parker worked at home, and Richard knew from his partner's surveillance report that it would be foolish to sit on the street and watch Parker's house. If he did that, he'd run the risk of Parker calling the police or sensing something was afoot and sneaking out the back. If Parker stayed home all day, fine. But if he planned an overnight somewhere, Richard might not see him leave and Pat would be out of luck. Whatever happened, Richard didn't want to hang around

Tampa very long. He was busy, and Pat must set the trap or get out of town. Besides, her nerves obviously couldn't take much more of this legal cat and mouse.

"Don't worry, Pat. I'll know where he is when it's time," Richard bluffed. "But just one day. That's it. If you can't get it done tomorrow, tough shit. I'm gone."

23

>>>>>>>>>>>>>>> Pat got up at six the next morning, sat on the carpeted steps, and cried. It wasn't just anxiety and fatigue. She felt totally alone with no one to confide in. She couldn't share her feelings with her daughters. They were part of her problem, and letting them know how desolate and frightened she was would only upset them more. She couldn't talk to Victoria about her feelings, either. Her attorney was swept up in the challenge and drama of the case. Pat thought she could have talked to Richard or Frank, who seemed to calm her just by their presence, but she could never manage a moment alone with either. Who else was there?

She waited until quarter to eight, then called Dr. Charles Crotty, the therapist who had helped her several times after she had found David, and who she knew would be in his office early. Unable to control her sobbing, she wasn't even sure he could understand what she was saying: ". . . biggest mistake of my life . . . girls on edge and fighting . . . they want to come home . . . they're scared . . . it's too late . . . I've done this to them . . . I'm pushing them into it . . . don't think I can make it . . ."

Dr. Crotty listened as he usually did, and Pat responded more to the kind and understanding tone of his voice than to what he actually said. She hung up feeling calmer and ready to face the day.

Richard had gotten up early, too. He drove out to Jim Parker's house and watched. He saw Parker's car in the driveway and, a few minutes later, a man passing in front of the window. Certain the man was Parker, from his photograph, Richard drove to the Holiday Inn where his partner, Rick, had stayed, and called Pat from the lobby.

"He's home," Richard said. "I'll be at the pool. Good luck in court."

Frank had asked his paralegal, Debbie Perez, to take care of the girls while Victoria, Pat, and he went to court to plead for a Writ of Ne Exeat. Debbie didn't know what to expect, but she had heard that Pat's daughters could be as restless as bees.

Victoria, true to form, burst into Frank's office dressed in a white suit, as fresh as if she had just returned from a vacation and ready to tear a hole in the courthouse. "Hi, Debbie," she called over her shoulder as she strode toward Frank's office. Pat, who looked exhausted, trailed a few steps behind; tagging after her were Christine, Andrea, and Marcia, the last two squabbling fiercely over a hair dryer. Oh, my God, Debbie thought.

While Victoria and Pat worked with Frank, Debbie tried to keep tabs on the girls. Christine, who looked quite grown-up in her high heels, was very quiet. Debbie was surprised because she had been expecting three noisy, gangly teenagers. She could see that Christine not only didn't want to be there, but was embarrassed at her sisters, who kept cracking loud jokes, mostly about Victoria's being a walking cosmetic counter. It was also clear to Debbie that they were trying to hide their fear under the string of wisecracks. They reminded Debbie of her own sisters—cute, lovable kids in grown-up clothes. She felt sorry for them because she sensed from the few serious comments they had let slip about meeting their father that they were expecting a ride into the sunset with full orchestra. Debbie knew better.

After the girls had explored the office and worn a path to the ladies' room, Debbie suggested lunch. Leading them into Frank's office, she pointed to a golden arch thirty floors below and two blocks away. The girls caucused, then agreed to eat and go back to the beach house to wait. With a sigh of relief, Debbie watched them argue their way out the door.

While the girls were having lunch, Victoria, Frank, and Pat were filing court papers. To hear their plea for the Writ of Ne Exeat, the clerk sent them to Judge Vincent Giglio, who was free. It was three o'clock. Pat held her breath in the hallway while her attorneys went into the judge's small chamber to present their case. After reading the motion with a stony face, Giglio listened to their brief argument, then asked, "Is there any reason why bond should be more than one thousand dollars?"

The motion before him requested forty-two thousand dollars, the amount of the arrearage. Knowing they had won, both Frank and Victoria argued for more than one thousand dollars, pointing out that if the court set bond too low, Jim Parker might pay on the spot, then flee.

"Ten thousand," Giglio said when they finished. "And good luck."

The order Judge Giglio signed directed the clerk to issue a Writ of Ne Exeat against James C. Parker, ordering him to post a $10,000 cash bond, stay in Florida, and attend the child support hearing Pat had requested. If Parker refused to or could not post the bond, the Writ further ordered the sheriff "to arrest him and confine him in the Hillsborough County Jail and to bring him before a judge of this Court within twenty-four hours of his confinement or at the Court's earliest session."

While Pat, Victoria, and Frank stood in the hallway savoring their victory, Judge Gonzalez walked by. No one had to tell him Bennett had won. "Yep," he said, "that Writ of Ne Exeat is a *mean* thing! But it's the way to go."

Pat rushed to the nearest phone. She had been checking in with Richard every couple of hours all day. The last time she had talked to him, he told her Jim Parker was still at home, and that he had seen him standing in his yard watching a construction crew. But Pat hadn't spoken to the girls since noon because there had been nothing to report. Now there was. Within the hour, she and Victoria would be asking the sheriff to arrest their father, and she wanted them to be dressed and ready. She phoned Debbie, who told her the girls had gone back to the beach house to wait. Pat called there.

"Christine took off," Andrea told her. "We don't know where she is."

"But why?"

Pat began to panic. Without Christine and her car, Andrea

and Marcia were stranded an hour's drive from Tampa. It *would* be Christine who'd disappear at the eleventh hour, Pat thought. She had never wanted to come in the first place.

"Christine's pissed at Marcia," Andrea explained. Apparently Marcia had spilled water on Christine while she was sunning herself on the deck, and Christine had got so angry, she dressed and drove off.

"Did she say where she was going? When she's coming back?

"We don't know where she is, Mom," Andrea said.

"Well, I'm going to see the sheriff right now, so sit by the phone!" Pat ordered. "When Christine comes back, go straight to Frank's and wait there."

Pat then called Richard, who was sitting by the swimming pool in the Holiday Inn in Lutz. "Christine's gone," she said. "No one knows where she is. Would you go get Andrea and Marcia if she doesn't come back?"

"It's too far," Richard said. "We'd never make it back here on time."

Pat was in a state of shock as Victoria led her down the polished terrazzo hallway and through the double glass doors of the Hillsborough County Courthouse Annex to the sheriff's office. Captain Richard Frazier stood up to greet them. A big man— six feet tall and two hundred pounds—he wore gold-rimmed glasses and had unusually large hands with neatly manicured nails. His voice was soft and kind, but a little raspy from too many cigarettes over too many years. And he spoke with the slow drawl of a native Floridian.

Dressed in a short-sleeve tan shirt with brown slacks and without a badge or gun, Captain Frazier didn't seem like a sheriff. But one look at the wall behind his huge glass-topped desk and you knew he was a lawman and proud of it. A Florida state flag hung on a pole next to the Stars and Stripes. To one side of it was his favorite picture—a color photo of Tampa in 1938. Although he had had many offers, he wouldn't part with it. Directly behind the desk hung certificates from the FBI National Academy and the Bureau of Prisons.

During his thirty years as a lawman, Frazier had done just

about everything: riding patrol, chasing pimps while on the vice squad, investigating homicides as a detective, and preventing prison riots as a warden. He was mighty proud of the fact that he had once made it into *Time* magazine. For the last sixteen years, he had commanded the civil division of the Hillsborough County Sheriff's Office. With regular hours and no street work to keep him on edge, it was the easiest job he had ever had and he liked it.

As Frazier eased back in his chair and listened to Pat's somewhat incoherent story, he felt touched. The woman was decidedly different from most of the wives who walked into his office begging him to arrest their no-good husbands. It wasn't just her tears, which he knew weren't the crocodile variety often used to soften the heart of an old sheriff. From what he could tell of her story, she had walked through hell to find her former husband, and he sensed in her a moral outrage that appealed to his Christian ethic. But whatever she was doing and for whatever reasons, he concluded, it was so important to her that she wouldn't waste his time by melting into a puddle and dropping all charges once he arrested this James C. Parker.

Victoria read Captain Frazier as easily as a billboard. Detecting a rather old-fashioned wisdom and chivalry clinging to his speech and manner, she went to work on him. In her best Virginia drawl—soft and lilting with just a touch of deep Dixie to match his—Victoria launched into her own five-minute version of the Bennett story. When she finished, she handed Frazier the Writ of Ne Exeat, stressing how important it was to arrest James Parker that very night because if he suspected his former wife was looking for him, he'd run again. The papers she and Pat had filed were public record, she pointed out. Someone in the courthouse who knew Parker might alert him, or a reporter who covered the court might sniff out the story and call him for a comment.

A father who prided himself on providing for his children, Frazier had little sympathy for Parker. The more he heard about how the man had treated his daughters, the more he wanted to help the woman in tears. In his mind, James Parker had violated the laws of the land and the rules of the Lord, and belonged behind bars for both. As he studied the writ,

Frazier was impressed, and his respect for the lady lawyer from Washington grew by the minute. That Writ of Ne Exeat was a mighty powerful piece of paper and plenty hard to get.

Pat watched as Victoria played on Frazier's sympathies like a master cellist. The more Pat listened to her attorney's stroking, the more impatient she became. After waiting sixteen years to face David, every extra minute was agony. She had three emotionally charged daughters, a writ in hand, a private detective on hold, and an attorney who didn't know what time it was. Pat was so close now, all she needed was Captain Frazier to send a deputy to Lutz, thirty miles away. Every minute of chitchat and flattery was a luxury she could no longer afford.

As Captain Frazier swiveled in his chair, a cigarette dangling from his lips, Pat noticed a curl of smoke drifting lazily up from beneath his seat. God, that was all she needed—fire engines and hoses, while David skipped town!

Victoria saw the smoke, too. "Captain Frazier," she said calmly, "I do believe you're on fire."

Frazier uncoiled himself just as calmly and began brushing his pants legs. "Looks like I'll have to buy me a new pair," he drawled. "I do this about once a week."

Pat had to laugh in spite of herself, and the tension momentarily drained from her body. What in the world am I doing here? she asked herself. I'm facing the biggest crisis of my life, and here I sit, watching slapstick.

"Don't worry none, purdy ladies," Frazier said after he put out the fire on his pants leg. "We'll get that desperado inside of an hour."

Spread out on Frazier's desk were Rick Hager's photos of James C. Parker. When he sat down again, Frazier studied them a moment, admiring Rick's work.

"Who took 'em?" he asked.

"A private detective," Pat said.

"D' ya think he might like to move down to Tampa?" Frazier smiled as he called a deputy into the office. "Look at these pictures the PI done took," he said. "You think you kin get this boy?"

The deputy nodded. He was a trim young man with dark hair and a mustache to match. On his tan shirt hung a silver star and a name plate. To Pat, he seemed so nervous that she wondered if he even knew how to fire the gun hugging his leg. Not sure exactly where the tiny town of Lutz was, the deputy went to the outer office to check a county map. A few minutes later, he was back.

"Lutz isn't in Hillsborough," he announced. "It's more than a mile into Pasco."

"Well, darn it!"

With disappointment on his face, Captain Frazier explained to Pat and Victoria that if Lutz were just over the county line, he could still arrest Parker there without getting into a jurisdictional skirmish. But under the circumstances, the Pasco County sheriff would have to do the arresting. He was sorry, but there it was.

"His name's Jim Marsee and you'll find him in the courthouse in Dade City," he told them.

Victoria checked her watch. It was just after four.

"The office closes at five," Frazier said.

Pat turned pale. Dade City was thirty miles away. Victoria had just wasted more than an hour finding and stroking the wrong sheriff. Now, as they got ready to make a dash through Tampa to Dade City, she still didn't know whether Christine had returned to the condo. If she simply sped off into the rush hour with Victoria, the girls might miss seeing their father.

While Pat and Victoria ran for the pay phones in the lobby, Captain Frazier called the Pasco County Sheriff's Office. Like good neighbors, Hillsborough and Pasco frequently did favors for one another. Since Deputy Sheriff Jim Marsee was out of the office, Frazier left a message: "Expect two ladies with a Writ of Ne Exeat. Keep the door open. It's important to me that you arrest him immediately."

While Frazier was leaving his message for Marsee, Victoria was paging Richard at the swimming pool. "Drop everything and race over to Dade City," she told him after she explained the latest legal wrinkle. "Hold the sheriff until we get there." On the phone next to her, Pat was ringing the beach house. No answer. All she could do was pray that the girls were on their way to Frank's.

After making their calls, Pat and Victoria raced back into Frazier's office. He was waiting, ready to push them out his private door, which opened onto the parking lot. "Lady lawyer,"

he told Victoria, "you better fly . . . But don't you worry none—
you ladies are too purdy to get arrested for speeding in *my*
county . . . North on the freeway to the Land O' Lakes exit
sign, Highway 54 . . . "

Victoria and Pat dashed to the white Lincoln parked just
outside. "Hold tight!" Victoria yelled as they took off down the
street behind an escort car and onto the freeway a few blocks
away. Tooling along at eighty miles an hour, they passed the
escort, who waved them by like a flagman at the Indy 500.

Victoria was having fun, and her driving scared the anxiety
right out of Pat. "Don't worry," Victoria said. "If we get stopped,
I'll just ask the officer to lead us right to the Pasco County
Courthouse!" She wove in and out of the rush-hour traffic until
she saw the Land O' Lakes sign and the Zephyrhills exit. Then
she screeched off the freeway and down the ramp to Highway
54. Which way—right or left? Neither Pat nor Victoria could
remember. There were no road signs, and no time to check a
map.

Across the highway sat a country store with a pickup parked
out front and a driver sitting inside munching a sandwich.
Victoria cut across the road and slowed down just enough for
Pat to jump out. She ran over to the truck and rapped on the
window.

"Which way to Dade City?"

"East on Fifty-four to Zephyrhills," the driver said. He
pointed right. "About ten miles. Turn left onto Three-oh-one.
There's a sign there that says Dade City—about nine miles."

"Where's the Pasco County Courthouse?"

"Can't miss it, lady. Keep driving right into town. Big gray
dome on the right side."

Pat pointed east to Victoria, who did a quick U-turn. With
the door hanging open and the car still moving, Pat jumped
back inside. It was after four-thirty. Victoria stepped on it
again, this time racing down a two-lane blacktop that rolled
first through pines, marshes, and pastures, then sliced through
a suburban sprawl of pizza parlors, trailer parks, and cheap
motels.

As the Lincoln bounced over a little crest, they saw a road
gang about a mile away, working on what looked like a bridge
over a patch of swamp. Sawhorses blocked the left lane. In the

right lane stood one man holding a stop sign and another signaling with a red flag. Refusing to slow, Victoria began flashing her lights and tooting her horn while Pat stiffened in fright.

The flagman frantically tried to wave them to a stop. When he saw they weren't about to, he flagged the left lane to a halt. The other worker flipped his sign around to Slow. The Lincoln sped over the bridge like a souped-up squad car. The column of waiting cars slipped by in a rush of wind, and Pat let out a sigh of relief.

As Victoria drove through Zephyrhills, Pat shouted, "There's the sign—Dade City—turn left at the light!"

24

>>>>>>>>>>>>> Sitting by the pool, bored, with nothing to do, Richard was relieved when he finally got his marching orders from Victoria. He listened to her story about the wrong sheriff in the wrong county courthouse and took it as a bad case of prebattle jitters. Typical Victoria, he concluded after he hung up. Melodrama at its best.

Richard eased into his rented Cadillac and leisurely drove to Dade City just a few miles from the Lutz Holiday Inn. He circled the courthouse, parked in the rear across the street from a string of police cars, then discovered he didn't have change for the meter. He didn't need to be a former cop to know that the easiest place to collect a ticket was right outside a police station. Hoping his luck would hold, Richard bounded up the stairs of the courthouse looking for a sheriff and a couple of quarters.

The Pasco County Courthouse was a relic of the old Florida—before snow-hating yankees had invaded. It was a two-story red brick building with gray cement steps and a clock in the dome. Inside, its ceilings were high and its terrazzo floors chipped. A long bulletin board papered with notices ran down one wall just above the white wainscoting. And at one end of the wide hallway, a double staircase with worn marble steps wound to the second floor, where Deputy Sheriff Jim Marsee was getting ready to go home to a clam and lobster supper.

Marsee was exactly what Richard expected. Smooth and quiet with a big gut. Richard liked Florida lawmen, whom he found pleasantly different from the cops around Washington. Florida police usually respected PIs and cooperated with them. Washington cops didn't—and who could blame them? Good PIs ran their own show, chose their own cases, made more money, and led lives filled with less danger and more predictability.

After introducing himself, Richard showed Marsee his license, stating that he was a former D.C. special-operations policeman who had been wounded five times. He explained why he was in Dade City and told Marsee two women were on the road somewhere between the courthouse and Tampa with an arrest warrant. Since he planned to leave town that night, Richard was as anxious for Marsee to arrest Jim Parker before dark as Pat and Victoria were.

"I know it's a lot of trouble, Sheriff," Richard said. "And I know it's almost time for supper, but I wish you'd help me out. These women are driving me nuts. We both know the guy will be there tomorrow. But *they* don't believe that. My client will get herself a heart attack if you don't arrest the man tonight."

Marsee was as sweet as pecan pie. Captain Frazier's message had not caught up with him yet, and he wasn't fond of PIs who more often than not came in, stirred the pot, then walked away leaving a mess for the sheriff to clean up. Although Richard seemed responsible, it was almost quitting time and Marsee wasn't eager to make an after-hours arrest for anyone. He told Richard he would wait until the ladies came with the paperwork so he could judge for himself what this was all about.

Richard got change from Marsee's clerk, bought an orange soda from the soft-drink machine downstairs, and walked out of the courthouse toward his parking meter. He was in the middle of the empty street when he caught a white gleam out of the corner of his eye. He heard tires squeal and jumped aside just as the white Lincoln cut the corner of the curb and screeched to a halt. Doors flew open. Victoria and Pat jumped out and began running up the courthouse steps. "Hurry up, Richard," Victoria shouted. "It's five o'clock!"

Richard followed, sipping his soda. By the time he reached the courthouse door, Victoria was already racing up the stairs at the other end, the clicking of her high heels on the marble echoing in the nearly empty hallway. Richard and Pat took the elevator. When they walked into Marsee's small, shabby office, Victoria was standing in front of the glass service window. Behind it, Marsee was studying the Writ of Ne Exeat.

"In fourteen years, I ain't seen anything like this piece of paper," he said. Since it came from Hillsborough County, Marsee wasn't even certain it was valid in Pasco. And Pasco County regulations required him to run the warrant by his superiors before attempting an arrest. He couldn't do that until the next day. "I'm on my way home for supper. I'll take care of this in the mornin'."

"We need to get it served tonight, Sheriff," Victoria purred, her big brown eyes pleading with his. "We need your help. You're the *only* one who can do this for us."

Marsee came out from behind his glass shield and walked over to Pat, trying to size her up. He considered himself a good judge of character, and the lady impressed him as serious. She had been chasing this James C. Parker in Fairfax, then Hillsborough, now Pasco. She had come all the way from Washington with an attorney and that in itself was unusual. In Marsee's experience, it was difficult to get an attorney just to walk across the street for a client. And the lady and her attorney were smart enough to get a Writ of Ne Exeat so the man couldn't run again.

Marsee decided to bend the rules. He'd try to arrest Parker that night without authenticating the Writ of Ne Exeat or settling the jurisdiction question first.

While Marsee was deciding how to handle Pat's case, the office clerk had been eavesdropping. Sensing Marsee's ambivalence, she got up from behind her desk and came over to him. "Deputy," she asked, knowing full well the answer, "is this a child-support case?"

"Yes, it is," Pat nearly shouted.

"Well, then," she told Marsee, "go get that bastard!"

Marsee let out a guffaw. He had been paying child support himself for almost ten years, and not only did he not owe anything, he was paid up two years in advance. He turned to Victoria, straightened to his full height, then let his knees buckle to bring himself down to her level.

"I'm gonna get this boy," he announced.

Pat was so relieved she had to bite back a giggle.

Marsee asked Richard if Jim Parker had a history of violence. When Richard said he didn't know, Marsee said he wouldn't make the arrest without backup. Not wanting to give him an excuse to put off the job until morning, Richard volunteered.

"I'll go right on out there and wait," he said. "If you can't get help, I'll back you."

Marsee thanked Richard. "You be there, but I'll go in alone," he said. "If you see a big ol' fat deputy flying out the door, you know I'm losin'. You jump right in, you hear?"

Marsee turned to Pat and Victoria. "You ladies go on out to the jail and sit. I'll bring 'im in for you." Then, after giving them directions to the jailhouse a few blocks away, Marsee closed up the office and left.

Victoria smiled in triumph. Not only had she just saved the day, she had had fun doing it. In fact, she had had so much fun that she had worked up a Texas appetite. "I'm starved," she told Pat. "Let's eat."

They walked across the street to the Crest Restaurant. Pat phoned Debbie from there to see if she had heard from the girls. For all Pat knew, Christine could be in Orlando now, leaving Marcia and Andrea still standing on the beach.

"They're on their way," Debbie told Pat. "Frank'll drive them to the jail when they get here."

"Christine too?"

"Yes, Christine too."

Pat was so relieved to have all three daughters on their way that she even managed to enjoy her dinner. The hardest part was almost over now. Unless David tried to kill himself or shoot it out with Deputy Marsee, the girls would finally get to meet him. She felt one twinge of regret, however. They would have to see him for the first time in jail.

I have no choice, she told herself. It's that or nothing.

Richard sat in his Cadillac down the street from Jim Parker's house waiting for Marsee to show up. It was growing dark. His camera with a 200-mm lens was loaded and ready to capture the arrest on film, but there were no street lights. And a flash would never work from so far away.

Richard was doing a slow burn. He knew Pat and Victoria were eating dinner somewhere, and he suspected Marsee had gone home for his supper as well, otherwise he would have been there by now. Everyone seemed to be getting something from this arrest but him. Marsee and Victoria were getting paid, Pat would have the satisfaction of seeing her former husband behind bars, and her daughters would finally meet their father. But him? He got to foot the bill himself for the car he was sitting in, the motel room he slept in, and—if he found time to eat—the food. To top it all off, unless Marsee hurried, Richard would miss his plane to Sarasota.

To make matters worse, Richard knew he couldn't just keep sitting on Parker's empty street. Somebody might call the cops on him and that's all he'd need to make his evening complete. Arrested while waiting for the police. His partner Rick would have a good laugh over that one.

Richard got out of the car and rang the doorbell of a house near Parker's. "Please don't be concerned," he explained to the man who answered. "That's my car over there. I'm supposed to meet a real-estate agent here who's going to show me a house. But she's late."

The man nodded knowingly and Richard went back to his car. This time, he stood outside to make it look as if he was really waiting for someone. He glanced at his watch and, without effort, looked genuinely steamed. Every now and then, he could see Jim Parker or a woman pass by the front window. Richard was worried that Parker might decide to take a ride somewhere, maybe for a six-pack, and he'd have to follow. If that happened, it would be just like Marsee to come by and, when he didn't find Parker, go back home for the evening.

As Richard's anger reached the boiling point, Jim Marsee pulled up to Parker's house in an unmarked car. A squad car with one uniformed officer inside tagged behind. Marsee hadn't gone home to eat as Richard had suspected. Since he couldn't be sure whether James Parker would try to flee or would arm himself, Marsee had decided not to go in alone, no matter what. To get backup, however, he had needed the approval of his supervisor. Then he had driven out to Land O' Lakes to pick up another deputy. That had taken almost two hours.

Marsee, who was casually dressed, and the policeman got out and walked up to Parker's front door and knocked. A man in his forties answered wearing Bermuda shorts and no shirt. He let the lawmen in.

"Good evening, Mr. Parker," Marsee said as he pulled out

his ID card. "I'm Jim Marsee with the Pasco County Sheriff's Office. I need to talk to you briefly."

As Marsee explained why he was there, he watched Parker's face so he could anticipate any move the man might make. He noted that Parker was surprised at his arrival but did not seem surprised by the reason. When he called Parker by his real name, the man didn't wince.

"Obviously, there must be some mistake," Parker said.

His wife came into the room. "What's this all about?" she asked her husband.

Parker gave her a vague explanation and told her he'd have to go with the sheriff to clear it all up. He'd be back soon. She began to cry.

"I need to change," Parker told Marsee.

The deputy sheriff followed Parker upstairs and stood in the open doorway as Parker put on a shirt, pants, and a pair of shoes. Marsee watched carefully. Parker might pull a gun and try to shoot himself. Under these circumstances, men were unpredictable.

Marsee followed Parker back downstairs, cuffed him, and led him to the unmarked car. He told his backup he could go home, then reached for his car radio. First, he called Central Communications. "Ten-fifteen," he said after identifying himself. "Ten-fifty-one" (prisoner in custody, en route). Then he called Warden George Carpenter at the Pasco County Detention Center saying he was on his way and asking Carpenter to open the back gate.

Richard watched the arrest with mixed emotions. He was happy for Pat, and relieved that Marsee had finally come. But through the bay window, he watched a woman enter the room, and he could imagine what she must be feeling.

He tensed when Parker left to get his shirt. Unable to see Marsee follow, Richard was appalled at the lawman's apparent carelessness. Any minute he expected to see the back door fly open and Parker race to his car for a quick getaway. By the time Marsee realized he was gone, Parker would have a head start—maybe he would even pull it off. Richard quickly slid back behind the wheel, ready to chase Parker if he tried to slip away. But the man returned a minute later buttoning a shirt.

When Marsee finally drove off with Parker, Richard glanced back at the house. The woman was still standing in the doorway, a silhouette against the soft living-room light. On her left arm, she held a child. She continued to stare down the street long after Marsee had taken her husband away.

The Pasco County Detention Center was a white box surrounded by a seven-foot chain-link and barbed-wire fence. Like the courthouse, it was an old building with chipped white tile walls and, above them, gray painted cement. Sergeant George Carpenter was the deputy warden in charge that night. When Victoria explained who she and Pat were and why they had come, Carpenter led them into the warden's office to make them feel comfortable. It was a slow night in the jailhouse and the drama of Pat's story caught Carpenter's imagination—a wife about to face a husband who had deserted her sixteen years ago; daughters about to see their father for the first time. Within fifteen minutes, all the guards and clerks knew the Bennett story, and there was a buzz of anticipation in the air that both Pat and Victoria could feel.

"Would it be okay for my daughters to talk to their father?" Pat asked Carpenter on one of his visits to the office to see how she was holding up. "They brought their photo album along so they can show him pictures of their childhood."

"If he wants to see them," Carpenter promised, "I'll arrange it." He wasn't so sure the man would. Handcuffs right after dinner, without warning, would shock the talk out of most men.

Warden Carpenter was so solicitous that Pat couldn't believe her luck. She had come to Florida convinced that justice would be hard to find there. After all, wasn't Florida the state where the old-boy network was alive and doing well? Yet every official she had dealt with—Judges Gonzalez and Giglio, Captain Frazier, and Deputy Sheriff Marsee—had been fair, if not actually kind. And now Sergeant Carpenter and the prison staff were warm and concerned. It was ironic: she was getting more cooperation in Florida based on a sixteen-year-old court order from another state than she had ever received in Virginia.

Half an hour after Pat walked into the jail, Richard called.

"They got him," he said. "He should be there soon. Good luck!"

"Aren't you coming?"

"This is your moment, kid," Richard said. "You don't need me there."

All in all, Richard felt pleased. He had just been part of something he knew was important—at least to the mother and three daughters, if no one else. And professionally, he was satisfied by how quickly the collar had gone down. No superfluous motion, just one clean move like a gymnast's routine. Richard checked his watch. If he hurried, he'd catch his plane for Sarasota after all.

Recognizing how anxious Pat was once she learned that Marsee was on the way to the jail, Warden Carpenter unlocked the door to the clerk's office and told her she could wait there so she wouldn't miss anything. Through the large glass window that separated the office from the intake section of the jail, she could see all the way down the hallway to the back door through which Marsee would lead David to be booked. Pat's mouth was as dry as bread crumbs. In her purse was the letter she had written David. She was certain that Warden Carpenter would agree to deliver it to him before David talked to his daughters.

Convinced that the next hour would be the girls' only chance to see their father, Victoria was nervous, too. She held David's FBI fingerprint card in her hand in case Parker denied he was David. Like Carpenter, she doubted he would want to talk to his daughters. Since Warden Carpenter had given her permission to use the prison phone, Victoria called Frank's BMW. "Step on it," she told him. "I don't want them to miss this."

Pat began to cry again once she realized her daughters would not be there when the back door opened. If the girls were lucky, they would have a few minutes to see their father through the window while a guard fingerprinted and photographed him before taking him to his cell. If they missed that as well, and if David refused to talk to them, they might never get the chance to actually see him. And *seeing* him—just that—was important to them.

Victoria tried everything she could think of to keep Pat's

mind occupied. She chattered, brought coffee, cracked jokes. Nothing worked. Every time Pat heard a noise, she jumped to the glass window. Doubts began to nag at her again. Maybe David had escaped. What if he wouldn't admit he was David? Maybe the girls wouldn't make it on time. What if they went to pieces? Maybe she should have let them live with their fantasy father instead of pushing them toward their real one.

Her own emotions were in a swirl, too: she felt sorry for David; she hated him; she was ready to forgive him; she wanted to see him punished. Pat was angry at having so many conflicting feelings.

She heard feet shuffling and chains jingling even before the back door swung open. She jumped up and stood by the window, Victoria next to her, her nose almost pressed into it so she wouldn't miss anything. Her heart was pounding. She shivered. Her palms were sweating.

Deputy Sheriff Jim Marsee led David in. His hands were cuffed in front of him, he shuffled down the corridor like an old man, head bowed. As he entered the booking area, he looked up. David studied Victoria's face first. His eyes were wide and filled with confusion. Then he looked at Pat.

Without flinching, her eyes held his. No fear or shame. They didn't plead or question as they would have done sixteen years ago—they challenged. "David, I know who you are," they said. "I know what you did. You got away with it all those years. No more. I'm here and I'm not going away."

In a silent, powerful, confrontation her eyes locked on his until he looked down. It was over.

Pat stood at the window and watched an officer book David. A guard lead him away to be deloused. She sat down and a nervous giggle overtook her. She was trembling uncontrollably: She had done it. This man wasn't the man she had married and had been afraid to meet. He wasn't the man she had written the letter to. *That* David was her fantasy husband who still lingered in her mind. She had been so concerned that her daughters might not be able to make the leap from fantasy to real father that she'd been blind to how a fantasy David had persisted in her in spite of her common sense, in spite of the photographs, in spite of everything.

At last she felt free. She slipped the letter to her fantasy

David back into her purse. The letter sounded foolish now. Whatever she had intended to say to him, she wanted to no longer.

Pat turned to Jim Marsee. "What did he say when you arrested him?"

"Nothing," Marsee said. "His wife asked him, 'What's this all about?' And he said, 'I'll explain later.' Then I told him the charges."

"Did he deny anything?" Pat was still worried that the FBI might have sent her the wrong fingerprint card.

"He didn't deny or admit anything."

"What did he say on the way here?"

"He said he didn't want to discuss it. He was very quiet."

"Did he deny who he *was*?" Pat asked.

"Nope!"

Pat threw her arms around Victoria and they both began to laugh out of sheer relief. "We did it," Pat nearly shouted. "We did it!"

25

>>>>>>>>>>>>> The traffic on Highway 301 was light. Not that it made any difference to Frank, who always drove fast and who didn't need Victoria to tell him to step on it. After a full day in federal court, he was tired, but still deeply concerned about the girls and more than curious. He could only imagine what it would be like to be a teenager about to meet your father for the first time. But he didn't have to imagine what it would be like to be a runaway father and have the sheriff knock on your door during dinner waving a Writ of Ne Exeat. A mean piece of paper that, no doubt about it.

Frank could tell that the girls were scared, and he did his best to keep their minds off their father. He cracked jokes whenever he could or picked up on their juvenile humor, trying hard to be one of the gang. Christine was quiet most of the time, somewhat embarrassed by her sisters' behavior. Andrea, clutching the photo album, did most of the talking.

When the car phone rang, Frank was never so glad to hear from Victoria. Within a minute, she managed to turn the BMW into a moving phone booth with everyone shouting. "Did they arrest him?—You hear that? They got him!—Is he there?— Let me talk to Victoria—No, let *me* talk to her—Come on, Frank, give me the phone!"

When at last they hung up, Frank could feel the girls' relief. They now knew that nothing could stop them from finally seeing their father. Frank also sensed they were taking David one step at a time, almost as if that was all they could handle emotionally. Just *seeing* him was uppermost. Talking to him would come later. More relaxed, knowing their father was there at the jail, they changed the conversation to their favorite topic—their mother's attorney. For the next half hour, they roasted Victoria.

Victoria had given Frank directions to the Pasco County Detention Center. Frank had barely turned the motor off before the girls flew out of the car and down the walk to the jailhouse door, Andrea clutching the photo album. Warden Carpenter let them in and Pat, Victoria, and Frank (as well as most of the jail staff) stood back while the three girls peered through a small glass window set in a steel door separating the visitors' section from the prisoners' section. Through it, they could see the fingerprinting room. The timing was perfect. An officer had already taken David's photo and was just beginning to ink his fingers.

The window was too small for three heads, and Andrea and Marcia, who were more aggressive, kept nudging Christine away. "Let me see," Christine kept saying. "Let me see!"

Pat watched with concern, expecting an emotional outburst. Her daughters were excited. It was almost as if they were looking at a new baby through the window in a maternity ward. It didn't seem to bother them that they were seeing their father for the first time in a jail while he was being fingerprinted. What he was doing and where he was made no difference to them. They were totally absorbed in just looking at him, taking in every detail. He was finally real, standing right there before them. Pat was surprised: no one was crying. In fact, the girls were smiling and seemed happy. Suddenly it seemed worth all the energy, pain, and expense for just that moment. A two-minute look at a runaway father through a tiny glass window.

Andrea was quiet, her wall of indifference down for a brief moment. Christine looked at her father, but then stood back to let her sisters have the window to themselves, as if to say, "What's the big deal?" Pat couldn't tell what she was really thinking or feeling. Marcia couldn't tear her eyes away or stop chattering nervously.

"Look, Mom," she said, as if to herself. "I have his nose."

Pat laughed and sighed all at once. In spite of all the threats to back out and all the "I don't cares," her girls had come, they had seen, and they had conquered their fear. They'll be all right now, she thought. No matter what David says or doesn't say, they can handle it. He is no longer a mystery. He's the middle-aged man who fathered them and who's just as scared as they are.

After a guard led David away, Warden Carpenter went to his cell to tell him that his daughters were at the jail and wanted to talk. When he returned, Carpenter told Pat, "He said he doesn't want to see them while he's in jail."

The girls didn't seem upset. They seemed to have had enough excitement for one day. In a way, Pat was relieved as well. It would be easier on all of them if the girls talked to their father privately in the courthouse before or after his upcoming hearing.

"Mom," Christine suggested, "what if we sent our pictures in to him?"

Christine meant the wallet-size photos of themselves they had intended to leave with their father after they had finished talking to him.

Pat collected the pictures, wrote the names and ages on the back, and gave them to Warden Carpenter, who took them to David.

"He wants to keep them," Carpenter said when he returned. Pat smiled. It was Jim Parker's first admission that he was David.

Parker's business partner, John Reynolds, hurried into the detention center shortly after David had been booked, asking to see Victoria and Frank privately. They went into a conference room and closed the door. Thinking Reynolds was David's attorney, Pat waited outside the conference room worried that her lawyers would make a deal without her as they had done in her nightmare, or that Reynolds had brought ten thousand dollars with him and would spring David immediately. If he got out, she was convinced he'd run.

When the meeting was over, Victoria explained to Pat who Reynolds really was. "He wants to give us three thousand dollars to leave town," she said. "He said, 'You don't want to destroy his business, do you?' "

Pat took the question as a threat: If you destroy Parker's business, how will he pay you? But the offer was laughable, not just because it was so meager, but because if she accepted it, David would avoid facing a judge a second time, just as he had sixteen years before. In her mind, David had to keep that date. She had come to Florida prepared to settle *in* court or *after* court, but not without a court.

"You're not considering that offer, are you?" Pat asked Victoria.

"No way!" Victoria said.

Reynolds introduced himself to Pat. He seemed cool, and if he was worried about his share of the business, he didn't show it.

"Did you know anything about this?" she asked him.

"No," he said. "I had no idea he wasn't Jim Parker or that he had three daughters."

"Does he have any money?" Pat asked. She was more worried about his having enough cash to post bond than his ability to pay his children what he owed.

"He should have," Reynolds said. "We did very well last year."

Pat was almost afraid to ask the next question. "Does he have any children?"

"A two-year-old boy," Reynolds said.

"No!"

The rush of sympathy Pat felt for David's wife and child was even stronger than her own shock. But despite her feelings, she still refused Reynold's offer. She had come all this way for her day in court and the papers had already been filed. The situation had become more complicated with yet another child who could be hurt.

It had been a long, draining evening and Frank, for one, was ready to put it behind him. With a sense of great relief, he left the girls with Victoria and began the drive back to Tampa alone.

Pat, her daughters, and Victoria sat outside the jail in Victoria's Lincoln Town Car waiting to see if John Reynolds would spring David. It was already eight-thirty and David had been in the jail since seven. Reynolds eventually came out with a message. "I saw Jim," he said. "He wants to see the kids, but not at the jail. Can we arrange something?" Once again, Pat saw the offer as a threat: Drop the charges and he'll talk, otherwise . . .

When David didn't walk through the door by nine, they took off for the beach house, stopping at a Roy Rogers on the way. Victoria called her parents with the news, and Pat phoned her mother.

Everyone felt good. Victoria was pleased that the legal strategy had worked so far. Pat was pleased that David was beginning to pay for what he had done. And the three girls were amazed to have actually *seen* their father.

"Did you see how shook up he looked?" they asked each other. There was no bitterness or glee in their voices. They didn't seem especially glad that their father was being punished, just fired with curiosity.

"What do you think he felt like?"

"I bet he sure was surprised when he saw the sheriff!"

"Maybe he was glad he finally got caught."

The more Christine, Andrea, and Marcia talked about the man they had just watched through the small glass window, the more they wanted to hear his voice, even if he only said a few words so they'd know what he sounded like. Would he have a deep voice? Would it sound frightened?

By the time they pulled up to the beach house, the girls were already planning what they wanted to say when they met their father at the courthouse in the next day or so. Talking to him was a real possibility now, not just a fantasy. Now they had a real father. Hadn't they just seen him? Now they had things to say, questions to ask, and answers to demand.

After settling the girls in at the condo, Pat told them they could have one long-distance phone call each. "Just one," she warned. Then, in a mood to celebrate, she and Victoria took off for the Adams Mark Hotel in Clearwater Beach. Still flying high, they laughed and giggled like schoolgirls as Victoria burned up the beach road. This time, she got caught.

"You know you were doing forty in a twenty-five-mile zone?" the officer asked Victoria after he pulled them over.

Pat jumped in before Victoria could try her wide-eyed Southern belle routine on him. "Officer, I can explain," she said. "This is my attorney and . . . " She condensed the entire sixteen-year saga into three minutes, and when she had finished, the officer was studying her curiously.

"Lady, I've heard a lot of stories in my day, but never one like this before. Still, I can see you're both all wound up. I'll let you go with a warning this time. Have a good time, relax— but slow down."

They thanked him, and when his tail lights had disappeared,

they burst out laughing so hard they couldn't stop. They had talked Jim Parker straight into jail, and now they had talked their way out of a ticket. Evidently nothing could stop them.

Pat and Victoria stayed at the Adams Mark until two-thirty the next morning, dancing with two doctors who were in Clearwater for a convention. If someone had told Pat back in Washington that a few hours after seeing David she would be light-hearted, she would have scoffed. Now here she was in a classy beach hotel having a good time at the moment she had feared would destroy her. The evening had turned into a celebration of life. Sixteen years of doubt and fear were finally over. She had left those anxieties with David in the Pasco County Detention Center.

Terry was right, she thought. You had to face it to get it behind you. And until it was behind you, you couldn't get on with your life. Well, she had taken the plunge, and by God, the water wasn't so cold after all.

26

>>>>>>>>>>>>>> The next day, Thursday, attorneys for both sides drew the battle line. David Rankin, Jim Parker's counsel, filed a motion to reduce bond. Victoria filed one to increase it. A hearing was set for Friday afternoon. Meanwhile, Parker sat in jail, waiting for the wheels of justice to grind Pat down.

Victoria had drawn Judge Julio Gonzalez. But since he had advised Victoria on the case and would open himself up to conflict of interest if he heard the motions, Gonzalez had recused (excused) himself. The hearing shifted to Judge Vernon Evans.

Victoria cornered attorney Rankin in the hallway before he went into Evans's chambers. "I don't think your client knows who my client is," she warned. She could tell from Rankin's motion to reduce bond that Jim Parker wasn't going to go down easily, and she didn't want him or Rankin to get the impression that they could bully Pat. "I think he thinks she's still the little girl he left on welfare. Well, let me tell you—she *isn't*."

Pat told her daughters to wait in the hallway during the hearing, which would be over in less than thirty minutes. She thought David might be present and didn't want emotions to cloud the issue. The girls could talk to their father afterward if he was willing to see them, she said. They didn't object.

It was a small, private hearing room and Jim Parker wasn't in it. The atmosphere was icy and everyone seemed nervous, including Judge Evans. If he had any sympathy for Pat and her daughters, his voice and manner hid it well. "What do I have to do to get this man out of jail?" he asked even before he heard the arguments.

Rankin pleaded that there was no reason for Jim Parker to run. He had been living in Florida since 1972 and, except for business trips, had remained in the state where he had deep personal and economic ties. (Rankin was mistaken: Parker had left Florida in 1976 and hadn't returned until 1981.) Parker and his wife had just bought a house, he argued. And besides owning a "substantial" and ongoing business, he had "numerous assets" in Florida. Why would he want to leave them behind?

Rankin went on to point out to Judge Evans that the Writ of Ne Exeat posed a jurisdictional problem. It was issued in Hillsborough County and served in Pasco. Although he challenged the legality of keeping Jim Parker in jail, Rankin did not make a formal motion to vacate the writ.

Since Frank was in federal court that day, Michael Echevarria, an attorney who shared his office and who had been helping Victoria over the past few days, pleaded for Pat. He argued that not only did Parker have a history of running and hiding, but he was counting on Florida's reputation as a haven for fugitive fathers, as well. Since Parker was such a poor risk and since he owed his children forty-two thousand dollars in back child support—not to mention current support—ten thousand dollars was not enough to encourage him to stay home. Echevarria asked Judge Evans to raise the bond to forty-two thousand dollars.

Judge Evans said he would study the written motions, consider the oral arguments and case law, and make his decision that afternoon. He would call the winning attorney and let him know what it was.

Even though David was still sitting in the Pasco County Detention Center, his wife and son had come to the hearing. Like his daughters, they waited for news in the hallway. Marcia, in particular, had a hard time keeping her eyes off her half brother. "Mom, look!" she said to Pat after the hearing. "There's our brother. He's so cute. He looks like us."

Although Marcia wanted to run over to the baby and ask his mother if she could hold him, she knew better. How could they talk even, with this lawsuit? She began to feel a twinge of jealousy toward the baby as well as guilt. If she had been a boy, her father would never have run away. He hadn't abandoned his new family, had he? Was that because he had a son instead of another daughter?

Everyone went back to Frank's office to wait for Judge

Evans's verdict. Sensing they had lost, they expected Evans to lower the bond to one thousand dollars. Parker would come up with the money, get out of jail, and put on his running shoes.

They didn't have long to wait. About an hour after the hearing, Judge Evans called David Rankin with his decision: he was issuing an order to vacate the Writ of Ne Exeat itself, making the question of raising or reducing the bond moot; James C. Parker was free to go home.

Rankin called Frank's office. Although no one was surprised that Rankin had won, no one had been expecting Judge Evans to grant what Rankin had never even asked for—a dismissal of the writ itself. The wording of the decision that Judge Evans called "Order Granting Motion to Vacate Writ of Ne Exeat" was vague. First, there never *was* a motion to vacate; second, the order never explained why it was being vacated. It simply stated, "The Court finds that the evidence presented at the hearing would require vacating of the order in and of itself."

Wasting no time, Victoria grabbed the phone and called the Tampa FBI with a warning that James Clinton Parker, who was wanted in Virginia for criminal desertion and non-support, who owed forty-two thousand dollars in back child support, and who was under court order to pay current child support, might try to flee as he had done before. Would bureau agents keep an eye on him? It was a long shot, but what the hell. Then she called The American Heritage Life Insurance Company, which had paid David's foster parents over eleven thousand dollars after the state of Virginia declared him legally dead. She told a claims officer that David was still alive and might try to play possum again. Shouldn't American Heritage put someone on his tail? If the company lost him again, it would never get its eleven thousand dollars back from David's foster parents, because it could never prove he was still alive.

By the time she got to reporters, Victoria was red hot. Frank didn't want her to attack the court—she, after all, could fly back to Washington the next day, but he'd have to deal with the repercussions. But Victoria had sharpened her tongue for Judge Evans. After accusing him of dealing "in a very, very light-handed and limp-wristed way with a man known to have avoided the courts," she came one word short of calling him incompetent. "It could turn out to be a very grave indiscretion," she warned.

Although Jim Parker got away with a light slap on the wrist, he wasn't happy either. He told the *St. Petersburg Times*, "It was a case of false arrest. It was thrown out in Hillsborough County and somebody's going to pay. They're going to have to stick to their story and somebody's going to pay."

And when the *Washington Post* caught up with him, he said:

It's been devastating. I'm rather angry they would still be pursuing me after all these years. It would seem that after a mistake I made twenty years ago—well, what good is it going to do now, other than persecute me? All they came for was vengeance. . . .

I wouldn't give them the satisfaction of seeing me with leg irons and handcuffs. I think that is a vindictive thing their mother did to try to parade me in front of them like that. . . .

We had a separation, and before I could ever do anything as far as her child support, she ran me out of town. Every time I got a job, she would call up screaming at my employer. I couldn't keep a job. I couldn't support myself, let alone them. . . .

After such a long time hiding from that woman, trying to get my life together, I really didn't feel that I had the right to intrude on their lives. . . . I don't think money is the primary thing. From all appearances, all they are trying to do is discredit me. . . .

It's affecting my family, my business, it's affecting me now. It's been mud and dirt and hurt and vengeance, that's all. And that's all it's been between me and that woman for twenty years. That's why I've gone to such extremes to hide from her.

Pat was disappointed but not shaken by Judge Evans's order to let David go. It was only round one; more bells would sound. She had accomplished what she had set out to do—establish Parker's real identity, have him arrested, confront him, and give her daughters the chance to see him. Victoria had already filed Pat's Petition to Establish a Foreign Decree as a Florida Judgment. Pat and David—either through the court or through their attorneys—would settle on how much of the forty-two thousand dollars David would have to pay. Eager to put the whole emotional mess behind her, Pat wanted to be reasonable. Not exactly a perfect ending, but a satisfying one.

If Pat wasn't upset, her daughters were. "How could they just let him go?" they demanded. "It's not fair!"

Naïve and inexperienced in the law, they couldn't understand Judge Evans's reasoning. Their father had abandoned them and avoided child support for sixteen years. He was wanted in Virginia for criminal desertion. He had committed bigamy and might have criminally assumed the identity of another person. Why did the judge let him go after just two nights in jail? They couldn't grasp the concept that justice and the law were not the same thing.

That night at about eleven o'clock, Pat crept out of bed, sensing something was afoot because it was so quiet. She went downstairs. Marcia had the telephone receiver in her hand and was about to call her father. Without saying a word, Pat sat on the couch waiting to see what would happen. What harm could a phone call do? If they were ready to talk, why not let them? Hadn't Terry advised them to think only of themselves, not of their father's feelings? Too bad if he had had a rough two days. Too bad if it was late and he might be upset by the phone call.

"Can I speak to my father?" Marcia asked Jim Parker's wife, who answered the phone.

"He's just been through a terrible ordeal and can't talk now," she said. "Wait a couple of days and he'll talk to you then." She hung up.

Andrea was angry. No one had the right to hang up on them, especially Parker's wife. He should have enough guts to answer his own damn phone. She dialed and got a similar message. Not one to be put off easily, she called again.

"Which one is this?" Parker's wife asked.

"Andrea," she said. "Look, I've been waiting sixteen years to talk to him and I'm not going to wait another day. If he's not man enough to come to the phone, then I'll stay here in

Florida until I see him. And I won't stop calling until he talks
to me!"

"Just a minute!"

Pat raced upstairs to wake Victoria, then picked up the
only other extension. Both she and Victoria listened to the
conversation.

"I just want to ask you one question," Andrea told her
father when he got on the phone. She wasted no time—it was
a question that had been on her mind ever since she realized
he had abandoned her. Deep down she knew there was no
answer that could possibly satisfy her, but she had to ask it
anyway: "Why did you do it?"

David blamed Pat, saying she had had him fired from his
job four or five times and then run him out of town.

Andrea wouldn't buy that. She was willing to concede that
her parents had had problems and that her mother might not
have been the easiest person to live with, but that was all. She
went after her father with rapid-fire questions, not even waiting
for the answers: "How could someone force you to leave? She's
not stronger than you. You're bigger than she is. You mean to
tell me that you let *one* little woman ruin your home, your
family, your children? Any marriage can fail, but that's no
excuse to just get up and run. You're a coward. A wimp!"

Andrea's anger poured out, not loud or volatile, but through
the fierce insistence of her questions. She saw through her
father, found his excuses thin, and recognized his evasiveness
as a sign of weakness. She had him on the mat. This time, *she*
held the power to hurt. She struck out, not wildly but with
short and painful jabs. And she knew exactly what she was
doing.

"I had no choice," David said when she kept asking why
he had run away. His voice sounded weak and defeated.

"What do you mean, you had no choice?" Andrea
demanded.

Silence.

"What do you mean? That's no answer!"

Silence.

Andrea moved on. "Did you ever feel guilty?" she asked.
What she wanted was to hear him say he was terribly sorry,

and would she forgive him? But Andrea was smart enough to realize that he really wasn't sorry. Embarrassed, yes—at having been caught. Scared, yes—of facing the consequences. But guilty? No. If he had felt guilty, he would not have been able to live with himself for seventeen years knowing what he had done to three children. Nor would he have been able to marry Lenora, leave her, and marry again.

When he didn't answer directly, Andrea's anger flared. "Don't you see what you've done?" she asked.

"Don't you *see?*" she pressed.

Silence.

Andrea moved on. "Didn't you ever wonder what we looked like all those years?" she asked. "Didn't you ever want to see us?"

Andrea knew what she wanted to hear. That he had missed her and had wondered about her all the time—what she looked like, if she resembled him in any way, how she was doing at school. Although she knew she would never get the answers she wanted, she was driven to keep asking these questions.

David told Andrea that he had thought about his daughters often, but that he hadn't wanted to intrude on their lives. He accepted full responsibility for what he had done, he said. If his daughters thought of him as a good-for-nothing father, he could accept that. When he left Virginia for Texas in 1969, he said, he was so depressed that he could hardly remember that year. For the first ten years, he thought he'd never be found. Then later he began to figure it was a possibility. During the last year, however, he had had a feeling they would find him somehow. He was too old to run now, he said, and would face his responsibilities.

Andrea wasn't satisfied. His answer sounded lame and insincere. If it had been *her* daughter left behind, Andrea knew she would have thought about the child every waking moment.

The issue was important to Andrea. It was one thing to be abandoned, but quite another to be abandoned and never thought of again. That was double rejection and twice as painful. So she asked again, "Didn't you ever want to see us?"

When she heard her father circling the question and choosing not to answer her directly, she struck out at him again. "I don't think you're listening to me," she said. Then she began to lecture him on what it was like to be abandoned.

Pat and Victoria listened to Andrea and David on the extension upstairs. Forgetting for a moment Terry's advice that her daughters were to tell their father whatever they wanted, and not be concerned about his feelings, Pat felt Andrea was talking too much and listening too little. She grabbed a pencil and a paper plate and scratched, "You're not letting him talk. You're lecturing him." Then she gave the plate to Marcia, who ran down the stairs to deliver it to her sister.

Andrea read the note, but didn't take her mother's advice. She continued asking questions and, when she wasn't satisfied with the answers, poured out her own feelings. If it sounded like a lecture, then her mother didn't have to listen. This was *her* father and *her* phone call. If her mother wanted to hear more of David and less of her, she could have the phone next.

Andrea's "whys" came so fast there was hardly time to answer them. Some she asked more than once.

"Why did you leave us?

"Why didn't you contact us?

"Why didn't you pay child support?

"Where did you go?

"You knew we were on welfare. You knew that and you *still* took off.

"Did you know what I went through?

"Weren't you even curious about us? What we looked like? Didn't you even wonder if we were dead or alive? What we were doing? You didn't even know if we were starving to death!"

"I take full responsibility," David said.

"You take responsibility! What kind of answer is that?" Andrea demanded.

David went on the offensive, but as far as Andrea was concerned, he was wasting his time. After explaining how he had been strip-searched in jail and treated like a criminal, he asked, "Why did your mother have to have me arrested? If all you wanted to do was talk to me, all you had to do was call."

As Pat listened on the extension, she found David getting

to her the way he used to when they were married. In spite of herself, she felt sorry for him and his wife and what they were going through. Tears began to well up.

But not in Andrea. So the police had treated her father like a criminal. Well, what the hell did he expect? He *was* one in her book.

"If we called, you would have run away again," she said coldly.

"No, I wouldn't. . . . It was a very cruel thing for your mother to do. No way am I going to give her the satisfaction of seeing me in chains and handcuffs."

"Why didn't you just pay the child support?"

"I couldn't. Your mother would have had me arrested."

"You could have sent it from anywhere and no one would know."

"No, she would have found out and come after me. She was always one step behind me. I kept looking over my shoulder the whole time."

Andrea was so angry by this time that she landed a low blow. Knowing how her father had favored Christine, she told him how his old friend Bill came over to the house to help Christine. She knew the jab would hurt, and although she felt bad about tossing it, she couldn't resist.

"Bill fixes Christine's car," Andrea said. She spoke more slowly now, giving each sentence a chance to sting. "Bill and my mom went out on New Year's Eve. . . . He comes over almost every day. . . . Bill and Mom are good friends."

In the end, Andrea hung up the phone neither satisfied nor angry, just disappointed. She felt nothing for her father, just as Pat had felt nothing for David when she saw him in jail. Her indifference surprised her. If he had said the right words, like "I'm so sorry, I'm glad you found me," or "I love you, please forgive me," and if she had believed him, she would have wanted to try to build a relationship, even if that hurt her mother. Now, as far as she was concerned, her father had talked but had said *nothing*.

Andrea realized that for weeks she had been setting herself up for either total acceptance or total rejection. What she had gotten was neither, and she felt as lukewarm to her father as he had sounded to her. With a curious weightless feeling, she realized he wasn't worth hating or loving. And she didn't want anything in between.

All during Andrea's conversation, Marcia was fidgety, and with good reason. She had had two dreams the night before that told her exactly where her heart was. In the first, her father walked into her house. Everyone was at home as if waiting for him. He was gorgeous and smiling, and under his shirt he was wearing a Superman suit. He gave her and her sisters a hug and said he was sorry. In turn, they each told him that they forgave him. Then he looked at her mother. She, too, forgave him. Marcia woke up feeling warm and loved.

In her second dream, her father was standing on the corner fifty yards from the cul de sac where her house stood. He was stalking her with a knife, threatening to rape and kill her. She hid in the bushes, shivering from fright. Although her mother and sisters knew he was after her, they couldn't help her. He went from door to door asking for her. When he finally came to her house, he went inside to wait for her. She couldn't hide in the bushes forever and she couldn't go home. Marcia woke up from the second dream in a state of panic.

Besides her anxiety about talking to her father, Marcia was also angry at Andrea. She kept telling her sister, who seemed to be on the phone forever, "Hurry up, I want to talk. You can get back on later." She was afraid that Andrea was being too tough on her father and that he might not want to talk to her.

When she wasn't trying to coax her sister off the phone, Marcia was upstairs with her mother and Victoria, trying to listen on the extension with them. But she found it difficult to concentrate with three ears to one receiver and a constant flow of comments: "Did you hear that?—Can you believe he said that?—Tell Andrea to ask him this!" As far as Marcia was concerned, the phone call was private business between her, her sisters, and their father. It was the big chance everyone had been promising her. Here he actually was—on the phone—and she couldn't hear, concentrate, or even feel what she wanted to feel without being coached!

Marcia left the bedroom after half an hour and sat next to Andrea at the table, waiting and making up the final list of questions she wanted to ask. She didn't want to repeat Andrea's questions. But she hadn't been able to catch all of her father's answers, and some questions were so important to her that she would never be satisfied with what he had told her sister. She wanted him to answer to *her*. What worried her was that she might lose control of her emotions, and she didn't want to give him the satisfaction of knowing that he could get to her that deeply.

"Hi," Marcia began, "how are you?"

She was so nervous that she kept twisting the phone cord around her hands. But the deeper she got into the conversation, the calmer she became until she could hardly believe it was Marcia Bennett who was talking and listening. She had expected to cry, hyperventilate, perhaps be so overwhelmed that some-one would have to hang up for her. Instead, not only was she in control of herself, she dominated the entire conversation, becoming as patient and unrelenting as a prosecutor.

"Did you cheat on Mom?

"Did you ever come to see me in the hospital?

"Weren't you lonely? Scared?

"Did you give a crap about us?"

Unlike Andrea, Marcia waited for answers. If David tried to avoid her, she'd ask again, saying, "You're not answering my question" or "You're trying to get around this." When he wouldn't give her the answer she wanted, she suggested one: "Well, you could have done this or that, couldn't you?" When she felt there was no more to squeeze from the question, she methodically moved on to the next.

Marcia asked her father about his boyhood, his parents, and his foster parents; about Lenora, his current wife, and his son. She and her father even laughed a few times. And when the time felt right, Marcia began to talk about what had been eating away at her for as long as she could remember.

"I always believed you were dead," she said. "And when I knew you were alive, I wanted to call you right away. But Mom wouldn't give me your phone number. I grew up believing that it was *my* fault that you left." She was crying now, not hysterical tears, but quiet ones springing from deep pain. "I thought that if I had only been a boy, you would have stayed.

I believed that, all the time I was growing up. I'm over it now, but that's what I used to think."

"How could it be a child's fault?" David said. He seemed close to tears himself. "Well, it wasn't your fault, I assure you."

"You have a son," Marcia said, still crying. "And that's *my* brother. Promise that you won't ever leave him like you left us. Promise!"

"I'm too old to run," David said.

Christine was next. Her voice was soft and warm and she was very nervous. "I missed you," she said.

To Pat, it sounded as if Christine had been holding back those three words for a long time, and she heard her daughter crying inside. So Christine was not indifferent after all. Missing her father for sixteen years and never hearing from him was like being rejected over and over again. Pat began to understand her oldest daughter's pain. Yet in spite of herself, she was annoyed at Christine for what seemed like forgiveness without even a show of anger.

"I remember you," Christine said. "I remember when you left. You gave me a ginger ale, then got your toy car set from under the bed."

"I still remember you," David told her. "I remember what you smelled like. I remember holding you. I thought about you every day. And I missed you, too. I want to see you. I want to see all you girls."

But after asking her father some of the same questions her sisters had asked and hearing the same answers, Christine gave the phone back to Marcia, convinced she still didn't care about her father, and that it hadn't been worth the energy and money to find him. If she wanted to meet him sooner or later, she told herself, it would only be to satisfy her curiosity, nothing more.

Still not satisfied, Marcia began asking the same questions all over again. What she was aching to hear was, "I lost so much when I left you. I love you. Can't I start being your father again? It's not too late. We still have a lifetime. I can't make up for what I did, but I can try. . . . " But her father didn't say that. The more he talked, the more he sounded as if he didn't care about her or what he had done to her. And the more Marcia listened, the angrier she became until, like Andrea, she began verbally pounding him. And when she sensed he was crying silently, she felt good. She wanted him to suffer.

"Look, you don't have to talk to me if you don't want to," Marcia finally said. Her voice was threatening.

"I'll talk as long as you want," David said. He sounded tired and beaten.

"That's not an answer," Marcia objected. "Do you want to continue talking to me?"

"I'll talk as long as you want."

"Look, I really don't see the point in all this," Marcia said. "We've been on the phone for three hours and you haven't said anything about being sorry or that you even *want* to talk to us. I'm going to hang up. Good-bye!"

Marcia ran upstairs to her mother. Pat was proud of her daughters. For three hours, they had said exactly what was on their minds, and each had unburdened herself of a special pain. Andrea had said how angry she was at being abandoned and, more than her sisters, demanded to know why. She wouldn't let her father off easily. Marcia had told her father how she had blamed herself for his actions all those years. Although she said she no longer felt guilty, Pat knew she did. And by telling her father how much she had missed him, Christine had admitted how deeply she had been hurt. She knew, even if she wouldn't say it to her mother and sisters, that she was pushing her father away so he couldn't hurt her again.

"I feel s-o-o good, Mom," Marcia said softly when she joined her mother in the bedroom. "Like the biggest burden has been lifted from my shoulders."

27

>>>>>>>>>>>>> Jim Parker didn't run. Instead, he decided to fight with the weapon of Pat's choice, the law—in the arena of her choice, the courtroom. Thirty days after Pat petitioned to have Florida recognize Virginia's child-support order, David's attorney hadn't lifted his pen. Technically, he didn't have to, for Pat's own attorneys had made a procedural error in serving James Parker. Pat would have to refile, serve David again, and wait another thirty days for a response.

Back in Washington, Pat wasn't terribly discouraged at the new delay. Filled with second thoughts about her legal strategy, in the light of Judge Evans's order to free James Parker, she was getting jittery about facing David in Hillsborough County, where she might draw Evans a second time.

But if Pat wasn't discouraged, she was angry. Her feelings of guilt, hurt, and anxiety disappeared, almost as if the face of her anger had frightened them away. Relieved that she had finally let go, she understood in a new way what Terry had told her daughters: before they could put the past behind them, they would have to express their rage.

What sparked the eruption was David's decision to use the system to avoid supporting Andrea and Marcia, who were still minors. Once she had found and exposed him, she had honestly expected him to begin paying current child support at the rate the court had ordered sixteen years before until he and she could renegotiate the amount before a judge. But it became clear to her back in Washington that not only had David chosen to stand in contempt of court as he had in 1969 when he ran away, but that he also intended to fight her on arrearages down to the last dollar. In 1969 he had hidden behind the name of another man. Now, in 1985, he was hiding behind the skirts of the law.

Well, if David wanted a fight, she'd give him one he'd never forget. Never again would she allow him to intimidate her the way he had when he walked out. Never again would he use her fear and guilt to keep her meek and humble. She would not allow him to punish his children a second time nor run from his responsibility again. If a battle was what he wanted, a battle to the finish is what he would get, win or lose. If he believed thirst for vengeance was driving her, as he told the *Washington Post*, so what? Of course she wanted to see him pay. She would even cheer if a Florida judge sent him to jail for a year. And if he was so foolish as to ever put his foot in Virginia again, she would send the sheriff after him for criminal desertion and nonsupport faster than he could say Jim Parker. As sweet as these thoughts were, however, it was not simple vengeance that fired her. She was fighting for her dignity and self-worth. For the right to hold up her head proudly and say, "No one can step on me and my children—no one!" It was justice she wanted most now. And next to dignity and justice, vengeance ran a poor third.

Before her Florida experience, Pat had been prepared to settle for five hundred dollars a month current child support for Andrea and Marcia, and ten thousand of the forty-two thousand dollars in arrearage to cover her travel and legal expenses. No longer. She began to rethink the motion Frank and Victoria had filed for her in Hillsborough County. And she talked to Judge Valentine about her anger, the Florida hearing, and her legal options. By mid-March 1985, two months after Judge Evans had let David go free, she made her decision.

She would seek a hearing in Pasco County, not in Hillsborough. For one thing, she didn't want to get into a jurisdictional skirmish that could cause more delay and expense. For another, she didn't want to risk drawing Judge Evans, before whom she was convinced she would never get fair treatment. She had done some checking on how Evans had ruled on other child-support cases, and the pattern she had found disturbed her. Since she couldn't fight him, protected as he was by the bench, she would avoid him.

Next, she would seek a judgment based on the now seventeen-year-old child-support order in Virginia, instead of in Florida, then ask Florida to enforce it. She had enough experience in the Juvenile and Domestic Relations Court in Fairfax to know that no matter which judge heard her case, he or she would at least grant a judgment for the full forty-two thousand dollars in back child support. Florida, on the other hand, had a history of whittling arrearages down to almost nothing just to clear the docket. In a way, Pat wouldn't have blamed Florida if it did that to her. If Virginia didn't take criminal desertion and nonsupport seriously enough to extradite, why should Florida clog its court with an order for huge arrearages that might be difficult to collect?

Finally, she would ask the Virginia court to include attorneys' fees and investigative expenses in the judgment as well as interest on the unpaid child support. Recovering legal and court costs should not be a problem, since attorneys routinely requested them. But to get interest in support cases was unusual. Pat had done enough legal research at the IRS law library on her lunch hours to feel confident that she would at least get a much better hearing on that issue in Virginia than in Florida.

At first, Victoria opposed Pat's plan. She had no argument with filing in Pasco County instead of in Hillsborough, since she wasn't eager to face Judge Evans again, especially after describing him as "limp-wristed" to the *St. Petersburg Times*. But legal sense told her that it would be easier to enforce a Florida judgment in Florida than a Virginia judgment in Florida. Besides, since she was about to leave for a vacation in the Sunshine State, she could file the papers in Pasco County at little cost. But Pat wouldn't budge.

Two weeks after Pat decided to begin the fight in Virginia, David offered through his attorneys to settle out of court—a single cash payment of five thousand dollars within ten days and two hundred dollars a month in current child support for Andrea and Marcia for two years, until Marcia turned eighteen. The offer only served to strengthen Pat's resolve to dig in and do battle in Virginia first.

Victoria made a counteroffer: two hundred dollars a month in current child support and a lump sum of between ten and twenty thousand dollars. Until both parties settled, she suggested, Jim Parker should begin sending the two hundred dollars a month the court had ordered in 1969, "showing his good faith in the event that we do reach an amicable settlement."

When Parker refused to send the two hundred dollars a month or settle for more than five thousand dollars, Victoria drafted a Petition and Affidavit for Rule to Show Cause in which she asked that the Fairfax County Juvenile and Domestic Relations Court summon David to prove that he should not be held in contempt of the 1969 support order, enter a judgment for $42,793 in arrearages plus $34,696 in interest, and grant Pat investigation costs and reasonable attorneys' fees.

Victoria filed the petition in mid-May. The court ordered David to appear on July 11, 1985, one year after Pat had found him in Tampa. Two days before the July hearing, Rankin responded to Pat's petition, arguing that James Parker could not pay the arrearage because he didn't have the assets, and that Virginia no longer had jurisdiction over the case because Pat Bennett had already begun legal proceedings in Florida.

Pat, Victoria, and Marcia, who had insisted on going to the hearing, sat in Judge Michael Valentine's courtroom at nine in the morning on July 11. No one seriously expected James Parker to be present because there was still a valid warrant for his arrest on charges of criminal desertion and nonsupport, and the jail was just down the corridor.

All Pat and Victoria knew for sure was that Judge Valentine would not be hearing their petition for a judgment because he had advised Pat on the case from the very beginning. Shortly after nine-thirty, Valentine called out Pat's name and told her to go to Judge Jane Delbridge's chambers.

"Oh, shit!" Victoria said. She had never argued before Delbridge and didn't know what to expect.

Pat waited on a bench outside Judge Delbridge's small hearing room until eleven. Every now and then she would steal a peek through a window in the door in the hope of catching a glimpse of the woman who could make or break her case. Over the last twelve months, Pat had discovered what most attorneys learn after their first week in the pit. Blind justice is a myth; judges, good and bad, are the reality.

It was eleven-thirty when a bailiff finally ushered Pat, Victoria, and Marcia inside. The room was empty except for a bailiff and Judge Delbridge, who sat up high behind a wooden barrier, like a bishop in a pulpit. Victoria went right to work.

After explaining the facts of the Bennett case, she told Delbridge what they had tried to accomplish in Tampa and why they were back in Fairfax. All the while, Pat watched Delbridge, hoping to read something in her face. But there was little to see. Delbridge listened intently to Victoria's story and when she asked a question, her tone was as dispassionate as a lawbook.

When Victoria rested her case, Judge Delbridge peered down at Pat for the first time, then leaned forward. "There's no court reporter here," she said. "Now tell me—how did you find him?"

Pat relaxed and walked over to the bench. As she began her story, she immediately felt at ease; she was simply talking to another woman. She told Judge Delbridge all about the Social Security hearing and Lenora's marriage certificate. How she found Lenora and her conversation with her. How she called Safeco in Seattle to confirm that David had worked for the company, and then how she phoned state insurance license offices in the South until she scored in Tallahassee. Then she told about Richard and Rick and the photographs. About subpoenaing David's fingerprints from the FBI and his personnel records from Safeco, which led to the Rutgers University transcript. And she explained how, through subpoenaed information from Rutgers, she had found the man she believed to be the real James Parker living in Oregon.

"You ought to consider becoming a private eye," Judge Delbridge told Pat when she finished. "You're very good and you'd probably make more than you do now."

Judge Delbridge's decision that afternoon didn't surprise either Pat or Victoria. She granted a judgment for the full $42,793 in arrearages, then asked Victoria if she had prepared a list of Pat's investigative costs and whether she had calculated the interest schedule from 1968 to 1985. Pat had done both. Promising to study them, Delbridge then asked if Victoria had brought a written analysis of decisions where the court had granted interest on arrearages in support cases. Victoria had not.

"Would you do a memorandum?" Judge Delbridge asked.

Both Pat and Victoria felt good after the hearing. Not only did they get a judgment for the total arrearage, but they sensed from Judge Delbridge's questions that she would at least grant *some* of the court and legal fees. And since she had asked for a memo on interest, which amounted to almost thirty-five thousand dollars, it was clear Delbridge was at least open to granting interest if Victoria could satisfy her about the legal grounds for doing so.

Victoria submitted her Supplemental Memorandum two months later, in mid-September. Along with it, she appended a breakdown of Pat's actual child-support expenses from 1968 to 1985, which Pat had worked out in great detail. They came to $359,000. Had David paid the two hundred dollars a month the court had ordered during that same period of time, his share of the actual support would have come to 12.1 percent.

Two more months crawled by after Victoria had submitted the interest memorandum, and Pat still had no word from Judge Delbridge. It had now been one and a half years since she had found David, and Andrea had just turned eighteen. Unable to stand the tension any longer, Pat wrote Delbridge a letter. After explaining the history of her court battle and how two of her daughters had already reached majority with a third one almost there, she said:

> I never anticipated in June 1984 that pursuing this issue would leave me so emotionally exhausted and financially burdened. I've mortgaged my house, borrowed from every possible source, and struggled not only to support my family by myself, but now to collect the child support owed. If I didn't believe this to be so important, I would give up just as so many other women have.
>
> Judge Delbridge, I respectfully request that my case be given priority, and that a decision be rendered concerning the issues as presented at the hearing on July 11.

Ten days later, on Saturday, November 23, Pat pulled into the driveway with her cousin Joe from San Francisco in the front seat. She had just driven back from Philadelphia, where Joe had attended a business meeting. He was planning to stay the weekend.

Marcia was waiting.

"You have the judgment!" she screamed. Instructed to open

any mail that looked important while her mother was away, she had read the letter from the court. "It's here."

Pat turned pale. Judgment? Was someone suing her? For what? Pat grabbed the envelope Marcia was waving and tore out the judgment. She screamed, then kept shaking her head in disbelief while Joe stood in the driveway thinking all the Bennetts must be crazy.

Jane Delbridge had given Pat everything she had asked for down to the last penny—$79,403.52 for arrearage and interest, $15,388.44 for current fees for Victoria Gordon, $6,100 for Frank de la Grana, and $5,181.62 for investigative and other expenses. She had been so angry and discouraged, feeling that the whole snail-paced child-support system was stacked against her. She had been beaten and bruised in the courts for one and a half years. Now this! The victory tasted as sweet as candy—$106,073.58 worth.

28

>>>>>>>>>>>>>> The following Monday, Pat took off from work and spent the day at the courthouse getting triple-sealed, certified copies of the judgment for Frank de la Grana to register in Pasco County. First, she obtained the signature of the clerk of the circuit court verifying that her copy of the judgment was true. Next, a signature from the judge of the circuit court verifying that the clerk's signature was valid. Finally, a second signature from the clerk attesting the validity of the judge's signature. That took half a day.

While scurrying around the courthouses, Pat met Judge Jane Delbridge in the ladies' room. Not wanting to compromise Delbridge by discussing the case, Pat merely looked at her and said thank-you quietly. There was a flicker of recognition in Delbridge's eyes, and Pat thought she saw the trace of a smile at the corner of her mouth, but she couldn't be sure.

"Good luck," Judge Delbridge said.

Not realizing at the time just how much luck she would need, Pat gave copies of Delbridge's judgment to Victoria, who, in error, sent them by express mail to Mike Echevarria. They sat in his office for a month before Frank finally found them and requested the Pasco County Circuit Court to register the judgment. Once again, David Rankin had thirty days to respond or the judgment would be binding in Florida. On the thirtieth day, Pat called the court to see what Rankin had done, if anything. The court told Pat it had misplaced her file and that James Parker had not been notified of the judgment. It was now the end of January 1986 and Pat had just lost another sixty days.

When the second thirty-day period had passed without Rankin contesting, Virginia's final judgment for $106,000 became active in Florida. Pat now had two ways to enforce it.

214

She could file a petition with a court of equity asking it to
determine how much of that amount and when he should pay.
If he didn't pay, he would stand in contempt of the Florida
court. Or, she could hire a collection attorney to ask the circuit
court for writs of execution to attach Parker's assets (certificates
of deposit, savings accounts, cars, stock, bonds); to place liens
on his assets so that if he ever sold them, part or all of the
money would come to her; and to garnish his wages. Either
choice would be expensive and thorny.

If Pat asked a court of equity to enforce the judgment, she
would have to subpoena Parker's financial records to prove he
could pay what she was asking. And Rankin would have acres
of legal territory in which to stall or maneuver, if that was what
Parker wanted.

If she hired a collection attorney, each time Pat wanted to
attach, place a lien on, or garnish an asset, her attorney would
have to ask the court for a separate writ of execution, and
Parker would be notified of her request. That would buy him
enough time to bury assets where Pat could never find them.

Frank, Victoria, and Pat all agreed that enforcement
through a court of equity was the better choice. The principles
on which that court was founded—morality, fairness, justice—
had their roots in the ecclesiastical courts of medieval England.
And since the moral obligation to support children was more
basic than the legal obligation to do so, Pat and her attorneys
felt that the court of equity, with its broad discretionary powers,
would handle her case simply, fairly, and quickly. If everything
went smoothly, Pat could ask the court to force David to pay
or go to jail. Given his last brush with Warden Carpenter, she
was certain David did not relish the thought of doing more
time.

But before Frank could finish writing his Motion to Enforce
a Foreign Judgment for the court of equity, Pat learned that
David was leaving for Texas. Afraid he might be planning to
run away again, now that he faced a valid $106,000 judgment,
she asked Frank to take his sworn deposition quickly.

The meeting took place in Frank's office in mid-April, five
months after Judge Delbridge had reduced the arrearage to a
judgment. Rankin's associate, Mark Kelly, represented James
Parker. Although Frank's main purpose in deposing Parker

was to uncover how much money he had and where it was, he also asked some relevant background questions and received some puzzling answers.

"What's your date of birth?" Frank asked. Pat had instructed him to pose the question because David/Parker had been using three different ones.

"July or August of 1944," Parker said. "I'm not sure which."

"Any particular reason why you're not sure?"

"I'm an adopted child."

When he joined the Marines and when he married Pat, David had given July 17, 1944, as his birth date. When he married Lenora, he changed the year to 1943. And when he applied for a job at Safeco a few years later, he gave August 30, 1944—the same birth date as James Parker from Rutgers University.

Frank then asked David when he had abandoned Pat, but Mark Kelly objected. This was a deposition in aid of execution of a money judgment, he argued, and therefore the question was irrelevant. He instructed Parker not to answer.

After David had admitted marrying Lenora in Dallas in 1969, Frank asked if he had divorced Pat first. Once again, Kelly advised him not to answer on the grounds that the question was irrelevant and possibily self-incriminating.

Next, Frank began asking Parker where he had worked, beginning in Florida in the early 1970s.

"I sold clothes in a men's clothing store," David said.

"How long did you do that for?"

"Year and a half."

"And after that, what did you do?"

"I was an insurance adjuster."

"Under what name?"

"James Parker."

"Is your name legally James Parker?"

"Yes."

"When did you change it?"

"Around 1969, 1970."

"What state?"

"Texas."

"What city in Texas?"

"Dallas, I believe."

"Did you have an attorney perform this for you, or did you do it yourself?"

"I had an attorney."

"Do you remember his name?"

"Smith."

"First name?"

"Lynn or Glenn, I'm not sure."

Frank continued taking Parker's employment history. "How long did you work at the Safeco Insurance Company?"

"Three to four years."

"As an adjuster?"

"Yes." Parker went on to explain how Safeco had transferred him from Jacksonville to Tampa to Baton Rouge to San Antonio, where he quit and returned to Jacksonville.

"What did you do after you left Safeco?" Frank asked.

"I had various jobs in and around the automotive industry."

"Such as?"

"Assistant service manager . . . Lee Chevrolet."

"How long did you work at Lee Chevrolet?"

"Approximately six months."

"What did you do after that?"

"I moved back to Tampa and I went to work for Ernie Haire Ford."

"In what capacity?"

"Body shop manager."

"How long?"

"Something over a year."

"After working at Ernie Haire, where did you work?"

"Bob Wilson Dodge . . . Body shop manager."

"How long?"

"Six months."

"After you left Bob Wilson Dodge, where did you go?"

"Back to the Ford dealer."

"How long did you work there?"

"About six months."

"Since leaving Ernie Haire Ford, have you worked in the capacity of an insurance adjuster?"

"Yes, I have . . . 1980 through the present."

"Where?"

"Custard Adjusters."

"How long did you work there?"

"1980, 1981."

"Any reason for leaving?"

"Yes, I got a franchise with another company . . . Frontier Adjusters."

"And have you worked at Frontier Adjusters up until now?"

"No," Parker said. "Approximately a year ago, due to the negative publicity, I lost my franchise."

"Frontier Adjusters took it away from you?"

"Yes."

"How are you presently employed?"

"With the Adjusters Claims Bureau of Tampa."

"How long?"

"One year."

"Since you lost your franchise?"

"Yes."

"Where is Adjusters Claims Bureau located?"

"In my home."

When Pat read the transcripts of David's deposition, she found only four surprises. She had not realized David had bumped around in the auto business after he had left Safeco. Had he not returned to insurance, she might never have found him. Second, she had never before heard that he had been formally adopted. She checked Virginia records and found out that his foster parents had legally changed his name to theirs but had never adopted him. Third, she hadn't been informed that he had lost his franchise with Frontier Adjusters because of the runaway father news stories about him. (She called Frontier. An executive told her that James Parker had not lost the franchise because of the publicity surrounding her case.) And fourth, she was surprised that David had legally changed his name. She asked the clerk of the county court in every city in which he said he had lived—Dallas, Houston, San Antonio, Baton Rouge, Jacksonville, and Sarasota—to check court records from 1969 (the year he ran away) through 1985 to see if the court had granted him a name change. She received certified reports from each clerk indicating no record of the name change.

Soon after Frank had finished questioning James Parker, Victoria and Pat began preparing for a second, more thorough, sworn deposition. But before they could subpoena David, Rankin asked the court for and received a Protective Order barring further questioning. There was nothing else to do but ask for a hearing. In mid-August 1986, three months after he had deposed Parker and two years after Pat had found him, Frank filed a Motion to Enforce the Foreign Judgment with the Pasco County Circuit Court. The clerk scheduled a hearing before Judge Ray E. Ulmer for October 13, 1986.

As she sat in the small hearing room waiting for Judge Ulmer to open the proceedings, Pat was nervous and disappointed. David wasn't present because the court had seen no reason to subpoena him. Once again, he had managed to evade the judge.

"What can we do for you, Counselors?" Judge Ulmer said as soon as he sat down. Aware that Pat had come all the way from Washington, he seemed friendly and anxious to settle the matter before him.

"For the record," Frank stated, "I would object to the defendant or respondent . . . not being present. I fear his lack of presence here today and the history that he has in the past of avoidance of child support is something that the court should take issue with."

Judge Ulmer nodded but did not respond. "Let's proceed as far as we can, gentlemen," he advised. "You have an opening statement?"

Frank outlined the Bennett story. "This is a court of equity and this court can do what it deems fair under the circumstances," he argued. "So we're asking the court not just to recognize the foreign judgment, but to go ahead and enforce it."

Rankin counterargued that a court of equity has no jurisdiction to enforce a foreign money judgment under Florida law because money judgments have to be enforced through a writ of execution or other collection means. "They are attempting to ask this court, sitting as a court of equity, to do something which it has no jurisdiction to do," Rankin concluded.

Never having practiced law in Pasco County, Frank was surprised that jurisdiction had become the focus of the hearing. In Hillsborough County, child-support matters were routinely handled in a court of equity. Frank was fully prepared to argue that Parker was David and that David was the father of Christine, Andrea, and Marcia, should he deny either fact.

"We're not here to enforce someone for failing to pay a *loan*," Frank argued. "We're not here to enforce [payment for] a car that was repossessed . . . We're here to enforce a judgment that arises from a formal order of child support, Your Honor. I feel there's a big difference."

"What do you want this court to do?" Judge Ulmer asked Frank.

"To enforce the final judgment of the Virginia court and to make the defendant pay a substantial portion of the outstanding judgment . . . And I think this court has the authority and ability to do so."

"All right," Judge Ulmer said. "I'm going to have to ask you gentlemen to drop me a brief on the jurisdiction. I'm not totally persuaded I have [it]. I do not customarily do that, but jurisdiction is an important prerequisite to my being able to do anything, and I have no intention of entering an order in this court that I cannot enforce."

Ulmer gave Frank five days to submit a brief arguing from Florida cases that a court of equity has the authority to enforce child-support payment under its contempt powers. And he gave Rankin five days to respond to Frank. Judge Ulmer would then study both briefs, call another hearing, and rule.

29

>>>>>>>>>>>>>> Christine, Andrea, and Marcia had come to
Dade City for the hearing, hoping to talk to their father. When
he didn't show up in Judge Ulmer's chambers in the Pasco
County Courthouse, they were angry. Most of the hearing,
which dealt with legal technicalities, went right over their heads.
With each passing month, they had grown less concerned about
arrearages—which they were not convinced their mother would
ever collect—and more interested in sitting down with their
father to hear what he had to say, face to face, under calmer
conditions. All this legal stuff was between their mother and
him. That Judge Ulmer had delayed their parents' final confrontation bothered them less than their father's not being
present at his own hearing. And though they wouldn't be
unhappy if their mother actually got $106,000, it wasn't the
most important thing to them.

After the hearing, the three girls stood in the courtyard
outside Judge Ulmer's chambers and stewed. It had been a
long time since they had telephoned their father from the
beach condo, and during that time their attitude about meeting
him again had changed. They were willing to give him one
more chance. Maybe he wasn't himself when he had first talked
to them after being arrested without notice and spending two
nights in jail.

Marcia still wanted to meet her father, even more than
when she had hung up on him in January 1985. In fact, she
had written him a poem and wanted to deliver it personally.
Christine and Andrea, both so disappointed in January, soon
began itching to look him in the eye at least once. Now, when
they felt they were giving him the benefit of the doubt, their
father didn't even bother to show up.

Outside the courthouse, Christine stayed close to her

mother and Frank, preferring adult company to that of her teenage sisters. Marcia and Andrea paced the flagstones in long, impatient strides. There was fire in their eyes. They walked over to Pat and Frank and announced, "We're going to his house to see him." That they didn't have a car or know exactly where he lived was inconsequential; this wasn't a time for logic. They strode over to Bob Jensen, a *St. Petersburg Times* reporter.

"I'm really ticked," Andrea told him.

"He couldn't face us," Marcia added.

Then back to Pat and Frank, saying they wouldn't take no for an answer. But both Pat and Frank, like Deputy Sheriff Marsee, cautioned them against walking in on David. Pat was still worried about possible violence; Frank didn't want to complicate a simple child-support case with a countersuit for harassment.

Despite threatening to see their father no matter what, the girls left Dade City for Tampa without a meeting. On the tense drive back to Frank's office, Pat could sense their anger.

Andrea was the most upset. She would not accept her mother's final decision not to allow her to see her father. She had come all the way to Tampa to do precisely that. Feeling left out and cheated, she exploded.

"I hate you," she yelled at Pat. "I hate you! All you think about is yourself and your money. I want to see him. I don't care about this stupid case. When we get to the hotel, we're going to rent a car and go!"

Christine and Marcia were shocked. Bitching was one thing, but such an outright attack on their mother, who had always stood by them, was a low blow they couldn't accept. Frank was so shaken he was ready to walk home. Pat was stunned and embarrassed, and only her pride kept her from crying. None of the girls had ever said that to her before. How could Andrea be so cruel?

After a long moment of silence, Marcia finally spoke up. "Shut up, Andrea. How could you say that? I love Mom."

The car phone rang—it was Victoria. Pat had never been so glad to hear from her. Each of the girls wanted to talk to the attorney, who managed to take their minds off their father for the rest of the ride to the city.

But when they reached Frank's office, the girls refused to let up. They wanted to call their father and force him to see them. How they would do that, they didn't know. But they'd find a way. As an attorney, Frank had no objection to their talking to their father or asking to see him. What Frank didn't want was for the girls to go out to Parker's house and beat the door down.

Somewhat reluctantly, Pat also agreed to the phone call and a meeting, but only if David agreed to meet them in a public place and if a third party sat nearby in case David tried something. After a few minutes of discussion, they had a plan: Christine, who was the coolest and least threatening, would make the call and invite David to the coffee shop in the Hilton Hotel, a few blocks from where they were staying. If he agreed, they would call him back later to set the time, after they had found a bodyguard.

"Hi, this is Christine," she began. Frank turned on the speaker phone so Marcia and Andrea could hear their father, too. "How are you doing?"

"Not too well," David said.

"Why's that?"

"I had a bad day," David said. "Someone's out to get me. Someone wants to destroy me—my business partner and my business."

Christine pushed her father's remark aside. "We'd like to see you," she said.

"I'd like to see you, too . . . hold you."

"We can meet you at the Hilton."

"Okay," he said. "I'll come."

"We'll have to call you back and set a time."

Pat and her daughters rushed to the Hyatt. After Pat arranged for a friend to be in the coffee shop when the girls walked in, Christine called her father back. "Let's meet at five," she suggested.

"No," he said. "I can't. My attorney advised against it. Everything I say will end up in the paper."

"Our attorney advised us against it, too," Andrea said. "But we're not wimps."

David hung up.

Jim Parker didn't know or understand his daughters. They

were determined to force him to meet them. Angry and frustrated, they ganged up on him, calling him thirty-two times over the next few hours until he finally took his phone off the hook in desperation.

Through it all, Christine was considerate and gentle. Controlled and understanding, she did everything but beg him to see her. In the end, she just gave up and sprawled on the bed while her sisters took over.

Andrea charged at her father like a Doberman. David was no match for her.

"We're your family," she insisted. "How do you suggest we go about this? There is no solution for us. We waited for seventeen years for you to appear on our doorstep. Our dreams and hopes did not include calling you and hearing you say you won't meet us. . . . You and my mother have your own thing to settle; we have ours. I told Mom before we came down here, 'This is his chance—he can take it or leave it.' Well, I mean it! If you can't come to visit, you've had your chance."

David still refused to meet.

"What are we supposed to do?" Andrea continued to pound. "You don't know what it has done to my life. Don't you see? . . . No, I am not yelling at you. . . . Do you know what it was like to see my father for the first time in jail? Do you know how it feels to be rejected a *second* time?"

David hung up.

Marcia grabbed the phone and dialed. "How come you won't see us?" she demanded. "I am *not* hostile. Why are you hostile to me? What did I do to you *ever*? You want to see Christine. Why not me and Andrea?—Damn it, he's hanging up."

It was a long and draining day for Pat. She sat in the semidark room, depressed and hurt. Sleep wouldn't come. Hands down, this trip was the worst experience she had had with the girls since she had found David over two years ago. And it wasn't over yet. Rejection had rubbed her daughters raw.

Christine had fallen asleep in Pat's bed as if nothing in the world bothered her. Andrea had finally drifted off as well. Marcia was still awake, crying softly.

Finally, Pat simply couldn't handle it anymore—her own

pain and Marcia's as well. She called her cousin Terry, allowing herself the luxury of crying now that two of her daughters were asleep. It was midnight in Minneapolis where Terry lived.

"Hell broke loose down here," Pat began, explaining what had been going on all day. "Terry, they're so hurt. Andrea yelled at me on the way back to the hotel, 'I hate you. I hate you. All you think about is yourself and your money.' They're so angry at me!"

"They should be," Terry said gently but firmly as if he meant it. "Look at it as they do. You married the asshole, didn't you?"

"Thanks a lot!"

"Their anger is healthy," Terry said. "Just try to understand, Pat. They don't mean it. But they don't have a choice. They can't say it to David because he won't let them. That leaves *you*. Let it go in and out. Let them say what they have to."

"Are they really angry at me?"

"Of course," Terry said. "You really *did* marry him, you know. Try to see it this way. Andrea's anger is her gift to you. If she didn't face it, it would smolder and prevent her from having a relationship with you. The more she accepts how deeply she's been hurt, the greater the possibility of forgiveness. Her relationship with you can't be built on her denying her anger at you. If she denies it, she'll drift away. Andrea has opened the door. You should be pleased."

Even though what Terry said was not very comforting at that moment, Pat had to admit it made sense. "Marcia's still very upset and can't stop crying," she said. "Will you listen to her?"

Marcia was eager to talk to someone other than her mother, and Terry was a good choice. "I just want to see him," she told Terry. "Just once."

"Once won't be enough," Terry said. He decided to tell her the hard truth. "You'll want more and more. It will never end because you'll never get back what you lost. You understand?"

"Yes," Marcia said. His voice had calmed her.

"You want to make him understand how you feel and how you hurt," Terry went on. "But Marcia, he'll *never* understand. If he could, he wouldn't have abandoned you in the first place. It would take a miracle for him to see."

"Well, I don't want to end up with someone who will do that to me," Marcia said. Her thoughts were running fast, trying to keep up with her feelings. "I have a very good boyfriend—and David has a little son, you know, my brother—I don't want him to grow up like David—I want to see my brother—"

Marcia started to cry again. Her emotion and confusion were almost too much for her. Terry listened and encouraged her to say whatever came to her mind. He recognized that she was still playing victim, trying to be loyal to her father, who had caused the hurt. She needed to stand up for herself and say, "The hell with you, Dad. You're simply not worth it. Get lost!" She was having a hard time saying that because she was afraid of the pain. It was much easier to punish herself than to attack her father.

But no matter how bad she felt, Marcia always thought of others. "You know, Christine never talks. I know she's hurting, too. But she never says it."

"Christine is probably more angry than anyone," Terry said. He was quick to turn the conversation back to Marcia. "Anger is *good*, Marcia. And you're beginning to feel it. Sooner or later you have to, in order to feel better, and right now it's important that you do. Let it out. If you can't tell your father how you feel because he won't let you, then write him a letter. Write him every day if you have to. Get those feelings out even if he doesn't answer."

"I wrote a poem to give him," Marcia said.

"Will you read it to *me*?" Terry asked. He was touched by how rejected she must be feeling. She had been courageous enough to compose a poem for her father—not, as it turned out, a tough, angry letter, but a poem that connoted care and thoughtfulness—only to have him deny her the chance to present it. Terry knew it was important for her to read the poem to someone. Better him than no one.

"All right," Marcia said.

What could have been going through your mind?
And what made you want to leave?
How could you have been so unkind?
This is still hard for me to believe.

It seems like you had it all so well,
A wife, a family, and a home.
Maybe you were hurting and no one could tell.
Is that why you felt that you had to roam?

The burden and responsibility had to be lightened.
Leaving was the only way you could have dealt.
So you ran away alone, you must have been frightened.
Didn't you think though, how your family felt?

Inevitably this was the way it had to be.
Through the years you would try to forget.
But you had to know you couldn't always be free.
Now, I'm sure running is something you regret.

You were gone for so long, sixteen years.
And you never figured you would get caught.
I'm sure, like me, you've had pain and tears.
But how do you feel now after being sought?

We found you after looking for just days.
There's no getting out of this, nothing for you to do.
If you try to get out of this now, there are no ways.
Well, Dad, it's over. Your running is through.

30

>>>>>>>>>>>>> Back in Washington, Pat was still shocked at Judge Ulmer's jurisdictional scruples. She had gone to Dade City expecting to settle everything in one hearing, prepared to some extent to argue that David could afford to pay off the whole $106,000 within three or four years. Looking back at several of Ulmer's courtroom comments, however, Pat sensed that the almost unprecedented size of the arrearage had frightened him into wanting legal certainty before moving ahead.

Well, if the law was muddy, Pat couldn't blame Ulmer for that. What angered her was that there could still be any legal doubt in the United States that child support was a moral issue as well as a legal obligation and, therefore, best enforced by a court of equity. To her, such legal myopia was just one more example of a system that cared more about fathers' pocketbooks than the rights and welfare of their children. Pat anxiously waited for the dust to settle on the debate so that Judge Ulmer could decide. She thought it would be a short wait. She should have known better.

As discouraging as the trip to Florida had been for Pat, it was not a complete waste. David had agreed out of court to pay two hundred dollars a month in child support for Marcia from October through January, when she would turn eighteen, and Judge Ulmer had signed an order reflecting that agreement. It wasn't the eight hundred dollars, which barely covered the airfare to Tampa for her and her daughters, that mattered so much. It was the psychological lift that the decision gave Pat, and the new legal door it opened.

When the first two-hundred-dollar check arrived, Pat sat at the kitchen table and stared at it. She felt good. David had actually paid something. After skipping around the country, avoiding the law, and running for cover under an assumed name for seventeen years, he had finally paid something. It *was* possible! And now, if Judge Ulmer either tossed her case out of court or enforced the judgment unfairly, she could invoke a little-known and even less-used regulation of the IRS code (#301.6305), which instructs federal agents to collect unpaid child support for mothers if requested to do so.

Based on a provision in the Social Security Act, the IRS code orders the district director to enter an assessment against the father as soon as the Office of Child Support Enforcement (OCSE) certifies the amount of arrearage owed. Then the code instructs IRS agents to go after the delinquent father "in the same manner and with the same powers" as they pursue delinquent taxpayers.

The state OCSE would determine the total amount of unpaid child support David owed, from 1968 to the date of Pat's request, and would fill out the two-page request form. Pat would have to forego attorneys' fees and court costs. The state OCSE would then send Pat's request via its central office in Richmond to the federal OCSE regional headquarters in Philadelphia, where the amount due would be certified. The regional OCSE in Philadelphia would send the certified request to the IRS southeast regional office in Atlanta, which handles Tampa. There, a tax specialist would enter the certified amount as an assessment against David and notify him to pay all of it within sixty days. If he failed or refused to pay, the regional office would assign a revenue officer to seize and sell David's property, levy bank accounts, and garnish his wages. If the IRS had reason to believe he might run, it could waive the sixty-day notice.

Whereas the court of equity granted judges leeway in deciding what was or was not fair, the Internal Revenue Code told its collection officer exactly what to do. Although he or she could allow payment through installments, the officer had "no authority to compromise a proceeding by the collection of only part of a certified amount." In addition, code provisions would yank the legal rug right from under David's feet, leaving him no platform to plead from. "No court of the United States," the code says, "has jurisdiction of any legal or equitable action to restrain or review the assessment or collection of certified amounts."

But in order for Pat to ask OCSE to request the IRS to collect for her, she must first have exhausted all other civil means, be able to prove that David could pay the arrearages, and have at least one minor child living at home and a valid court order for that child's support. The Juvenile and Domestic Relations Court had never ordered David to pay child support specifically for Marcia because he had run away just after she was born and before Pat could get him in front of a judge. The new Florida order for child support for Marcia, however, enabled Pat to qualify for the IRS collection.

By the end of October, and within two weeks after the hearing, Frank de la Grana and David Rankin had their briefs on Ulmer's desk. The next move was the court's. On December 8, two months after Pat had first appeared in his court, Ulmer issued a Notice of a Hearing, set for January 8, 1987. Frank subpoenaed James Parker to appear so that, win or lose, Pat's daughters would have one more chance to meet their father face to face.

To prepare for that final hearing, Pat began to subpoena Parker's bank and business records in an attempt to draw a clearer picture of his income and assets. She flew down to Florida just after New Year's and set up an office in her room at the Tampa Hilton. Using tax returns, canceled checks, savings account records, and the patterns of withdrawal and spending they indicated, she worked out a summary for Judge Ulmer and made up a series of exhibits. Fully armed and proud of her thoroughness, she was prepared to ask and argue for $30,000 to be paid within ten days and $2,000 a month for the next three-plus years, until David had paid off the full $106,000. If she had to settle for less, she told Frank, she would be reasonable.

For his part, Frank was amazed at what Pat had put together. If her analysis was correct, Parker had made as much or more money in 1986 than he had. Frank called Victoria to discuss the summary. "We're in the wrong business, Frank," Victoria quipped.

Pat's parents had agreed to drive their granddaughters to

the airport on the morning of the hearing. When they arrived at Washington's National Airport, everyone was frazzled. Marcia was tired and tense, Christine was sick with the flu. And Andrea was cranky.

While her daughters were in the air somewhere over North Carolina, Pat got a call from Frank, asking her to come to his office. Something had turned up. She hurried there at once.

"Bad news," he told her after motioning her to a chair. "The hearing's off."

"What do you mean, the hearing's off!"

"Ulmer's reached a decision."

The judge had paged Frank at eleven that morning in Clearwater where Frank was defending a client to say that he had read both briefs for the first time the night before. Based on the cases presented and argued, he had concluded that a court of equity does not have the jurisdiction to enforce child-support judgments. When Frank pointed out that his client and her three daughters had flown all the way from Washington for the hearing, Ulmer asked Frank to extend his apologies for any and all inconvenience.

"You're kidding!" Pat said when Frank finished. "Shit, the kids are on the plane! Why in the hell didn't he think of that before? That's why I made the kids wait until the very last minute before coming down."

"I told him that," Frank said.

"Well, you have to think of a way to still have that hearing— anything, I don't care what. I want David at the courthouse so the girls can see him."

"What's the use?" Frank said.

"I'm going to call Judge Valentine," Pat announced.

"Can you believe this?" she asked, when Michael Valentine came to the phone.

"Why are you surprised?" Valentine said. "You're in Florida. And they're wrong."

"The kids are landing right now. Can you think of anything we can do?" Pat asked.

"Go to the hearing, anyway," Valentine suggested. "Ask the court to reconsider. The judge hasn't signed an order yet. Make him give you the reasons for his decision. Whatever he says will form the basis for an appeal."

Frank was standing next to Pat during the conversation and caught the drift enough to know what Valentine was recommending and why.

"Okay," he told Pat after she hung up. "Let's do it."

Pat was too angry to be discouraged. Ulmer had no excuse for waiting until the night before the hearing to read the arguments for the first time, especially since he knew she would probably come down from Washington. She had just spent two thousand dollars in airfares and hotel bills to learn that she and her daughters shouldn't have bothered to come. She had taken a week of annual leave and had spent another two thousand dollars to subpoena records she would not be able to use. What did she have to do to make David face judgment on the real issue—of right and wrong—instead of just jurisdiction? What did she have to do to get justice?

They met in the same hearing room where they had sat four months earlier. Andrea and Marcia were present. Christine was back at the hotel, too ill to budge. Before Frank could challenge Judge Ulmer's oral decision, Mark Kelly, who represented James Parker, told Ulmer that his associate David Rankin had complied with the subpoena and had brought his client to the courthouse. But in light of Ulmer's phone call and decision, neither he nor Rankin felt Parker had to be present in court. "I have him in the [court] library," Kelly said. "I don't at this state of the proceeding understand the necessity for his presence. For that reason, I have asked him to wait over there."

Judge Ulmer agreed and Frank did not object.

Judge Ulmer, it turned out, had three legal problems with the Bennett case. The Virginia judgment didn't actually order Parker to pay $106,000; it merely stated that he owed that amount. Second, Bennett had not demonstrated that Parker could pay that much. And finally, the cases Frank had presented in his memorandum did not convince the judge that the court of equity actually had jurisdiction to enforce support judgments in Florida.

"I have a judgment here from the Domestic Relations Court of Fairfax, reducing the matter to judgment in the amount of $106,000 and some change," Ulmer began. "And there's no question but that it has been properly registered here in the

State of Florida and this court has jurisdiction of the matter now for that purpose. But I don't find where the man has ever been ordered to pay that amount."

Judge Ulmer's first problem was so thin that a second-year law student could have settled it for him. Pat Bennett stood before his court with a valid seventeen-year-old decree ordering David to pay, an outstanding warrant for his arrest because he hadn't paid, and a valid 1985 document from Judge Jane Delbridge called "Order," holding James Parker in contempt of court and entering a judgment against him, in part, for $79,403.52, "which amount constitutes the amount currently due and owing in child-support arrearages."

Judge Ulmer's second problem was a catch-22 of his own making. During the first hearing, he had not allowed Pat to furnish proof that Parker could pay until the jurisdictional issue was settled. Now Ulmer was arguing that he didn't have jurisdiction because Pat had not proved that Parker could pay.

"Unless he, at this moment as of today, has the present ability to respond to any lawful order that this court might enter," Ulmer said, "it occurs to me that I would be wasting my time and it wouldn't be worth the paper that it's written on."

Frank was unwilling to budge a centimeter. "Your Honor, I understand what you're saying," he argued. "But if you will recall—and if need be we can have the record . . . transcribed—at the previous hearing you basically cut off . . . my client."

"True."

"Once again," Frank continued, "we were prepared prior to our conference call this morning to come in here and to complete proving that gentleman's ability to pay. And if that had been done, then we would be in a position for the court to have jurisdiction to order him to make payment. But we were kind of cut off at the pass this morning . . . We can more than prove his ability to pay, Your Honor."

Frank went on to tell Ulmer that he agreed with the court's assessment that the Bennett case was unusual. "This is not your common everyday support case."

"Well, now, but for the amount of money involved it is," Judge Ulmer said. "That's an unbelievable amount of money alleged to be due."

Pat almost jumped out of her chair. How could Ulmer say "alleged" when he had already accepted the Virginia judgment as valid? It had been properly domesticated in Florida and David had never contested it. Pat sensed she was in deep trouble. Ulmer's statement was clearly biased.

Frank argued back: "I believe that this court is entering an order today or proposing to enter an order today, based on circumstances which have never come to light or have never been able to come to light."

Judge Ulmer gave an inch: "I'm not going to preclude you from any presentation of any evidence that you need . . . Number one, I think it would not be fair not to provide you an opportunity to make a proper proof. And I would never preclude someone from doing that.

"Number two, it very well may be that after you have made the presentation . . . you might very well be entitled to an order ordering this man to make these payments depending upon his present ability to pay. And if he does not do so then you may very well be entitled to the contempt-of-court powers of the court."

But before Frank could even begin demonstrating Parker's ability to pay, Mark Kelly turned Ulmer's attention to the judge's third problem—cases indicating that a court of equity in Florida did or did not have jurisdiction to enforce support judgments. Kelly summarized the cases he had presented that seemed to argue against jurisdiction. Then he, Frank, and Ulmer chased each other in a circle for ten minutes. In the end, ignoring his previous promise to allow Pat the opportunity to prove Parker could pay, Judge Ulmer said: "Okay, gentlemen, we might as well take the bull by the horns and get the matter resolved . . .

"I would find that the contempt authority of this court is not available for us to enforce a foreign judgment for child support as it has been presented to the court in this fashion. Now, if there are other matters that you wish the court to address in these proceedings, I will do so. But if your sole request for the court is to order this man to pay this judgment from a sister state, subject to the contempt powers of this court, I do not feel that I have the authority to do so. And that would be the ruling of the court.

"And I am more persuaded as to the correctness of this, having had the opportunity to be enlightened by counsel. And I appreciate your help . . . The only other comment—it is unnecessary for me to make, but I will make it—is that I am not pleased with this decision. But I don't make the law. I am sworn to uphold it as I see it."

The hearing was over in exactly thirty-five minutes. It had taken Pat Bennett two and a half years to get that far. She had spent fifteen thousand dollars in out-of-pocket expenses. And she had one bill from Frank de la Grana for ten thousand dollars and another from Victoria Gordon for fifteen thousand dollars. David had paid her exactly eight hundred dollars in current child support. Marcia would turn eighteen in twelve days, all but guaranteeing that Robert Horan would never reconsider extraditing David to Virginia to stand trial for criminal desertion and nonsupport.

Pat was so discouraged by Judge Ulmer's final decision that she could not even cry. But she never considered giving up. Hadn't she promised herself to give David a fight to the finish? Hadn't she vowed to see him face a judge? Once again he had wriggled away, protected by an old-boy legal network that made the victim look like the criminal. Now it was no longer David versus her. It was Pat versus the system—and the fight was on.

31

>>>>>>>>>>>>> When Christine had walked into the Tampa Hilton on the afternoon of the hearing, she headed straight for the queen-size bed. Her mother felt her hot, damp forehead and told her to skip the hearing. Although she wanted to go to Dade City to meet her father, Christine had to admit she felt somewhat relieved that she wouldn't have to. She also felt as foolish as she did feverish. She had come all this way only to sleep the afternoon and night away in an expensive bed. She had a reservation for a return flight to Washington the next morning so she would not miss work and school. Sick or well, she intended to be on that flight.

Andrea and Marcia made up for their sister's lack of energy. From the moment they had jumped out of Frank's car in the courthouse parking lot, they began searching for their father. "He'll be here, I *know* it," Marcia kept saying. She had brought along her poem, which she had recopied five times on white stationery so it would be in her best handwriting. It was folded inside an envelope addressed "James Parker."

Andrea and Marcia made the courtyard outside Judge Ulmer's hearing room their command post. Every five minutes they would charge out to the parking lot, looking for their father's car.

"He's here," Marica told her mother after one foray. "I saw his car. I know it's his."

"There's a baby seat inside," Andrea nodded. "Maybe he's in the coffee shop with Kelly." A friend checked for her, but he wasn't there.

Shortly before three-thirty, Marcia and Andrea had followed their mother into the hearing room to wait for Judge Ulmer. When they heard Mark Kelly tell Ulmer that James

Parker was waiting in the court library in case he was needed, they were somewhat relieved and satisfied. They at least knew where he was hiding this time. With growing impatience, they waited through all the jurisdictional hair-splitting for Judge Ulmer to rule in their mother's favor, then order Jim Parker before the bench.

But Ulmer ruled against their mother and walked through the hearing-room door to his chambers. At once Andrea and Marcia shifted their attention to cornering their father before he drove off. "You check the parking lot," Marcia told Andrea. "I'll take the library."

Noting that Jim Parker's car was still in the lot, Andrea rushed back to her mother. "He's still here, Mom," she announced. "We're going to go talk to him."

"Of course," Pat said. "If he wants to."

Frank turned to Mark Kelly, who was standing nearby, and asked if it would be all right for Pat's daughters to talk to their father. Kelly agreed, and Frank thanked him. Pat knew he didn't have to grant permission, since the case was still in litigation. He had done the compassionate thing and she was grateful.

In the meantime, Marcia had reached the library. It looked empty. She began walking down the center aisle, which cut through rows of bookcases. After passing two rows, she found her father sitting behind a table in a research alcove. Dressed immaculately in a three-piece blue suit, he was flipping through a book as if to kill time while waiting for someone. Seeing him there stunned her for a moment, for she had half expected him to be on his way home by this time.

"Take a seat," David told her.

Marcia placed the envelope with her poem on the table and immediately backed away. "No . . . no," she said. Frank and Pat had so worried her about jeopardizing the case that she was afraid she would get in trouble. Besides, her father's invitation surprised her. So far, he had always resisted talking to her.

"Wait a minute," David said. "Don't go. I want to talk to you. Please—take a seat."

"Let me go get Andrea first."

Marcia disappeared around the bookshelf and out of the library as quickly as she had come, almost running across the stone courtyard to Andrea and her mother.

"Come on," she said to her sister. "He wants to talk to us. Okay, Mom?" They raced to the library, where David sat looking fidgety and nervous.

"Will you sit down?" he asked.

"Are you going to talk to us?" Andrea said.

"Why wouldn't I?"

"Christine's not here," Andrea said. "She's sick."

Both Andrea and Marcia could read the disappointment in their father's face. They knew Christine was his favorite and sensed that he had only agreed to meet them because he wanted to see Christine. Ever since they had first talked to him, he had not bothered to disguise his preference for her and it hurt. They sat down across the table from him.

"You look like me when I was a boy," David told Andrea. Then he turned to Marcia, "You look more like your mother."

At that moment, Marcia had the strangest experience of her life. After two and a half years of wanting and dreading this meeting, she looked straight into her father's eyes as her mother had done in the county jail and realized that she no longer wanted to talk to him. Her feelings of anxiety, fear, and anger seemed to dissolve. All she wanted to do was go home and put her father and her past behind her. No longer feeling a need to listen to him try to explain away his behavior, she had only one question to ask.

"Did you love my mother?"

"Of course I did," David said.

Drained from the strain of anticipation and lack of sleep, Marcia rested her head on the table and waited for Andrea to finish her business with David. I want nothing from him, Marcia thought. He means no more to me now than a stranger on the street. He is not my dad—or even my father.

Andrea, too, had been surprised that her father had waited to talk to them. She felt it was out of character and wondered why. It didn't take long to find out. She began with the string of questions she had already asked him over the phone in the beach condo, but he stopped her after a few minutes, saying he didn't want to talk about the past. Suddenly, Andrea no longer felt the need to press him. A strange kind of indifference she had never felt before had smothered her anger. She couldn't quite believe it. This indifference was real, not the kind she had frequently put on like armor to protect herself from disappointment. Here she was, sitting across the table from her father and feeling no emotion at all—not even the need to ask one more "why." She had absolutely no curiosity about what he had done during the past seventeen years or how he had felt.

It's gone, Andrea thought. There's nothing there anymore. Not even a possibility.

David widened the gap between Andrea and himself by his blatant attempt to use her to get Pat to drop the suit against him. He began to make promises to Andrea about what he would do for her once the child-support matter was settled out of court. At one point, he admitted that he intended to make sure her mother wouldn't see a nickel of his money, and that he would continue to bleed her pocketbook by legal tactics until she gave up.

Recognizing the game for what it was, Andrea played along for a while, then said, "So you want me to tell my mom that if she drops the suit, you'll give us an allowance each month, help us through school, and give us spending money—okay, I'll tell her."

Marcia had been listening to all of this. Suddenly, she felt so used that she wanted to get away as fast as she could. She could take no more. "This whole thing is beat!" she said. "I'm tired and I want to go."

From the look on her father's face, Marcia could see that her remark had cut him, and she was glad. She wanted him to suffer. "Here, this is for you." She shoved her poem, which lay unopened, across the table.

Andrea and Marcia stood up to go. David remained seated. Eyes red, he looked tired and close to tears. They both sensed he wanted something more from them. They could see it in his face.

Andrea felt a stab of sympathy for the man sitting in front of her and was tempted to walk around the table and give him a hug. She knew that was what he wanted. But then she thought, I don't owe him a thing. If I deny him a show of affection, I will be punishing him. And I want him to feel how much being rejected hurts.

Marcia also recognized that, for the first time, her father wanted a sign of forgiveness from her. But she didn't feel anything for him and had nothing to give him. She wanted to go home where she belonged.

"I don't know what to say," David finally volunteered, breaking the tension. He seemed awkward just sitting there.

"How about goodbye?" Marcia suggested.

Andrea and Marcia turned their backs on David and quickly walked out of the library.

Part Four

>>>>>>>>>>>>>>>>>>>>

Justice

32

>>>>>>>>>>>>>> On the legal battlefield, time was on James Parker's side. Marcia would turn eighteen in less than two weeks. That would only complicate Pat's strategy.

Florida law was not clear on whether a judge could order a father to pay arrears of child support after the child had reached majority. And to make matters worse, if Pat wanted the IRS to collect arrearage, at least one daughter had to be a minor on the day she made her request. So the day before Marcia's birthday, Pat signed the petition for an IRS collection, then filed away the rest of the paperwork until she could decide what to do about Judge Ulmer's decision.

On the one hand, Pat wanted to fight. She was convinced that Ulmer had been unfair and had made a legal error. Her case against him was strong and the issue was important. To crumble now just because one elected judge either didn't know the law or feared male-voter backlash was foolish. Women had been doing that for the past century. It was time to take a stand.

On the other hand, justice was expensive. Pat had taken out a second mortgage on her house, owed at least twenty-five thousand dollars in legal expenses, and had borrowed heavily from her parents. It was clear she couldn't afford an appeal. And attorneys were not standing in line to take her case pro bono.

If Pat itched to beat Judge Ulmer at his own game, so did her parents. Being private people who didn't relish dragging family matters into the limelight, they had not encouraged their daughter's search. Although they never doubted that the law would deal firmly with David if it ever caught up with him, they didn't believe he was worth the inevitable emotional and

financial strain. And they couldn't understand Pat's need to
face David and her past before she could get on with her life.
But the more they watched the law at work, the more shocked
and disillusioned they became. To them the issue was clear:
David had abandoned his wife and children; abandonment is
against the law; therefore, David must face the law. Judge
Ulmer's decision struck them as irrational, and they were
angrier than their daughter, who had long since learned the
painful difference between the law and justice.

"Your daddy wants you to appeal," Pat's mother told her
when she returned from Tampa. "We'll help."

That was all Pat needed to hear. She called Frank, but he
was not convinced she could win; her daughters had all turned
eighteen. Next, she contacted the Tampa law firm of Pippinger
and Tropp, who, she was told, was good on domestic relations
cases. Asking her to send the relevant court documents, the
firm told her that if it decided to take the case, it would require
a five-thousand-dollar deposit.

Pat told Pippinger and Tropp that she was looking for an
aggressive attorney who understood the national significance
of her case and who was not afraid of publicity. Explaining
that she was financially exhausted, she asked how the firm
intended to spend the retainer and what the total cost of the
appeal might be. Two days later, Pippinger and Tropp turned
Pat's case down, saying it was primarily a collection matter and
that the firm rarely took collection cases.

Not knowing where else to turn for legal help, Pat finally
decided to write her own brief and argue her own case. It was
the only thing she could afford, and she had nothing to lose.

She spent most of her free time in February and March of
1987 researching child-support decisions, writing a fifty-page
brief, and answering the brief written by James Parker's
attorney, Mark Kelly. Gene Bennett read her final drafts.
Finding her casework and legal logic thorough, he suggested
a few stylistic changes. Then, with nothing to do but wait for
the oral argument before the Second District Court of Appeal
in Tampa, Pat turned her attention back to the IRS collection.

Although the Internal Revenue Service pursues delinquent
fathers much more aggressively than the courts, it gets fewer

than one hundred child-support collections a year because it requires a summary of the father's assets. Nine out of ten mothers who know about the IRS collection option and who apply don't know their former husbands' assets or how to find them. Pat did.

When she walked into the Fairfax County Office of Child Support Enforcement (OCSE)—the first step on the IRS collection ladder—Pat had 151 pages of James Parker's financial records, which she had subpoenaed for the hearing before Judge Ulmer, including personal and corporate bank account statements and canceled checks, 1982–85 tax returns, loan applications, credit card information, and property transfers. Based on these certified documents, Pat submitted a financial analysis of Parker's income, known assets and liabilities, and net worth. She asked the IRS to collect the unpaid child support to date. That amounted to $80,303.52.

Pam Powers, the Fairfax County OCSE case officer, concurred that Pat had submitted enough asset information to satisfy the IRS and that the eighty thousand dollars-plus she requested was accurate, given the judgment against David. Powers sent the documents and forms to her district office in Richmond by overnight courier. Then the bureaucratic wheels began to turn:

—At the end of April, a month later, Richmond certified Pat's request and mailed it to the OCSE regional office in Philadelphia for final approval.

—At the end of May, a month later, Philadelphia sent the approved certified request to the IRS Service Center in Atlanta, which covers Tampa.

—At the end of June, a month after that, the IRS notified James Parker that he had sixty days to come up with either $80,303.52 or a payment plan, or the service would begin collecting it from him.

Pat had requested that the IRS waive the sixty-day notice, as the code allows when there is reason to believe that "assets are in jeopardy." But the IRS apparently had declined to do so. Convinced that David would use the grace period to bury his assets and prevent IRS collection, Pat began to pump herself up for her oral argument in Tampa.

———

Pat's mouth was dry as she sat on the bench facing Judges Campbell, Danahy, and Threadgill in the Second District Court of Appeal on July 8, 1987. Three years earlier, almost to the day, she had found David. Now she had twenty minutes to argue her case against him. For days people had been offering her advice—a blue dress would be perfect; don't hide your nervousness; let them know you're not an attorney and would appreciate help; keep it simple.

Even though she was afraid of making a fool of herself, Pat could appreciate the irony of the moment. She had started out simply expecting Fairfax County to extradite David to Virginia to stand trial. But Commonwealth Attorney Robert Horan had blocked extradition. Now, three years and more than thirty thousand dollars later, she was sitting nervously before three black-robed judges still looking for justice. It was a page right out of Dickens.

Even more ironic, all Pat had ever wanted was to face David in court and give her daughters the chance to do so as well. Now she found herself waiting for a chance to force the state of Florida to settle a question that affected other people's lives: can a Florida judge hold a father in contempt of court if he refuses to pay a judgment issued in another state?

Using different interpretations, both Pat and Mark Kelly had picked apart the *same* Florida court decisions in their briefs. Now the task of the three judges about to hear the oral arguments was to evaluate their legal logic and decide what the Florida courts had meant in those earlier decisions.

A handful of visitors sat in the four rows of theater chairs in the back of the courtroom. Frank de la Grana was there to wish Pat well and a few journalists were hunched over their notes. Standing confidently at the walnut podium, Mark Kelly spoke as if addressing an appeals court was something he did every day. But from the moment he opened his mouth Judge Campbell began challenging his legal reasoning. Quickly sensing he was getting nowhere after a few critical exchanges, Kelly changed his tactic. Since Marcia had reached majority six months earlier, he argued, James Parker was no longer required to pay arrearages according to Florida law.

Without denying his argument, Judge Campbell inter-

rupted Kelly again, pointing out that *age* was not the issue
before the court.

"I understand, Judge," Kelly said. "But even if we do send
it back [to Ulmer] we're going to have to reach that inquiry."

"We don't jump those hurdles up here that haven't been
jumped in the trial court yet," Campbell said, almost promising
another legal battle ahead.

Blocked a second time, Kelly summarized his position,
telling the court he'd be pleased to answer further questions.
There weren't any.

For her part, Pat chose to address the social problem rather
than the fine points of the law she had already raised in her
brief. Clutching the podium, she briefly told the court in a
quavering voice how David had abandoned her and his three
children, and how his foster parents had had him declared
legally dead in Virginia. Sixteen years after he had run away,
she said, she found him in Florida living under an assumed
name. After a warrant had been issued for his arrest for
criminal desertion and nonsupport, she had asked Fairfax
County to have him extradited, but the commonwealth attorney
declined to do so because desertion was only a misdemeanor
in Virginia. At that point, Pat explained, she had two choices—
file a URESA [Uniform Reciprocal Enforcement Support Act]
action or seek a judgment. She rejected URESA because she
was told it would take two years.

"Three years later here I am," she said.

Judge Campbell smiled.

To save her time, Judge Danahy summarized her story.
"What you finally did was to get the judgment in Virginia for
all of the arrearages?" he asked.

"Correct."

"And you brought that judgment to Florida?"

"That is correct."

"You went to the circuit court here in Florida to enforce it
. . . through what we call equitable-type remedies, including
contempt?"

"That is correct."

"[Judge Ulmer] refused that and that's why you're here?"

"That's why I'm here."

Judge Threadgill then took over. "What would you ask the

trial court to do to [Parker] for not paying the hundred and six thousand dollars?"

"I would like to see the case sent back to the lower court to have another hearing," Pat said. "And for the court to order him to pay whatever the court deems that he *can* pay."

"In failing to pay?" Threadgill asked.

"He would be subject to contempt and imprisonment."

"Jail?"

"Yes," Pat said. "Unfortunately that is one of the only ways some child support can be collected."

If Judge Ulmer's decision was correct, Pat argued, Florida law was contradicting itself. On the one hand, the law required that arrearages like David's be reduced to a final judgment, before a court of equity could enforce collection. But once they were reduced to a final judgment, it was saying that a court of equity had no jurisdiction.

Calling child-support enforcement in the United States a national disgrace, Pat pleaded with the court to help by at least clarifying Florida law. "The decision of this court," she emphasized, "has a very far-reaching effect when you consider the fact that [a large] percentage of the Florida child-support cases are from out of state."

Pointing out that the Tenth Annual Report to Congress ranked Florida close to last for child-support enforcement, she said it was generally accepted in Virginia that if you were a father and wanted to hide from the law, Florida was the place to go. If the court let Ulmer's decision stand, she argued, it would be opening the door to runaway fathers from all over the country.

Pat recapped her own story. "In this eighteen-year time frame, this man has changed his identity," she said. "He has committed bigamy. He has failed to support his children. He has never once gone before a judge to answer . . . There is no amount of money—even if he walked in here today with a check for a hundred and six thousand dollars—that would repay the emotional damage and scars left on my three daughters."

Pat closed by quoting Senator Daniel Patrick Moynihan: "The quality of a civilization may be measured by how it cares for its elderly; just as surely, the future of a society may be forecast by how it cares for its young."

Recognizing the importance of the issue, the Second District Court of Appeal moved with unusual speed. A month after the oral arguments, Pat got a call from the clerk of the court saying she had won. Although she felt a deep sense of satisfaction, Pat was neither surprised nor terribly excited. She had never doubted the logic and strength of her case. After all was said and done, she had merely won the right to buy another ticket to Tampa to pick up the hearing where Judge Ulmer had left it.

The last paragraph of the appeals court's unanimous decision requested the Florida Supreme Court to rule on the decision, whether Parker appealed it or not. If its decision was correct, the Second District Court felt it was important that it be the law in the *whole* state, not just in five of the state's twenty judicial circuits. For Pat, that meant still another trip to the bench.

"This court," Judge Campbell wrote, "certifies to our supreme court as a question of great public importance, the following: Do the circuit courts of this state have jurisdiction to enforce a foreign judgment for arrearages of alimony or child support by means of equitable remedies including contempt?"

No one was more pleased with Pat's victory than Florida's Department of Health and Rehabilitative Services (HRS), which was responsible for prosecuting runaway and deadbeat dads. Florida's reputation for coddling runaway fathers embarrassed HRS and made it look as if it wasn't doing enough to help out-of-state mothers. But without the threat of jail, the fathers HRS was prosecuting were not about to open their wallets. If the Florida Supreme Court upheld the Second District's decision, HRS could quickly dispatch a stack of cases. It immediately petitioned the supreme court with an amicus curiae brief in support of Bennett.

"The issues raised by this appeal are important and far-reaching," William Branch and Chriss Walker, attorneys for HRS, told the supreme court. "This court's decision will literally impact upon millions of persons within and outside the State of Florida."

The supreme court accepted HRS as the amicus curiae for Pat Bennett.

Recognizing the national significance of the Bennett case, the Legal Defense and Education Fund of the National Organization for Women (NOW) also petitioned the Florida Supreme Court for leave to join as amicus curiae. The organization argued that the Bennett decision was not only important for children of other states whose fathers lived in Florida, but for children in states where the law—like Florida's—needed clarification.

"The poverty rate for female-headed single-parent families is nearly three times the national average," NOW attorneys Kathy Chinoy and Sally Goldfarb argued in their motion to the supreme court. "This trend has disastrous implications for American women and children. . . . The National Advisory Council on Economic Opportunity has estimated that by the year 2000, if current trends continue, virtually all of the Americans living in poverty will be women and children in single-parent families. Inadequate child-support enforcement is a major cause of the spiraling poverty rate among women and children. . . . The question currently before this Court directly addresses this issue."

The supreme court granted NOW's request to appear as an amicus curiae for Bennett as well as a request from the attorney general of Florida and, ironically, the attorney general of Virginia. John Rupp, Virginia's senior assistant attorney general, argued that his office took a "strong position in support" of the issue, which was important to Virginia children whose fathers lived in Florida. What Rupp didn't say, however, was that the Virginia warrant for David's arrest was still valid, that David was still charged in Fairfax County with criminal desertion and nonsupport, and that, in this particular case, the attorney general was not taking a "strong position in support" of extradition.

But extradition was the furthest thing from Pat's mind. It was time to prepare for a new hearing in the Pasco County Court, which would now center around two questions—one legal, the other practical: Did Florida require a delinquent parent to pay arrearage if the child was no longer a minor? And did James Parker have the ability to pay the $106,000 judgment?

If the court ruled that Parker didn't have to pay because Marcia had turned eighteen, it made no difference how much money he had; he was home free.

33

>>>>>>>>>>>>> Christine drove from Tampa to Dade City half-listening to her mother and Richard Froemming chattering in the back seat, and wondering what she was doing back in Florida. From her sick bed in the Hilton six months earlier, she had listened with total indifference to Andrea and Marcia describe the meeting with their father in the courthouse library. At the time, she had not felt even a twinge of jealousy or sadness. The only emotion that penetrated the wall she had built between herself and her father was a sense of satisfaction that her absence had disappointed him. At least, that's what her sisters had told her. And even though Andrea and Marcia seemed to have settled the score with their father, Christine wasn't convinced he had been worth the energy and money. Now, half a year later, as she drove to what she hoped would be the last in a string of ridiculous hearings, she still wasn't convinced.

Whatever her feelings, Christine's appearance belied her facade of indifference. She wore a simple but striking black dress that made her look even taller than she was and high-lighted her pale skin and long, thick auburn hair. Around her neck hung a single sapphire on a chain, a gift from her fiancé. Even if she couldn't admit that impressing her father was important to her in some strange way, she had evidently dressed up for him.

If Christine wasn't sure why she had come to Florida, Richard Froemming knew why *he* was there. Even though the private detective hadn't investigated anything for Pat in the past year, he had followed her case closely and had given her advice whether she asked for it or not. When Pat suggested he come to the hearing as her bodyguard, Richard took her seriously. During his first month on the street as a Washington cop, he had learned that domestic violence can be as vicious as it is unpredictable. And although he joked during the drive to Dade City about a courtroom shootout or knife fight, his adrenalin was flowing. As soon as the car pulled into the courthouse parking lot, the wisecracks stopped. Richard walked a few steps behind Pat and refused to carry her briefcase filled with bank records, so that both his hands would be free. And when Pat and Christine entered the courthouse coffee shop, he cased the place quickly, then made certain the door was in sight the whole time they were there.

Half an hour before the hearing, David Rankin, who was representing James Parker, handed Pat a stack of documents she had requested six weeks earlier. The papers, especially Parker's financial affidavit, were important for her case against him. Using that sworn statement as a foundation, Parker had to prove he was too poor to pay the $106,000 arrearage. Acting as her own attorney, Pat's job was to destroy the credibility of that affidavit.

"You made one mistake," Rankin said as he handed her the pile of documents. "You asked me to mail them to Virginia. Remember that for next time."

Although Florida's Rules of Civil Procedure required that Rankin either produce the documents Pat had asked for or file a motion arguing they were irrelevant, he was not required to mail them outside Pasco County and he hadn't.

This was not the first time Rankin had interpreted the rules in his client's favor, or ignored them altogether. Florida law had also required him to submit the same financial affidavit to Judge Ulmer at least ten days before the first hearing more than a year ago. Not only did Rankin fail to do that, he actually chided Frank de la Grana for being late in submitting Pat's companion affidavit. At that earlier hearing, when he noted that Parker's financial statement was not in the court file, Judge Ulmer had ordered Rankin to produce one within five days. Again, Rankin failed to do so. For the current hearing before Judge Cobb, Florida rules also required Parker to submit to the court the same financial affidavit he gave to Pat, and to do it at least ten days before the actual hearing. Yet Rankin gave the court its copy at the same time Pat got hers.

Naturally, Pat was eager to study the elusive document even

if she had less than thirty minutes to do so. What she found in Parker's three-page sworn financial affidavit rocked her. She had spent weeks analyzing his subpoenaed corporate and personal bank records, including canceled checks. According to those records, Adjusters Claims Bureau, which employed Parker and which he co-owned, had paid him around $85,000 a year during 1986 and 1987; and Parker had at least $16,000 in bank accounts in his wife's name. From that information, Pat was expecting Judge Cobb to order Parker to pay at least $25,000 within ten days and $2,000 a month until he had retired the full $106,000 judgment.

But Parker's affidavit claimed that his corporation paid him around $26,000 a year in salary and rent, that he had no cash, and that his current liabilities totalled $166,000. Something was very, very wrong. If canceled checks showed that the corporation had been giving him around $85,000 a year, what had happened to the other $59,000?

Judge Wayne L. Cobb's court was so small that the ABC cameraman pointing a lens across the only table in the room could barely move. A dozen chairs for spectators lined one wall. Christine sat quietly on one of them behind her mother, facing her father just a few feet away.

"Good morning, Mr. Rankin," Judge Cobb began. He looked serious and anxious to dispatch the case once and for all.

"Good morning, Your Honor."

"How are you?"

"Fine."

"Mrs. Bennett, you are still representing yourself?"

"Yes, Your Honor, I am."

The court swore in James Parker, and David Rankin argued first. After establishing that Parker's financial affidavit bore his true signature and was a true statement, Rankin asked, "Are you the sole source of income to your family?"

"Yes, I am," Parker said. His voice was firm and unemotional. If he was nervous, he didn't show it.

"In the event you were incarcerated . . . would there be any form of income which your family might have benefit of?"

"None."

"Have you recently been contacted by the IRS?" Rankin asked.

Pat froze. She knew that the IRS had begun the collection process at the end of August, nearly four months ago. But she had no idea what it had taken so far, if anything.

"I have," Parker said.

"Did they explain to you why you are being contacted?"

"Yes. They are attempting to collect this judgment."

"Have you paid the Internal Revenue Service money as a result?"

"Yes."

"How much?"

"Six hundred sixty-five dollars and some change."

Pat was not totally surprised at that piddling sum. Parker's bank records pointed to a flurry of money transfers and withdrawals days before the collection began.

"Did you enter into some negotiation with the Internal Revenue Service with regard to [monthly] payment of the outstanding debt?" Rankin asked.

"They wanted five hundred dollars."

"After they had an opportunity to review your financial condition at this time, did they come up with a lesser sum?"

"Yes."

"Had you agreed to pay that lesser sum?"

"I signed an agreement to pay two hundred fifty-six dollars a month. . . . First payment is due on the nineteenth of this month."

"Your Honor," Rankin concluded, "that's all I have of this witness at this time."

"Mrs. Bennett," Cobb asked, "do you have any questions?"

"Yes, I do."

Judge Cobb's question sounded unreal to Pat. Even in her wildest courtroom fantasy, she had always watched a judge humiliate David as he stood before the bench. Never had she dreamed of actually having the power to force him to answer questions she herself would ask. Ever since she had decided to represent herself before Judge Cobb, she had worried about falling apart in court or becoming so emotional that she'd forget why she was there and what she had to accomplish. She had even talked to Dr. Crotty about her fear, and he advised her to write out her basic questions and stick to the script. Then, when it was time to ad lib, he told her, she'd be warmed up.

But Rankin destroyed that game plan when he introduced the IRS collection, forcing Pat to ad lib her initial cross examination of Parker. Without realizing it, Rankin had done her a favor. She was so determined to expose the IRS collection issue as a legal red herring that she forgot to be nervous. From what she knew of Internal Revenue Service procedures, she doubted that the IRS would settle so quickly for $256 a month— only $56 more than the court had ordered David to pay eighteen years ago.

"Do you have a copy of that agreement you made with the Internal Revenue Service?" Pat asked Parker.

"I do not," Parker said.

"Would they not have given you a copy of an agreement?"

"I asked for it and they indicated that it had to be approved."

"So it has not been accepted as yet?" Pat said.

"Well, as I understand it, it hasn't been accepted. It has not been approved."

Having made the point, Pat began questioning Parker about his salary. He didn't know it, but in the briefcase at her feet Pat had copies of all the checks Adjusters Claims Bureau had made out to him; and outside the courtroom, she had a bank officer waiting to attest to the validity of those canceled checks.

"How does the corporation pay you?" Pat asked.

"By check . . . twice a month."

"How much?"

"One thousand dollars each payday."

Pat had noted that Parker owned a 1985 Mercury, which cost seventeen thousand dollars. She wondered if he was making the three-hundred-dollar-a-month payment or whether his corporation was doing it for him.

"Does the corporation pay for any of your . . . business expenses?" she asked.

"Yes."

"Your car payment?"

"Yes."

"They make your car payment?" Even she seemed surprised. "Whose name is the car titled in?"

"It's jointly held in my and my wife's name."

Having established that Parker was indirectly receiving thirty-six hundred dollars a year from his corporation in car payments—over and above salary and rent for an office in his home—Pat began probing Parker's equity, since ability to borrow helps the court determine what a father can and should pay.

"Have you received any loans since January 1985?" she asked.

"I have borrowed from the corporation."

"How much?"

"Somewhere in the neighborhood of sixty thousand dollars."

Pat was momentarily stunned. So Parker wasn't denying that the corporation had given him around eighty-five thousand dollars a year. He was simply alleging that all the money over and above his twenty-four thousand dollar salary, rent, and odds and ends was loans. Pat doubted that was true. But without proof, she had a weak case.

"Have you made any payments back?" she asked.

"Yes."

"Would you have canceled checks for the payment of the loan?"

"Yes."

"Was this sixty thousand dollars one loan or many loans?"

"Many."

"Do you sign a note with the corporation?"

"More than one kind," Parker said. "Some . . . are short-term loans . . . payable quarterly, and others were long-term loans."

"Does [your partner] borrow the same amount that you have?"

"Yes."

"So you both have borrowed roughly sixty thousand dollars . . . within the same time period?"

"Yes."

"Why do you not consider [the money] salary?"

"Because I borrowed the money and it will have to be paid back sometime."

"Can you prove you are making payments to the corporation?"

"I think I've done that already."

"Do you have any of those records with you?"

"No, I do not."

It was a stalemate. Although Pat had asked Rankin to produce Parker's corporate records six weeks before the hearing, Rankin had argued that they were irrelevant and did not furnish them. They turned out to be not only relevant but the one piece of evidence that could weaken or destroy his case. Naturally, Parker did not bring copies of the notes payable he swore he had signed, or the canceled checks proving he had repaid some loans. If Pat had received Parker's financial affidavit on time, she could have fought for those records and subpoenaed Parker's accountant to explain his bookkeeping to the court.

With no further option than to leave a doubt in Judge Cobb's mind as to how much money Parker was actually making, Pat moved on to Parker's assets. He had told Marcia and Andrea in the courthouse library that he was burying his money where their mother could never find it. Bank records showed that he had kept at least sixteen thousand dollars in various accounts, but that he began withdrawing and moving the money around just before the IRS sixty-day grace period was up.

First, Pat established that within days after his arrest on the Writ of Ne Exeat, Parker had transferred his share in a co-owned property, cashed several co-owned certificates of deposit, and transferred a duplex, which, he claimed, belonged to his wife and her family.

Next, Pat got Parker to admit that he had spent nearly twenty thousand dollars in home improvements during the past year and had purchased a new TV for thirty-two hundred dollars—not exactly the spending habits of a poor man.

Finally, Pat tried to prove Parker was hiding cash. But he swore he no longer had any savings or checking accounts anywhere, and that the cash he had once had was either spent on home improvements, used to pay off a bank loan, or levied

by the IRS. In short, James C. Parker claimed he was stone
broke and deeply in debt.

"Does your wife have any [accounts]?" Pat asked.

"She may."

"You don't know?"

"I believe she has a checking account."

"Where would the money come from?"

"My pay."

"Does she have a money market account?"

"She did at one time. I'm not sure she still does."

"Does she have a savings account?"

"I don't know."

"You don't know!" Pat was getting frustrated. "Have you
opened any new bank accounts in the last six months?"

"I have not."

"Do you deposit your check, or does your wife deposit it?"

"More often she does."

"And you do not know to which account that check
goes?"

"Since the IRS levy, the checks have been cashed because
I don't have an account."

Requesting time to examine Parker again, Pat rested for
the moment. Rankin then took a few minutes to reestablish his
client's credibility, focusing on the sixty thousand dollars in
loans from the corporation.

"Prior to making those loans," he asked Parker, "did you
consult an accountant?"

"Yes . . . he arranged it and made the loan papers."

"So that in his opinion, it was a loan from the corporation?"

"Yes."

As her only witness, Pat called Sandra Mitchell, a records
custodian at the Sun Bank of Tampa Bay. Noting that the
Parkers had closed their money market account and savings
account just before the IRS collection was to begin, she asked
Mitchell, "How much was in the money market account?"

"Fourteen thousand, seven hundred forty-four dollars and
eighty-eight cents," Mitchell said.

"And the money withdrawn from the savings account?"

"One thousand, five hundred sixteen dollars and fourteen
cents."

"That is roughly about sixteen thousand dollars withdrawn from both accounts in August of 1987?"

"That's correct."

Next, Pat asked Mitchell to review the canceled checks written to James Parker from Adjusters Claims Bureau from January 1986 through November 19, 1987. For the first time, Parker seemed nervous. He conferred with Rankin several times as Mitchell read the bank record. Pat called the court's attention to March 1987 as Mitchell slowly read the numbers: $8,000 . . . $815 . . . $815 . . . $1,000 . . . $1,000 . . . $2,500.

"Excuse me," Pat interrupted. "What was the amount on the first check?"

"Eight thousand."

"Thank you."

Mitchell continued down the month-by-month list until she came to October 1987, six weeks before the hearing. "Would you read the amounts . . . very slowly please?" Pat asked.

"One thousand dollars . . . one thousand dollars . . . two thousand dollars . . . one thousand dollars . . . two thousand dollars . . . one thousand dollars."

That amounted to eight thousand dollars in six weeks. Under Pat's probing, Mitchell testified that several recent checks had been deposited into another account at the Florida Federal Savings and Loan. Parker had just sworn there were no other accounts.

Recalling Parker after Mitchell's testimony, Rankin quickly established that his client had used most of the fourteen thousand dollars in the money market account to repay a bank loan, and that the large checks Mitchell had read off were the loans Parker had testified to earlier.

Once again, Pat returned to the loans in her recross examination. "You stated earlier that you had [received] approximately sixty thousand dollars in loans from your corporation," she asked.

"Yes."

"But the income level that you state for your corporation for 1986 is negative one thousand, three hundred thirty-four dollars; and for 1985, [a negative] twelve thousand, one hundred fifty-two dollars. How are you able to borrow sixty thousand dollars from a corporation . . . doing so poorly?"

"I can't explain that. I'm not an accountant," Parker said, once again denying that the sixty thousand dollars was salary.

Pat pointed out that she had carefully traced the money traveling in and out of his bank accounts before he had cleaned them out. It amounted to $78,298.22 over a one-year period.

"Two thousand a month is what you say you make," she argued. "How can you deposit seventy-eight thousand dollars a year in three accounts?"

Parker said that because he was moving the money around, she had counted it three times.

"Do you have another bank account?"

"I do not."

"Why did those checks say 'for deposit only,' " she asked, referring to the other account, "and [can you give] the account number of Florida Federal Savings and Loan?"

"I can't answer that."

"Is the account in your wife's name?"

"My wife has no account."

"Is it in another name?"

"I have no hidden accounts," Parker said, losing his composure for a moment. "I have no Swiss bank accounts. I have *no* hidden accounts, Ms. Bennett."

Pat was getting nowhere. She was convinced that the sixty thousand dollars was a form of compensation rather than a loan, but she couldn't prove it. And she believed that Parker was hiding cash, but she couldn't find out where. Her frustration began to show. Judge Cobb stepped in after Rankin objected to her badgering his client.

"Ma'am," Cobb said, "you have been over this, and I think you are just argumentative at this time."

"Thank you," Pat said. "I have one final question . . . You met your two daughters, Andrea and Marcia, for the first time last January, is that correct?"

"No, that's not correct."

"For the first time since they were babies."

"That's correct."

"Did you tell your daughters at that time that you had money hidden in places that their mother would never find?"

The question hit like a slap in the face. Parker flushed.

"Absolutely not," he said.

"Do you know who this lady is here?"

Pat pointed to Christine sitting behind her. She had planned that question for weeks and had been looking for the right moment to slip it in. This might be Christine's only confrontation with her father, and Pat thought it best to force her oldest daughter to face him. She had not warned Christine in advance, sensing that surprise might help break down her protective wall of aloofness. Pat had no idea how the confrontation would turn out, and she relied only on her instincts and the knowledge that David could not hurt his daughter any more than he already had.

David looked across the table at Christine, then said without hesitation, "No, I don't."

"She's your daughter," Pat said.

The courtroom grew very quiet, and Judge Cobb let Pat have the one emotional moment of the morning.

"It's too bad you do not know who she is."

"It is," Parker said.

"That's Christine!"

Judge Cobb waited for a long second, then asked, "Any other questions, Mrs. Bennett?"

"No, Your Honor."

Christine had sat through the tedious hearing barely moving a muscle. Naturally, she wanted her mother to win her case and Judge Cobb to order her father to pay. But in cold reality, the money—whether it was a little or a lot—had little to do with her. She was no longer living at home and had been paying her own way for some time now. Furthermore, she had no overwhelming desire to see her father suffer. She neither hated him nor felt sorry for him.

But the more Christine listened to this middle-aged man with a raspy voice trying to squirm out of his obligations, the more she began struggling with a new set of feelings. Was this the man she had loved so much as a child? Who had always thought she was special? Who had apparently been disappointed when she hadn't come to see him in the courthouse library?

Was this the father she had carried around in her mind for eighteen years?"

Her mother's question "Do you know who that is?" both jolted and angered her. Her relationship to her father was a personal and private matter. Her mother had just dragged it into an open court before reporters and a television camera. All at once, she could no longer hide—from her father or from herself.

But if the question made her feel uncomfortable, the answer hit like a harpoon. After the initial numbness, tears welled up in her eyes. She fought them back. Her father didn't even know her! He had asked for her picture in the Pasco County jailhouse and she had sent one back to him. But it had made such a small impression on him that he didn't even recognize her when she sat six feet away. He didn't care about her. He never had. And he never would.

Why should she care about him?

The moment passed quickly for the court, and the hearing moved on to its inevitable conclusion. But for Christine, time stood still.

Rankin directed the court's attention away from money to the fine point of the law: since Marcia was no longer a minor, did her father have to pay the arrearage? Rankin had already argued that muddled issue in his written brief to the Florida Supreme Court and Bennett had answered him in her brief.

After listening patiently to both sides argue, summarize, and reargue, Judge Cobb called a cease-fire. "I don't require any further argument at this time," he said.

It was almost as if Cobb had made up his mind long before the hearing, but had allowed Rankin and Bennett to debate for the record. Throughout the hearing, Cobb had shown a great deal of patience. Most of the time, he overruled Rankin's objections, giving Pat every opportunity to proceed at her own pace. His message was clear: You waited a long time for this day. I don't want you to feel cheated. Although the court had set one hour aside for the hearing, he had allowed it to drag on for nearly three hours with only a single break to clear up several other cases waiting in another courtroom.

The financial question was simple enough. As far as the court was concerned, James Parker had proven he could not pay a lump sum of $106,000. His sworn financial affidavit, which the court accepted as factual unless proven otherwise, made it clear that he was making around $26,000 a year, that he had to support a wife and child on that income, and that he was more than $160,000 in debt, including the judgment.

For her part, Pat Bennett had proved that Parker's corporation had given him around $85,000 a year, and that he had at least $16,000 in cash a few months ago. But she had not proved that the $60,000 Parker identified as loans were not really loans, or that he still had the $16,000 cash.

Judge Cobb knew, however, that no matter how he decided the practical financial question, he would be criticized. If he came down hard on Parker, ordering him to pay a large sum up front and steep monthly payments, he would be accused of trying to squeeze blood from a turnip. If he tailored the payments to fit Parker's pocketbook as described in his sworn financial affidavit, he would be accused of coddling runaway dads. And then, there was the question of the ongoing IRS collection. If Parker had money buried somewhere, wouldn't the IRS find it for Bennett?

The age question was trickier, and Judge Cobb found himself on thin legal ice. Whatever he ruled—and rule he must—he would be challenged by either Bennett or Parker. Ultimately, the Florida Supreme Court would have to settle the issue. All he could do was what the taxpayers paid him to do—interpret the law as fairly as he could.

Cobb bit the bullet. "I find that this order by the Second District on Mrs. Bennett's appeal," he ruled, "survives children reaching the age of majority, that is eighteen, and that this court *does* have contempt authority."

Rankin seemed rattled. No matter what Cobb now ordered his client to pay, he had lost his case—at least for the moment.

"Is there some authority?" Rankin sputtered, his face sunburn pink. "I just don't see any case law. I would be glad—I certainly wouldn't argue with the court unless I—I just didn't see any case law that might support what the court is doing . . ."

Cobb explained his reasoning, in part agreeing with Rankin. "I believe the Second District [Court of Appeals] doesn't give me the authority to do it," he said. "But it gives me *direction* to do it, and I believe they understood. They are intelligent folks over there. They understood the children were getting near eighteen. They have the whole record, and they have said that contempt was the proper mode of enforcement. . . . I therefore find that Mr. Parker has had the ability to make payments on this support and has failed to do so."

Not only had Cobb studied the ruling of the Second District Court of Appeal; he had done his arithmetic. Noting that the $106,000 judgment was over two years old and that Parker had not paid the full amount of current child support during that time, Cobb recalculated Parker's bill and charged 12 percent interest on the unpaid balance. The total now came to $148,536.12.

"I'm going to find that his failure to make payments on this has been willful," Cobb continued, "and order him confined to the Pasco County Jail for a period of thirty days.

"I'm going to allow him to purge himself of that contempt by the payment of fifteen hundred dollars toward that arrearage and order him to pay one hundred dollars a week for the remaining arrearages when he's released. . . .

"Mr. Parker, I'm going to remand you to the custody of the sheriff to begin serving that sentence."

Parker seemed devastated. He kept his back to the television camera hoping it would go away. It wouldn't, and neither would the bailiff.

"We'll have to go now," the bailiff said after giving Parker a minute to compose himself.

As the camera rolled, Parker held out his wrists.

As soon as Judge Cobb walked out of the hearing room, Pat felt an overwhelming urge to run and hide. She didn't have the strength to face reporters. Nor did Christine, who ached to get back to the hotel so she could nurse her wounds.

"Let's go, Christine," Pat said. Brushing by the cameras, they hurried down the hallway and into the ladies' room. Pat was shaking so badly she held onto a sink for support. "Only fifteen hundred!" she sobbed. "I can't believe it! How am I going to pay my mother back? And what am I going to tell the press?"

Christine was pale and sick to her stomach. "They want to know how I feel about David," she said softly. "I don't *know* how I feel."

When they both calmed down, they agreed to tell the media that Cobb's decision was important for all women and children, and not to talk about their personal disappointments. After touching up their make-up, they walked out to the courtyard to face the cameras.

When the last question was asked and answered, Pat felt as alone as she had when facing David in the courtroom. Everyone, from Richard Froemming to the TV reporters, was calling Cobb's decision a big victory. Maybe it was. But she didn't feel victorious. Just exhausted and disappointed.

Back at the hotel later that afternoon, Pat tried to be happy and chatty over drinks with Richard and Frank de la Grana. And although she joined the small group that partied and danced until the early hours of the next morning, she was only going through the motions.

Pat and Christine had reservations for a two o'clock flight back to Washington that day. When they pulled up to the car rental office at the airport, Pat realized she couldn't leave. "You go on by yourself," she told Christine. "I'm not ready to go back yet. I'm exhausted and I need time alone."

Christine was relieved; she wanted nothing more than to be alone, too. Seated next to the airplane window and shielded by anonymity, she finally let out the tears she had held back for so long. Christine cried quietly all the way home and through most of the night. In Tampa, her worst dream had come true. She had always resisted meeting her father because she was afraid he would reject her once again. He had, and it hurt more than she thought it ever could. James Parker had shattered the image of David she had carried for most of her life and with it, any hope of a relationship with him. David *was* really dead after all.

While Christine was on her way home, Pat was driving around aimlessly. She found herself drawn to the sea.

It was late afternoon and chilly as she took off her shoes and began walking down a deserted beach. Waves lapped the shore, leaving a trace of foam on the wet sand, and the icy water on her feet lent the only reality to the dreamlike day. She walked until her car was a speck in the distance.

Away from everyone, she began to sob uncontrollably. She desperately wanted to leave David behind in Tampa where she had found him. She was tired of courtroom battles, exhausted from pushing and protecting her daughters, raw from facing her own feelings. But she was afraid she wouldn't be able to leave it all there—the bitterness, the obsession, the tiredness.

The more she let go of her emotions, the more she felt the tug of an indefinable sadness. She encouraged the new feeling until it enveloped her like a pool of soothing warm water.

She had never mourned David when he walked out seventeen years ago. By simply disappearing, he had denied her that right. Part of what drove her to find him and drag him before the bench, she finally understood, was the need to arrive at a ritual conclusion. She was burying David at last. Now the mourning that she had put off seventeen long years could begin.

She was ready to go home, to let the sadness run its course, to face the Florida Supreme Court. No matter what happened there, she had already won. She had conquered her fear. She had faced David. She would never dream of him again.

A small white seashell, washed up by a wave, lay gleaming in the sand. She stooped to pick it up, then found two more. David had proposed to her on a beach in Bermuda. Now she had buried him on a beach in Tampa.

Three shells were all she wanted to take home. Three shells, one for each of her daughters.

Epilogue

>>>>>>>>>>>>>>>>>>>>>>

James Parker's wife paid fifteen hundred dollars two hours after Judge Cobb's hearing and her husband was set free. Parker began missing his weekly payments four months later. With the threat of contempt, however, he quickly caught up.

The IRS is still trying to collect some or all of the outstanding arrearage.

Pat Bennett argued her case before the Florida Supreme Court on April 1, 1988. A decision is expected in late 1988. If she loses, Parker can no longer be sent to jail for contempt.

Washington, D.C., June 1988

Acknowledgments

>>>

More than fifty people, from judges to sheriffs, family friends to child-support experts, have contributed to this book through interviews, expertise, and guidance. Their cooperation has not only enriched the story of the Bennett family but has made it more objective and balanced. I wish to thank them:

Lorraine Baker, Andrea Bennett, Christine Bennett, Eugene Bennett, Marcia Bennett, Arlene Bierbaum, Philip Brophy, William Branch, George Carpenter, Kathy Chinoy, Charles Crotty, Bill Daniels, Marge De Blaay, Elizabeth L. Dribben, Michael Echevarria, Cheryl Fitzpatrick, Richard Frazier, Richard Froemming, Sally Goldfarb, Frank de la Grana, Richard Hager, Carl Hanfling, Ron Haskins, Margaret Campbell-Haynes, Nanette Hoback, Clegg Holliday, Jean Holzhueter, Joyce Jeffers, June Inuzuka, Maureen Kayes, Daniel Kellogg, John Kellogg, Mary Kellogg, Terry Kellogg, Jim Marsee, David Mees, Kathleen Meredith, Debbie Perez, Pam Powers, Jean Samson, Linda Schnatterly, Susan Sheehan, Viola Tesch, Michael Valentine, Chriss Walker, Jill Weber, Beth Weisberg.

I would like especially to thank Betty Murphy, president of the National Child Support Advocacy Coalition, for sharing her knowledge and experience and for evaluating the first draft manuscript; Diane Dodson, child-support specialist, for directing me to resources; Chriss Walker for reviewing the final draft manuscript; and my wife, Paula Kaufmann, for editing draft after draft.